The Self-Improver:
A Pilot's Journey
By
Nick Eades
ISBN: 978-1-8383868-6-3

Published By: -

i2i
PUBLISHING

i2i Publishing. Manchester.

www.i2i.publishing.co.uk

To my uncle, Flight Sergeant Jack Eades, Wellington Bomber pilot, killed in action, 1941.

To my wife Liz's uncle, Pilot Officer John Waring, Battle of Britain Spitfire pilot, killed in action in command of a Sunderland Flying Boat, 1942.

Acknowledgements

Life comes at you quickly, memories fade slowly.

When I first considered writing this book, friends immediately offered their advice. I decided to go ahead anyway. My earliest memories were stirred by my oldest friend, Peter Brown. I found him in 1959 after crawling through a hole in my garden fence. We ended up running a company and flying together. We are still best friends.

To Liz, who my dog, Roffey, found in a pub in 1986. She was trusting enough to fly with me and then, to marry me. Also, to our two wonderful boys, James and Robert, both of whom we could not be prouder.

The characters mentioned in the book have all contributed in one way or another to inspire me. Thank you to everyone who has helped me along the way.

Special thanks go to Lionel Ross, my publisher at i2ipublishing.co.uk for believing in my book and his senior editor, Mark Cripps, for all his hard work in getting the book ready for publication.

I would also like to thank the hugely talented Mike McCarthy for his illustrations. I have known Mike for over thirty years and only recently, discovered his hidden talent.

Lastly, special thanks go to Liz for proofreading the book and to Sally Pitiakoydis and Karen Sanders Young for all their hard work in making the book readable.

Contents

Prologue

Three Avenues

'The years thunder by
The dreams of youth grow dim
where they lie
caked in dust on the shelves of patience.
Before we know it, the tomb is sealed.
Where, then lies the answer?
In choice.
Which shall it be:
Bankruptcy of Purse
or Bankruptcy of Life'
Sterling Hayden

In the aviation world, the term Self-Improver has traditionally been a derogatory term used to describe a pilot who has not been trained in one of the more traditional methods. But why does the self-improver even exist? The overriding reason lies within the aviation world and its elitism. Only the best make-it to the rarefied atmosphere of the airliner flight deck. Many try, a lot fail. Aviation is elitist, not because it is a difficult career, although being a pilot does require a keen mind, discipline and some natural ability. However, rocket science it most definitely is not. Becoming a pilot is elitist mainly because of the enormous cost of the training. Ultimately, the men and women who make it to the flight deck are the best. Their initial training involves considerable personal cost and large amounts of time and energy, severely testing an applicant's will and ability. To even consider financing your own flying training takes a great deal of courage and a certain amount of wishful thinking.

At the time I started learning to fly in the late 1970s, there were three avenues into the world of commercial aviation. The best and most prestigious route was to apply to one of the major airlines for acceptance onto their training courses. This was the equivalent of going to either Oxford or Cambridge University. Only the very best and most suitably qualified candidates needed to apply and even then, the chances of a successful application were remote indeed. This route normally meant being sent to places such as Hamble, on the south coast of England, for a course lasting two years. At the end of this time, the successful candidate would be the proud owner of a Commercial Pilot Licence. Our budding aviator would have been taught to fly in exactly the manner that the airline sponsoring them required. This meant that the finished product, as far as the airline was concerned, was a pilot that had been trained from day one, to act, think and fly precisely as the airline required. Their careers were already fully mapped out. Four years later, they would be promoted to senior first officer and some five to ten years after that, depending on the all-important seniority list, they would be promoted to captain. Those pilots who flew the smaller, short-haul aircraft could achieve their commands in a much shorter timeframe than those who waited for the long-haul command on the largest aircraft. Waiting times to become a captain on these aircraft could be over twenty years in the larger airlines. Commands on the low-cost airlines could be achieved in a much shorter time frame.

The second source of potential pilots for the airlines were the armed forces. Military pilots would normally complete a short service commission of around twelve years in either the Royal Air Force, Army or Naval Air Arm. This would provide the airlines with a steady supply of highly experienced and well-disciplined aviators in their early- to mid-thirties at a fraction of the cost of training a new pilot.

There was, however, a third type of pilot, one the recruitment departments of the major airlines had been reluctant to consider, the aptly named, Self-Improver. As the name suggests, this was a pilot who, for whatever reason, had not been accepted into an approved training school or the armed forces. This group of aspiring pilots could further be subdivided into two categories. There were those who were able to afford the enormous cost of attending an approved flight training school, normally by the kindness of wealthy parents, or parents willing to re-mortgage their homes. Then, there were those who had to beg, steal or borrow the funds to pay for training by the hour. There would be no organised classes and structured training for this group. Instead, they had their noses pressed to the window peering in on those lucky enough to attend the hallowed flight training schools. They would then hang around the school gates, hoping to borrow unwanted notes to further their chances of passing the ground school examinations. Instead of a shiny new fleet of aircraft to train on, this type of self-improver would hang around and offer to clean the aircraft in return for a few minutes of flight time. I most certainly belonged to this sub-group. I was the lowest of the low on the aviation ladder.

How then, would such an intrepid aviator be able not only to gain the all-important commercial licence, but then convince a major airline to employ them ahead of their own candidates or the highly competitive military pilots? The following is my own path through the many varied, astonishing and occasionally frightening hurdles. Whilst by no means unique, my journey had many twists and turns that no approved course could ever replicate. In retrospect I would not have changed a single thing.

Chapter 1

A Poor Start

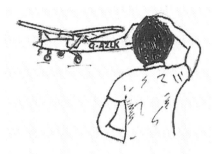

It was April 1974. I was sitting in a Cessna 150, registration number G-AZLK. The little two-seat high-wing training aircraft in its yellow and white livery looked very much at home as it taxied slowly but surely back towards its parking spot at the flying club at Shoreham Airport. Sitting beside me was Dennis McQuoid, a senior training captain with British Caledonian. We had just completed a one-hour flight to see if I had the aptitude to become a private pilot and hopefully and even more ambitiously, a commercial pilot. Initially, everything had gone well. I enjoyed walking around the aeroplane counting the number of wings, elevators, propellers and engines. As it was a tiny aircraft, I accomplished this task with a certain amount of accuracy. It was an unusually sunny day for April and as the little aircraft sat proudly on the grass airfield, the sun reflected from its metal skin and all looked well with the world.

To get to this point, allow me to fill you in with a little background. I had been brought up within a stone's throw of the sea and a couple of very long stone throws from the small grass airfield at Shoreham-by-Sea in Sussex. My family had a long and distinguished history in aviation. My Uncle Jack had been a pilot in the Second World War. He had a career flying Wellington

Bombers. His life was tragically cut short, a mile from the runway and safety at RAF Marham. He was twenty-one years old. Incredibly within five years our paths would cross, but more of that later. My other uncle was also in the Royal Air Force and retired as a group captain. He flew the first generation of jet fighters, a difficult and dangerous job at which he excelled and distinguished himself. His logbook included such aircraft as the Meteor, the Vampire, the Hawker Hunter. The man was an aviation god but also a humble and decent human being.

My father had also been in the Royal Air Force, having trained in Canada to fly large multi-engine transport aircraft. After the war, he left the Air Force to pursue a very successful career in commercial aviation and was a senior captain on the Boeing 707 also with British Caledonian Airways. My elder brother lived and breathed aviation and had begun to learn to fly on his seventeenth birthday. All of this set the scene for me to follow in these illustrious footsteps on that fateful day in April 1974. However, there was one major problem. I had absolutely no interest or desire to fly an aircraft. I felt that I was being pushed into something that did not interest me. At that time, I was far more interested in rugby, cars and women (in that order). Pushing this to the back of my mind, I tried to concentrate on taxiing our little Cessna across the bumpy grass to another patch of even bumpier grass which served as one runway at Shoreham Airport. For the life of me, I couldn't distinguish which bit of grass I was meant to be following and had great trouble understanding why the steering wheel refused to do its primary job and steer the aircraft. I had forgotten the pre-flight brief in which I had been told that you steer the aircraft on the ground by use of the foot controls, which on a car, would have been the brake and clutch.

Slowly, we made our way towards an area where we could check that the engine would probably keep going for most of the flight and nothing was going to drop off before we became airborne. Hopefully, we would stay intact until we were safely back on the ground. My instructor Dennis, ever the gentleman, asked me to put my hands and feet on the controls and follow everything that he did. Finally, they cleared us for take-off and G-AZLK bumped over the grass surface until the only way that I knew we were finally airborne was when my teeth finally stopped chattering. We climbed steadily towards the sea, the Eades' family house passing lazily under the left wing. Although this was not the first time I had been in an aircraft, it was the first time that someone had said, "You have control." I quickly learnt my first lesson as a would-be pilot, that you cannot look sideways out of the window trying to identify your house and have any hope of controlling an aircraft that seems to have a mind of its own. This was obvious to my instructor, as he quickly took back control after affirming, "I have control."

The rest of the flight followed a similar pattern of demonstrations on how to do something properly, quickly followed by my demonstration of how not to do it. I felt that I had rather dented my instructor's claim that anyone can be taught to fly. It was a rather quiet aircraft that taxied back over the grass on its journey to the clubhouse. It seemed obvious that, unlike the rest of my family, aviation was not in my blood. Apologising to both Dennis and my father, I had to finally admit that I much preferred cars and that aircraft did not excite me. I could see the surprise and disappointment on both their faces. It looked like my career in aviation was over before it had begun.

So, it was back to my first love, cars. I would often go to the local car auction and buy a sad-looking Triumph Spitfire or MGB sports car, drive, or as often as not, tow them home. Here, I would spend hours filling in rust holes, servicing engines and getting my proud purchase ready for resale in the auction the following week. I was barely seventeen and got an enormous amount of satisfaction from my small but usually profitable hobby. There were setbacks along the way. I usually only bid for cars that I could work on with relative ease and could turn a quick, if not large, profit. If I bought a car for four hundred pounds on a Monday and sold it a week later for five-hundred pounds, I considered it a successful transaction.

However, as I grew bolder, I looked at more exotic cars. One week, there appeared before me, what seemed to be an outstanding Lancia Fulvia. Here was a beautiful two-seater coupe in Ferrari red that was a real head turner. As can happen to any amateur, my heart took over from my head. As the bids climbed above my price range, I heard a voice offer way above the car's value. As the hammer came down, I was astonished and perplexed when I realised that voice was my own.

I was now penniless and the proud owner of a car I knew absolutely nothing about. Although the car looked good, it had one slight problem. It rarely started. As with most Italian cars built in the seventies, you purchased them for their aesthetic beauty rather than any expectation that they would start every day and become a useful means of transportation. Undaunted, I undertook servicing the engine, changing the spark plugs and checking the ignition system, which was an early and very unreliable electronic affair, probably designed by a committee and built by their children.

Unfortunately, this task was not made any easier when I could not find where the spark plugs were located on the engine. The more I looked, the more frustrated I became. Here was a car that had no spark plugs, no leads, no ignition system, no rotary arm. I might just as well have been looking at an alien spacecraft. There was almost nothing I recognised or could work on. Worst still, the car stubbornly refused all my efforts to start it. It drained battery after battery as the little Red Devil refused to show any signs of life. I resorted to what I knew best, brute force. Persuading my best friend Pete, I decided the best course of action would be to bump-start my Lancia. One obstacle to this plan was that I only had one car and that wouldn't start. Pete, unfortunately at the time, did not own a car. The answer seemed to lie with a lovely grey Rover 2000 sitting on my father's drive. He was out for the day, but I couldn't imagine him disagreeing with the use of his pride and joy in such a worthwhile and well-thought-out plan. With Pete driving the Rover and myself in the Lancia we reached twenty miles an hour, the agreed speed at which I would engage the clutch and bump start my car.

The plan worked perfectly until the point at which the Lancia's clutch engaged with its engine. Instead of a smooth transition from being towed to driving, the Lancia's engine reacted to this rude awakening by totally seizing. The piston heads took the top of the engine away from the bottom and in doing so, hit the bonnet, which flew open and blocked the windscreen. The poor Rover which, up to this point, had done nothing wrong, now had a two-ton anchor doing its best to stop it dead in its tracks. Luckily, there was no other traffic around as the Rover left most of the rubber from its tyres on the road before it came to a halt. The Lancia had left a lot more of itself scattered across the public highway.

Quickly assessing the situation, we cleaned up the road as best we could before any damage could occur to passing vehicles, luckily it was relatively quiet. We then partially secured the Lancia's bent and broken bonnet and towed what was left of my dream car home. Safely in the garage, I reopened the bonnet and peered inside. It's amazing what damage you can cause an engine in such a brief space of time. There were bits everywhere and the engine seemed to have literally split in two. Sticking out of the side of the engine bay, there were four small missiles. I prised one away and to my disbelief, discovered that they were the spark plugs I had been looking for. Only the Italians could hide them on the bottom side of an engine. My father could not understand why his car failed its MOT test the next week with four bald tyres. I never told him. That incident spelt the end of my budding career in the motor industry. An interesting aside though is the fact that there were many E-Type Jaguars going through the auctions. This was the time of the early seventies' oil crisis and cars that ate fuel were reduced in value so much that they became almost valueless. Every week, these beautiful E-types were being sold for just a few hundred pounds. After my Lancia adventure, I knew that I did not possess the skills to repair and service these beasts. However, I was convinced that if I could find a barn to rent where I could store these cars until the good times returned, then there was a fortune to be made. I tried to raise the capital to buy ten to twenty cars and pay for a ten-year lease on a barn. I estimated the cost of the project at around ten thousand pounds. I could not convince anybody at the time that E-type Jaguars would become a valuable investment. Today, a good E-type can easily be worth over two hundred and fifty thousand pounds. My interest in cars was fading, but enthusiasm for starting a business was awakened. All I had to do was to find out where that business should take me.

Chapter 2

University

Eighteen years old: Would-be car salesman – failed; would-be pilot - failed. In fact, I had failed at just about everything I had tried. I had no direction to follow and absolutely no idea of what I wanted to do or be in life. So, what did I choose to do? I did what my parents wanted. I went to university. Again, the curse of family traditions weighed heavily on my shoulders. My father had gone to Oxford University studying at St Edmund Hall and my brother achieved straight A's in all his exams and was studying for a degree at Christ Church College Oxford. Well, no pressure there then! I managed a motley collection of bare minimum passes in reasonably obscure subjects. Unsurprisingly, my applications to the top universities were met with the derision they deserved. Finally, through UCCA - the universities clearing system, used in dredging the bottom of the academic pool - they invited me to study economics at the University of Essex. My parents, friends and teachers were totally underwhelmed. I knew nothing about economics and had the same amount of interest in the subject, but still, how hard could it be - especially as a bit of politics and philosophy were thrown in? I was about to find out.

Whilst my university days were not a significant influence on my latter career, they were a springboard from which I failed to launch myself intellectually. However, there were two significant incidents which would be game changers in different ways.

Life at the University of Essex in the late seventies was a strange mixture of student militancy and academic anaemia. This was especially prevalent in my chosen subjects of PPE (politics, philosophy and economics). During my time at Essex, there were weekly mass meetings of the student body, protesting against just about anything the government supported. Feelings and emotions were running deep. As often as not, these protests ended with the local police force feeling a few collars of the normal suspects. I watched most of the action from the Student Union bar, wondering why people got so upset when there was perfectly good beer to be drunk. Due to my total lack of interest in anything political, it slowly dawned on me that perhaps studying politics was not the way forward. I attended no lectures on the subject, which left only economics and philosophy. Eventually, I would leave them as well.

The fundamental difference between being at school and being at university is that at the latter, it is up to the student to make sure they attend all the seminars and lectures and put in hours of self-study to achieve the required standard. This, I failed to appreciate until it was too late. To be fair to my lecturers, they had inherited a student with no great interest in any of the subjects thrown up by UCCA. I was there because there was nothing else on offer. It was that or go to work - heaven forbid!

My downfall came on that fateful day of the end-of-year examinations. As I rarely read anything on the public notice boards except for the rugby team sheets, I was blissfully unaware that we had to sit exams at the end of the year. Therefore, I was mistakenly secure in the knowledge that I had another two years of rugby and beer before I had to face the unpleasant prospect of an examination. I was now faced with the further unpleasant prospect of being thrown out of probably the only university in England that would have taken me. To fail in this exceedingly lenient environment was almost unheard of. Yet fail I would.

In my defence, I did not go down without a fight. I have always been good under pressure. Without it, I tended towards idleness and aimless wandering. Therefore, I set my sights on passing these examinations with the best score I could manage. I had two weeks of hard revision ahead to make up for a long year of intellectual abstinence. I begged, stole and borrowed all the notes my roommates had taken over the past year of lectures and seminars. They had been busy whilst I had slept in most mornings. I would often wonder where everyone was when eventually, I made my way into the kitchen around lunchtime. Now I knew! Who would have thought it?

There was a certain reluctance by some individuals to give up lightly the fruits of their labour. Some demanded beer, others money. However, the brightest amongst us was a wealthy teetotaller and subsequently very difficult to corrupt. I knew he had the information I desperately needed, but his inherent integrity and the fact that I had ignored him totally up to this point in time, meant that my pleadings fell on deaf ears.

At this point, Lady Luck raised, albeit briefly, her beautiful head. Our intellectual friend had fallen in love. Sadly, the lady of his affections had not reciprocated and blunt refusals had met his offers to take her out by bus, the lady was not for public transport. As he recounted his woes, a perfect solution to both our problems became apparent. Although I had given up my car auction career, I still dabbled enough to allow me to be the proud owner of a beautiful, red Triumph Spitfire. This little two-seater convertible sat proudly in the car park at the base of our accommodation block. Now, we both had something the other desperately needed. Everyone has their price (as they say) and tonight, the loan of my car for the evening secured me access to a mountain of invaluable notes. The deal was done.

That should have been the end of the matter. His night should have ended with a lingering kiss and I should have passed my exams with flying colours. Sadly, neither happened. After a long evening of study, not being used to any intellectual activity, I had gone to bed reasonably early and for once, totally sober. I was rudely awoken, some hours later, by loud and persistent banging on my door. After failing to drown out the noise with a pillow over my head, I gave into the inevitable and opened the door. Standing there with my car keys and a trickle of blood running down his face was my new best friend - a position he was about to vacate.

The problem with being a teetotaller is that when you try to impress a young lady with a bottle of the best Chianti, it's not a very good idea to have a glass or three yourself. This normally would not present a problem to a seasoned drinker like myself, but to a drinking virgin, it was the equivalent of consuming a bottle of spirits.

"I think I might have dented your car," were the only coherent words from him that I could make out. We looked at each other for a moment as I contemplated how hard I could hit him without causing permanent damage. At the same time, I imagine he was deciding on how fast he could run.

However, he convinced me it was more of a scratch than a dent and could be easily repaired. I opened my window to look into the car park below to see if I could spot anything amiss.

"It's not actually in the car park," he informed me. "I left it where I dented it. That seemed to be for the best." Demanding that he show me where my car was, we set out on a beautiful moonlit night along a deserted country lane.

A faint, blue, flashing light in the distance heightened my suspicions. This light became brighter as we made our way along the lane. Eventually, we came around a bend in the road and there in front of us, were two police cars with their lights illuminating the trunk of a large oak tree. At the base of this tree was a very sad looking Triumph Spitfire. I think both the police officers and I were quite impressed at the feat of going sideways into a tree and being able to walk away relatively unharmed from such a badly damaged sports car. After ascertaining that it wasn't stolen and that nobody had been hurt, the police officers were happy to leave it at that. No point in creating unnecessary paperwork. This was the seventies, after all. On the slow trudge back to the university campus, it suddenly occurred to me that there were meant to be two people in the car.

"What the hell happened to your date?" I inquired.

"Oh, we had an argument in the restaurant and she took the bus home," he explained.

After a few choice words from me, he took his notes back and sealed my academic fate.

The second significant event during my first and only year at university had occurred a few months previously. My father had invited me along on one of his South American trips. This involved a ten-hour flight to Recife in Brazil and then a few days later, a shorter flight to Rio for a week on the beach and excursions to the likes of Sugar Loaf Mountain and the famous Corcovado mountain and the statue of Christ. The trip lasted just under three weeks and I had had the time of my life. As my father was the captain, I was allowed to occupy the observer's seat in the flight deck on every flight. I asked the flight engineer semi-intelligent questions and surprised myself by understanding the answers. The more I probed, the more interested I became. I then moved onto asking the first officer questions about the actual flying of the aircraft and how it felt to operate one, so large and complex. Slowly, I understood just what attracted people to the world of aviation. I was having in-depth conversations, something that I could never have had with my father. It was with a heavy heart that I bade farewell to the crew and returned to university life.

Inevitably, the first-year examinations arrived. First up was a three-hour paper on politics, present day and the past. My crash course revision was paying some dividends and slowly, I ploughed through the questions, using abstract words to disguise the lack of facts and in-depth knowledge. Although this was not my principal subject, I needed to pass this exam to progress to pure economics in year two. At the end of the exam, I felt that I had acquitted myself reasonably well. Next, came the economics paper itself. I only hoped that there were some questions about John Maynard Keynes and Adam Smith. My plan was a little bit like roulette. Instead of covering a large percentage of the table, I selected just two numbers. If they came up, I was rich, but if either or both failed to materialise, I would lose everything. Therefore, I studied everything about these two men in the very limited time I had available.

So, it was with a certain amount of trepidation that I opened my examination paper. The document was several pages long. I read it, read it once more and to be absolutely certain, read it for the third time. I never had much interest in gambling and I was beginning to understand why. Still, I bravely wrote for three hours and tried my best to mention Keynes and Smith as often as possible. I left the examination with a sinking feeling in the pit of my stomach. Two down and one exam to go. Things could only get better. I had three days to revise for the last exam - philosophy.

Now, philosophy and I are not natural bedfellows. If I see a table and chairs in front of me, I tend towards the fact that they are a table and chairs. It seems highly unlikely that Descartes' evil genius would go to the trouble of destroying the world and then instantly recreating it and then plant false memories in my conscious and subconscious mind. My approach could be summed up by the phrase, 'if I can see it, touch it or smell it, then it's probably for real'. For this reason, I decided that my first lecture in philosophy would be my last. If anyone queried my absence, I could always fall back on good old Descartes and ask if my apparent absence was in fact something perceived rather than something actual. It seemed a good plan. After three days of intensive study, I presented myself in front of the adjudicator.

"Name?" she asked.

"Eades," I replied.

Her finger ran down the list of candidates. She tried again. Nothing, there were no Eades, nothing even close. I tried my best to be philosophical about this omission. They asked me to stand aside to let the approved candidates enter the room. Finally, I was called back to the adjudicator's desk. There followed a series of questions and answers which established that to sit the exam, you needed to have attended a minimum of half of the lectures. Eventually, the dean of my college was called to adjudicate. My argument was simple; I could prove that I had reached the required standard without the need to attend any lectures. The dean, an elderly and wise man, considered my case.

"Why," he asked, "did you not attend the lectures?"

Good question, I thought. As is often the case, my mouth came out with an answer before my brain had finished listening to the question.

"I lent my car to a fellow student, sir, to visit his very sick grandmother. Sadly, he crashed my car and was very lucky to walk away from the wreckage. Therefore, I had no means of transport. The lectures were on Wednesdays, the only day of the week that buses do not run frequently."

I hoped he didn't realise I lived on the campus.

"Very well," he kindly informed me. "You may sit the examination." This turned out to be a very short-lived reprieve.

I was the last person to sit down to await my papers. I was seated at the back of the room, next to a large window overlooking the Essex countryside. The weather was perfect with deep, blue skies together with the occasional white, fluffy clouds, a description that would lose me marks in my meteorological exam at a much later date. In the far distance, an aircraft's contrail painted its way across this idyllic canvas. I breathed a deep, contented sigh. What could go wrong on such a perfect day? I was brought back to the matter in hand with the fateful words from the adjudicator, "You may begin."

Now, as previously mentioned, I had burned the candle at both ends - and in the middle - preparing for this exam. True, it may have been better to adopt this approach twelve months earlier. However, I felt strangely optimistic as I turned the examination paper over. There was a time limit of three hours to complete the questions. It may have been true that I did not possess three hours of philosophical knowledge, but I felt certain I could waffle my way through. Reading the examination paper changed all that. There, on page one was the question - Is this a question? Discuss! Hmm, I knew vaguely that someone in the world of philosophy may have said something along these lines. Never mind, I will come back to that question later, I thought. I turned the page which revealed only the side I had already studied before being told to start the exam. No matter how many times I turned the single sheet of paper over, I could not find question number two. I, therefore, raised my hand to get the attention of the adjudicator. I politely pointed out that they had only given me the first page of the exam. Imagine my horror when I was informed that this was the exam. I could see the pleasure in her eyes as my head sunk towards my chest. This was revenge for my insisting on taking the exam. That the dean had overruled her decision was being softened by the sight of my discomfort. She turned and made her way back to her desk at the front of the hall. Even to this day, I remember the fresh spring in her step.

I now had three hours to write an essay on a quote I barely remembered. I looked around me and every other candidate had their head down, busily scribbling away. I had arrived at my Lancia engine moment. It defeated me, rightfully caught out in my vain and wildly optimistic attempt at beating the system. My eyes were once again drawn to the idyllic scene being played out through the window. As I watched another aircraft lazily paint its way across the sky, I finally made my mind up. I took up my pen and wrote in capital letters IF THAT WAS A QUESTION, THIS IS THE ANSWER. With that, I put my pen down, collected my things and with as much dignity as I could muster, I left not only the room but the university. I put my worldly goods into a very dented car and drove away. I never enquired as to the results of my exams.

Chapter 3

Aviation at Last, Well Almost

I had made my decision. Bridges were burned. There was no turning back. Five years after my first attempt, I was now committing myself to becoming an airline pilot, although that was the simple part. As far as my father was concerned, I had squandered my opportunity to learn to fly and I had not shown the commitment nor the aptitude to become a competent, let alone successful, professional pilot. There would be no help from that quarter. Fair enough, I thought.

One of the best pieces of advice I received was to make sure I was physically fit enough to get an initial Class 1 medical certificate issued by the UK Civil Aviation Authority, often referred to as the CAA. Without this document, I had no hope of flying as a career. Sadly, my brother, who had shown such promise and enthusiasm, had fallen at this hurdle. It was, therefore, with some trepidation that I arrived at the headquarters of the CAA in Redhill, Surrey. To get to this point, I had to work hard to save up hundreds of pounds to pay for this extensive medical bill. Every part of me was probed, prodded and X-rayed. They tested my senses, eyes, ears, nose and anything else they could think of. The entire process took up most of the day. When it was finally over, I was a physical and emotional wreck. The other would-be pilots and I were then shown into a small waiting room with those immortal words, "the doctor will see you soon."

It's human - well it's my nature - to study other candidates also striving to achieve something you so desperately want for yourself. There were six of us in the room, all waiting to be called individually, to learn our fate. I guessed that out of the group, there must be at least one person who was going to fail his medical, even if it was just to give the doctors and nurses something to talk about after we had all gone home. We were all male, Caucasian and in our late teens or early twenties. Not an unusual group of applicants for those days. I began studying the competition, which was of course how I saw them, as inconspicuously as I could. One of us would be going home bitterly disappointed and as I would not let it be me, I had to decide which of us it would be. The chap opposite me, sadly looked in good shape, so he would get through. My eyes gave each of these poor chaps a thorough going over. One was far too skinny for my liking while another had such large ears, I really couldn't believe that a headset would fit over them. One candidate had such bad breath that we all kept a respectable distance and hoped he didn't speak to us! With these uncharitable thoughts running through my mind, I called in to learn my fate.

Now, as with all things medical, as soon as a man or woman in a white coat stares at you across an enormous desk, you immediately revert to being an eleven-year-old in the headmaster's study. Misdemeanours were dealt with at a much lower level, only the hardened criminals made it this far.

"Do you understand what I am saying? Mr Eades, do you understand what I have just told you?" brought me immediately back to the room. I had heard something. However, my brain was still processing the news and for once, I allowed it to complete the process before my mouth took over.

I had heard the words failed and sorry and something about plenty of other careers where this would make absolutely no difference to someone's prospects. However, I could not understand why the doctor was confiding these details to me. Didn't patient confidentiality apply in these circumstances? Didn't his Hippocratic Oath prevent him from explaining why old Big Ears back there, or Quasimodo, had failed their medical? Did he expect me to have a cheap laugh at their misfortune? Well, I had higher standards than that. They could laugh all they wanted, after we had all left, but to do it now, seemed highly insensitive. Sadly, it was not the others that he was referring to: it was me.

"Well, if that is all, Mr Eades, I am once again, very sorry. The nurse will see you out." At this point, neither my brain, nor my mouth had anything constructive to add, so leave I did, thankfully not through the room containing the other candidates. I'm sure all of them had inspected me and had relaxed. At least I didn't have big ears and I didn't flinch when looking in a mirror. These thoughts only gave me a small amount of comfort as I slowly made my way back to the train station, my buckled Spitfire having finally gone to the scrap yard, with my chosen profession following in its tyre marks.

I received the full medical report a few days later. Everything had gone well until the comprehensive check on my vision. They had checked me for long vision, short vision, night vision, peripheral vision, colour vision and depth perception vision. I had excelled in every category. They then asked me to take my contact lenses out, damn. Now, until puberty, my eyesight had been excellent. Then, as my voice changed, so did my ability to see things. Apparently, this is not an uncommon problem and these days, can be completely reversed by laser eye surgery, unfortunately not an option to me. Basically, the muscle holding the lens of the eye at the correct angle cannot mature properly and the lens is gradually moved away from the optimal position. The eye itself is perfectly healthy. However, because of its lens being at an incorrect angle, the eye becomes out of focus.

There are two ways to correct this condition (known as myopia): The traditional way was prescription glasses. The other way was the alternative method of contact lenses. With traditional spectacles, the more short-sighted a person was, the thicker the lens became. They measured the amount of short-sightedness in diopters. A normally sighted person would have a zero-zero prescription. Away from this base line, a long-sighted person, who had difficulty in focusing on near objects, would have a positive prescription. This occurred in most people as they aged, hence the need to wear glasses as you got older. The aviation licensing authorities understood and accepted this natural decaying of vision with age, as long as it could be fully corrected with spectacles.

Short-sightedness or myopia, however, was not so easily tolerated by the CAA in the UK. Whilst old age glaucoma rarely resulted in prescriptions of more than plus three diopters, short-sighted myopia could be very different. The higher the prescription became, the thicker the lens became to correct the problem. At around minus four diopters, the lens becomes thick enough to create visual distortion around the very edge of the lens. Whilst this would cause no problems to the average wearer of spectacles of this power, the issuing authorities set minus four as the limit for any applicants of an initial first-class medical. My prescription was minus seven. I was, therefore, refused a medical certificate. I literally couldn't see that coming.

As previously mentioned, in the late seventies, an alternative method of correcting short-sightedness had become available, the contact lens. Initially, they were made of glass and were applied directly to the cornea of the eye. As I can testify, they were difficult to insert and remove and after a few hours, became so uncomfortable that they had to be taken out. Also, being made of glass, they were not permeable, which meant the eye became starved of oxygen. The eye tried to compensate for this lack of oxygen by carrying more blood in the capillary system in the eye itself and this resulted in the eye becoming very red. Looking like you had just got in from a night on the town was not the image the airlines wanted for their pilots. However, I had persisted with these lenses as I detested wearing thick, milk-bottle-type glasses. My saviour was the introduction of the soft, permeable lens still in use today. Suddenly, I was free of glasses and the pain of glass contact lenses. My sight was perfect and I could wear these new lenses all day without the slightest discomfort. Most of my friends were not aware that I wore contact lenses and I had mistakenly assumed that as I could see perfectly well, this would present no problems at my medical. This seemed to me an insurmountable problem. There was no way the authorities would change the rules for me and this would have probably been the case had I not been introduced to a certain Dr Peter Chapman.

In life, we are all occasionally lucky enough to meet the right person at the right time. It may be your future wife, a future employer or someone who changes your life significantly. For me, it was Dr Chapman. After my rejection by the CAA, I was understandably upset and depressed. It was at this point my father suggested that I speak with his own aviation doctor. They regularly check all pilots every six or twelve months and they normally remain with their own authorised medical examiner or AME, for many years, even to the point where one or both of them retire. Once you have successfully passed your initial examination at Redhill, you may have all future examinations carried out by these uniquely qualified professionals.

Therefore, with very little hope, I sat in Dr Chapman's waiting room. There were several fully qualified pilots going through their regular checks. How I envied these people. They were at the pinnacle of their careers and fully fit to fly the largest airliners in the world. I felt like a fraud sitting there as they assumed that I belonged amongst their ranks and was renewing my medical certificate. If only they knew.

Eventually, I was called forward into the great man's office. Dr Chapman was in his early fifties and was the head of British Caledonian's medical unit at Gatwick Airport. Why he was taking the time to see me, I really could not fathom. He was very busy dealing with a large and dynamic airline and responsible for ensuring their pilots were medically fit to continue their careers. I was a 'no hope, would-be' pilot who had already been rejected for perfectly understandable reasons.

As with many in his profession, Dr Chapman wore half-moon spectacles over the top of which he assessed me with deeply intelligent eyes. After a quick introduction, he looked down at some papers. He had my results in front of him and he would read, then look, look, then read. I wasn't sure if he meant me to say anything, so I kept quiet, which was probably just as well, as I had absolutely nothing to say.

Finally, he enquired as to my desire and commitment to become an airline pilot. In retrospect, he was making sure that if he was to go to a great deal of time and trouble to help me, then I would be equally committed. Luckily, I had convinced him.

As far as he was concerned, the CAA were very reluctant to consider, let alone accept, any advances in medical innovations. A certain conservative approach was no doubt a good thing from a licensing authority. Dr Chapman, however, felt that they should be receptive to new technologies. It was with these words ringing in my ears that I was given an even more thorough eye examination than the CAA subjected me to. When all the tests were complete, I was invited to wait whilst Dr Chapman reviewed the results. I think, in retrospect, there are basically two types of aviation medical examiners, those who look for reasons to stop you flying and those who look for reasons to keep you flying. Luckily, I was sitting in front of one of the latter.

Once again, peering over his spectacles, he informed me that as far as he was concerned, my eyesight was more than acceptable for a Class 1 medical certificate. However, as mine was an initial application, he did not have the authority to grant it. He then asked me the name of the doctor I had seen at Redhill. A smile slowly appeared on his face as I answered. "Leave it with me," were his parting words. I left Gatwick with a sense that something very unusual was about to take place.

Two weeks later, I received a letter from the medical department of the CAA informing me that my application was under review and could I attend a review board in Redhill at ten o'clock the following Tuesday? You bet I could!

Therefore, I presented myself in front of what looked like three very senior members of the CAA. They all looked at me with great interest and I felt a certain amount of suspicion. I was asked if I understood why there were certain limits placed on an application of visual acuity. I answered that I fully understood. Why then, I was asked, did I consider that I knew better than them and continue with my application. I thought hard and tried to find the words that would not only give strength to my case but would not alienate these men who held my future in their hands. All I could come up with was the fact that with my lenses in, I could see perfectly and could pass all their tests. Also, I assured them I would never consider flying without my lenses, just as a pilot who wore spectacles, would never consider flying without those.

I sat there whilst they conversed quietly amongst themselves. I could not hear much of what they said. However, I distinctly heard the name Chapman, repeated frequently. Eventually, the most senior person, maybe the chairman, cleared his throat and spoke directly to me.

"Mr Eades, we do not appreciate having our valuable time taken up in this way. You have failed to meet the required visual standards set out in document number, subparagraph ..." At this moment, I had stopped listening and was about to leave the room.

"However," that word got my attention, "we have been persuaded in this instance to grant an alleviation." They informed me they would grant me my medical certificate with a restriction that I was to be reassessed every six months, instead of twelve and that should my prescription deteriorate below minus seven diopters, then they would immediately revoke my medical certificate. They also informed me they fully expected this deterioration to occur within the next few years.

Despite these words of doom and gloom, I left Redhill the proud owner of my Class 1 medical certificate. From that moment on, I saw Dr Chapman every six months to renew this certificate. Years later, I could extend this renewal period to twelve months. Every time he signed my licence, he chuckled, as even many decades later, they still deemed my eyesight below limits without my alleviation.

"I can't believe we got you flying young man," were words he repeated on every renewal, even when I was in my late fifties.

As an aside, Dr Chapman continued to carry out my regular medical checks until he took early retirement at the age of ninety-two. He still lives near me and now runs a second-hand car dealership. I would definitely buy my next car from that man.

Chapter 4

Where to Begin?

I was now the proud owner of a Class 1 medical certificate. The euphoria I had experienced faded with the realisation that it was of little use without an actual private pilot licence.

As the seventies were drawing to an end, the UK's economy was not in the greatest of shapes. The trade unions held the country to ransom, the self-imposed three-day week was fresh in people's memory and the country was in the depths of the Winter of Discontent. Margaret Thatcher had yet to make an impact on the power of the trade unions. Perfect, I thought to myself: I have picked exactly the right moment in time to apply for an airlines' sponsored training course. Who in their right mind could turn away a short-sighted university drop-out with absolutely no flying experience except for an hour's instruction five years previously? The fact that several airlines were actually making pilots redundant because of the economic situation barely crossed my mind as I sat down to write to all the airlines that were lucky enough to have made my short list. Initially, I thought that I would choose just five. I didn't want to cast my net too wide and have to disappoint the airlines that I would have to reject. I posted these applications and sat back to await their responses. And wait I certainly did. It slowly became obvious, even to me, that these airlines were not interested in my application. In fact, they were so disinterested that they failed to even acknowledge my letters. I repeated this process with the five airlines on my reserve list. I still felt that this would result in my disappointing one or two of them, so I resolved that choosing me would be on a first-come, first-served basis. This seemed to be the fairest way for all concerned. With this resolve, my next bunch of applications disappeared into the mouth of the bright red post box at the end of the road. Once again, I sat back and waited and waited until it dawned on me that maybe, just maybe, I had nothing to offer any airline. Luckily, I had another plan, although I really had not expected to have to put this into action.

There was - and still is - a weekly magazine for all things to do with aviation. *Flight International* is an excellent publication, full of news and reviews from both the civil and military worlds. It is also probably the only publication that was habitually read from back to front. Now, this had nothing to do with the quality of the articles. They did not start with the least interesting and work their way to the end up with the best stories last. No, the magazine was consistently interesting from front cover to back. However, at the very back were the classified ads. Within these pages could be found all the latest pilot recruitment information and job opportunities. Also, there were details of any airline that were offering training courses. Out of work pilots could often be seen in their local newsagents pretending to browse the magazine shelves in search of a suitable purchase, when in fact, all they were doing was scanning the advertisements at the back of *Flight International*. Once satisfied that no suitable positions were available, they would return the magazine to the shelves and shuffle out to wait until the following Thursday when the next issue was published.

I wanted no part of this subterfuge. I knew full well that the newsagent needed to earn a living and by turning his shop into a public library, we were depriving him of his rightful income. Therefore, I entered the shop with my head held high and approached the magazine rack. After a minute, I could not find a single copy of *Flight International*. I looked for any magazine that appeared as though it had been read from the back to front, still nothing. The shopkeeper approached me, enquiring if I was looking for something special. I informed him that I was indeed, looking for something very special and before I could elaborate, as if by magic, he produced several publications that would probably have finished off my dear old grandmother. It worried me I was thinking of my grandmother whilst being subjected to images I had not previously even known existed. I turned a certain shade of red and quickly explained that these were not the magazines I had meant and asked him if he had any copies of *Flight International*.

His friendly expression suddenly turned to a distinct scowl as he enquired as to whether I was "one of them," who read but never bought. "Follow me," he barked, as he made his way back behind his counter. He then produced a copy of *Flight International* firmly sealed in a plastic bag. "You people never buy the magazine so I've sealed them all. You can't have a copy until you have paid for it." I was taken aback and was about to inform him that all along, it was my intention to pay for the magazine before reading it. However, the look on his face convinced me that this would be a pointless exercise so instead, I meekly handed my money over and left the shop as quickly as I could, hoping that no one was wondering why the magazine I had just purchased was in a sealed bag.

Safely home, I settled down to read. I was determined to read it properly, starting where the publisher had intended and eventually, ending up at the classified section. I got to page three before the temptation was too great. As quickly as I could manage, I scanned every entry, until I realised that there were literally no advertisements for pilot vacancies. Not one, nothing, absolutely no reference to anything even close. This did not matter to me as I was not a pilot. However, I had been told that companies sponsoring pilots also advertised in these hallowed pages. If there were no jobs for pilots, then it slowly dawned on me that no company would go to the expense of training someone they did not require. This had a serious effect on my plans. I was now twenty years old. My parents had allowed me to move back home after leaving university, although my father had clarified that I was to support myself. However, he did relent and informed me that whilst I was still pursuing a career in aviation, he would not charge me rent. The rest was up to me.

As a last roll of the dice, as far as *Flight International* was concerned, I placed my advertisement for sponsorship with a promise to repay the debt at a healthy interest rate as my career progressed. As expected, I did not receive any replies. The door to sponsorship had been firmly shut in my face. I had to accept the fact that there was no way any airline was going to pay for my training. Even Dr Chapman had given me this advice. He explained that no company was going to take a chance on spending a lot of money on training me while there was the risk that I could easily lose my licence if my eyesight deteriorated by even the smallest of margins. He asked me what I would do if I had two candidates in front of me equally qualified to start a course, yet one had a medical restriction, while the other did not. Which one would I choose? Even with my eyesight I could see his point. Therefore, I had to decide. I could choose another profession and immediately start to work towards qualifications for that career. This seemed the most obvious and sensible path to follow. I knew that I was not interested in office work, as mentioned earlier, I knew that I tended towards the path of least resistance. If I became a junior office manager, I could see myself staying at that level until I retired, a ghastly thought. I needed and craved motivation each day to perform at anything like my true potential. I really believed that only flying would keep pushing me forward each day. I had to find another way to fulfil my dream.

I made the decision that if no one else believed in me, then I would believe in myself and do it the hard way. I would self-sponsor and become what I much later learned I was referred to, always with a hint of disapproval, a Self-Improver.

Chapter 5

Private Pilot Licence: A Good Start, Nearly

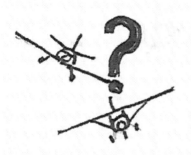

I needed advice and help, so I returned to the club where I had my first flight all those years ago. Mercury Flying Club. It was run by Ken Honey, a training captain on the BAC 1-11 at Gatwick. The training aircraft were mainly the Cessna 150s I had previously flown or the newer Cessna 152s (basically, the same aircraft but updated). They gave me a comprehensive breakdown of the costs involved in obtaining a Private Pilot Licence. This would require a minimum of forty - which normally meant at least forty-five - hours flying time. There was also the cost of ground school, books, charts and landing fees. At a very rough estimate, I was looking at a cost of well over two thousand pounds and this was just the very basic start of what was to come. I thanked the very helpful receptionist and made my way home.

Things did not look promising. Two thousand pounds was a lot of money. At the time, the average annual income for a family was less than five thousand pounds before tax and I was in no position to earn even this level of wage. I was at an impasse. Did I give in to the inevitable and look for another career? Or did I roll up my sleeves and accept any work that would help pay for my flying lessons? The flying club had given me the advice, correctly, that if I wanted any continuity, I should have at least one flight a week and more if I could afford it. Therefore, I needed a job that would pay me at least the average wage and I had absolutely no qualifications. Therefore, I discounted anything to do with the office or anything which might be termed nine-to-five employment. I needed to work as many hours as possible at something that would keep me close to the aviation world. The conclusion I came to was that I should apply to become an aircraft loader. This is literally what it sounds like. You load aircraft. It's the person you see putting your bags, hopefully, into your aircraft as you set off on your flight. They also load the cargo into the aircraft holds and at night-time, carry the next morning's newspapers into the correct aircraft. You worked shift patterns, normally eight hours at a time with four days working followed by four days off. The most exciting thing about the job was that there was plenty of overtime available and you could work for seven consecutive days if you needed to - and I needed to! It was hard manual labour in those days, something that held no fear for me.

Immediately, I applied and was delighted to be accepted: I had moved slowly forward. The best thing about my new job was that I was working seven days a week and earning good money, especially as I often worked twelve, instead of eight-hour shifts. I also got to drive little tugs powered by propane gas, which was great fun. I also thoroughly enjoyed the company of my fellow workers and was accepted once they realised that I would do as much manual labour as required. This allowed some of the more experienced guys to concentrate on the high loaders and other more complex loading machines. It also meant that on wet days, they stayed dry whilst I did not, still … needs must. The major drawback to this new arrangement was that although I was earning money to pay for my flying lessons, I had no spare time to learn to actually fly. I began to save up enough money to pay for four consecutive flying lessons over two days. Within a month, I had saved up enough to start what would hopefully, be my new career. With a certain amount of trepidation, I reported to the flying club, as instructed, at ten o'clock on a blustery day in the early spring of 1979.

With a banker's draft in hand, I secured my four initial lessons, all the books I would need to pass the ground school examinations and the all-important map which would allow me to find my way back to the airfield should I ever be allowed to take to the skies alone. Maybe, I had been a little hasty with this particular purchase. With all this completed, I finally bought my first ever pilot's logbook. This was a relatively small blue book published by someone with the name of Pooley. He seemed to have the market in flying logbooks covered as there were no alternatives to consider. Mr Pooley was probably a very wealthy man as his books were very expensive. I expect he completed his university degree. Still, no matter, I had to buy his book otherwise my instructor would have nothing to sign at the end of each flight. I would require at least forty of these signatures before I could apply for my licence. However, I was getting ahead of myself. I still had the minor matter of getting through my first flight.

Now, each flying lesson would start with a ground lecture detailing what we would practise in the air that day. These lessons varied in length according to which part of the syllabus we were attempting. You could not progress to the next part of your training until you satisfied the instructor that you fully understood each lesson and could perform the manoeuvre satisfactorily. However, today was purely an introductory flight, so they kept things to a very basic level, a place where I was always more comfortable.

Today's flight would be a simple demonstration of how each of the flight controls worked and their effect on the aircraft. The instructor held a small model aircraft aloft and pointed out the various flying surfaces and their effect. I was way ahead of him at this point and drew upon my previous flying experience three years earlier.

"Excuse me," I interrupted. "I thought we were going to be flying in a Cessna 152," I continued. I had remembered that these excellent little aircraft had their wings above the principal part of the aircraft. The model he held in his hands had the wings in a different place. I was proud of myself for noticing this and expected to be congratulated for my observation. He then informed me that this was not the aircraft we would fly in today, but the theory and the effect were the same. Without trying to be difficult, I enquired as to why the wings were in a different place if the effect achieved was the same. I was abruptly informed that high-wing and low-wing aircraft did not perform in the same way. Why then, I asked, do you have a model of a low-wing aircraft when we would shortly be taking off in the high-wing type? He stared at me for a moment or two, then left the small briefing room, closing the door behind him, a little too hard for my liking. My eyes wandered around the room and I picked up various aircraft instruments, probably salvaged from a low-wing aircraft whose pilot thought he was in the high-wing type, or vice versa. This was not a trap I was going to fall into. I felt a certain amount of satisfaction at this thought. The door reopened revealing my instructor, holding the original low-wing model.

"Sorry," he said, "the Cessna model is being used by another instructor, so we will have to stick with this Piper model." I later noticed this instructor and his pupil climb into the low-winged Piper, whilst we walked towards our Cessna. I hoped these instructors knew what they were doing, although it all seemed odd to me.

Despite all of this, I was determined to concentrate on everything I had been taught in the briefing room and do my best to remember as much as I could. We then walked all around our aircraft as I was shown all the controls and how to check they were secured properly. After this, we finally climbed into the aircraft and made ourselves as comfortable as possible in a very confined space. We then checked everything that needed checking before starting the engine, making sure there was nobody near our propeller. Once all our checks were completed, we spoke to the air traffic controllers and asked for permission to taxi. With this obtained, we taxied across the bumpy grass airfield to our allotted runway. I ensured that I understood how to steer the aircraft on the ground using the foot pedals, or to give them their correct name, the rudder pedals. Now that I knew these were connected to the nose wheel, it made sense that by moving these pedals left and right, the aircraft would also turn in that direction. This worked very well on the ground but had unexpected consequences when repeated in the air. More of that later.

Eventually, we had completed all our ground checks of the aircraft and engine systems. Unlike the larger aircraft, we did not have a printed list of the actions required, known as a checklist. The theory behind this was that a checklist was more useful if there were two pilots flying the aircraft. One pilot would read the checklist and the other would complete the required actions. Although there were two of us today, the Cessna, as with most small aircraft, was designed to be flown by just the one pilot. Therefore, I was told that all checks would have to be performed from memory. Never good at remembering things, at first, I was concerned that I would struggle to complete the right checks at the right time whilst trying to control the aircraft. Luckily, as this was my first flight, the instructor completed these checks on my behalf. However, he warned that he expected me to have learnt them off by heart before tomorrow's exercise. I felt this was asking a lot, especially as I had a twelve-hour shift of loading aircraft bags before my next lesson. Still, with all checks complete, we got our take-off clearance. I was asked by my instructor to taxi the aircraft towards the runway. He kindly informed me he would allow me to handle the aircraft for the take-off whilst he would carefully monitor what I did.

All instructors had a separate set of controls on their side of the aircraft as unlike cars, almost all aircraft have two identical sets of controls for each pilot. This allows each pilot to fly the aircraft, as you could imagine, a situation that would not work well on a car. The advantage of this is that you can have two pilots operating the aircraft without having to change seats. On multi-crew aircraft you have a captain and a co-pilot. On small training aircraft you have the pilot and pupil or passenger. The drawback to this arrangement is that you could have two pilots each thinking they are flying the aircraft. One may want to turn left and climb, the other may want to turn right and descend. If they both try to do this, the aircraft will carry on flying in the original direction until eventually, the stronger pilot gets his way. Now, this may well be a perfectly satisfactory way of deciding some things in life, such as a tug of war. However, it does not lead to a desirable outcome when flying an aircraft. It was drilled into me before I was allowed anywhere near an aircraft that if the instructor said, "You have control," I would immediately reply, "I have control." Then and only then, would I make a movement of the controls. If the instructor decided that things were getting a little too exciting, he would say, the pitch of his voice rising with the level of excitement, "I have control," would then take my hands and feet off of the controls and inform him, "You have control." This way, hopefully, both of us would have some idea of who was doing or not doing what. As incredible as it may seem, aircraft have been lost due to the fact that each pilot thought the other was flying it.

With this in mind, I manoeuvred our little aircraft onto the grass runway, pointing in roughly the correct direction. As I increased the engine power, we accelerated, slowly at first and then more quickly as the engine reached full power. I had been told to expect the aircraft to turn to the left on take-off as the propeller turned to the right. I knew this as the torque reaction and it always occurred opposite to the rotation of the propeller. Luckily, most aircraft had propellers that rotate clockwise or to the right when viewed from behind. Therefore, the aircraft always tried to go off the left side of the runway. This was corrected by moving the foot or rudder pedals to keep the aircraft straight. This could be a trap for the unwary, if it was not anticipated and it would not be long before I was to discover this for myself. Still, today was not that day. I kept the aircraft reasonably straight until we reached the correct speed when a little back pressure on the control column was all that was needed for the aircraft to leave the ground and return to its natural element.

It was my first ever take-off and it felt wonderful. Concentrating on keeping the nose of the aircraft at just the right angle: too low and we would not climb and the speed would increase; too high and the speed would become dangerously low and we would eventually run out of flying speed and stall the aircraft. An aircraft is designed to fly, it likes to fly and it is very good at flying. Sadly, it is normally the inexperienced pilot that stops the aircraft from performing well in the air by over-controlling. This means that the new pilot is trying too hard and making too many movements of the controls. An aircraft properly trimmed to fly straight and level will continue to fly that way until the controls are moved. This was demonstrated to me by my instructor and quickly, I learnt the valuable lesson that to fly smoothly and safely, one makes early, small, minor inputs rather than large ones later on. If all else fails, just let go and the aircraft will sort it all out for you. With this in mind, I released my death grip on the controls and the blood slowly made its way back towards my knuckles. The rest of the hour-long flight literally flew past as I learnt how to turn, climb and descend using the control column and rudder pedals. Far too soon, we were lining up with the little grass runway as my instructor allowed me to follow him through on the controls as we sank gently onto the bumpy surface. I was allowed to taxi the aircraft back to the clubhouse and with a last check on the controls and engine, we switched everything off. As we sat there, the only sounds were the cooling clicks from the engine. All seemed well with the world.

We returned to the briefing room to discuss what we had just learned in the air and to make sure I understood what had gone well and what had not gone so well. My instructor then went to retrieve the model aircraft and emphasise the points he had just made. He reached for the little low-wing Piper model. However, I was way ahead of him and suddenly produced the Cessna model from my flight bag. The door opened and there stood the instructor from the Piper. "Anyone seen my model?" he impatiently barked. We both shook our heads as I quickly returned it to my bag. As the door closed, we looked at each other and smiled.

"I think we are going to get along very well," he said. "See you tomorrow! Oh, and don't forget to learn all your checks." It had been a good start to my flying career, I thought.

The next few weeks followed a very similar pattern, load bags on aircraft for six or seven days in a row and then take a day off to learn to fly. It was hard work, the physical demands and long hours of loading followed by hours of studying for my ground exams. My first goal was to be allowed to fly the aircraft without my instructor sitting next to me, a situation known as going solo. On average, this normally took between ten and fifteen hours of instruction. You also had to pass two of the ground examinations before they could allow you to fly by yourself. These were the Air Law and Radio Operator's Licence exams. It made sense to make sure that a pilot could not take to the skies alone if he did not understand the rules of the air or how to operate his radio using the correct phraseology. Therefore, I made sure that I had these exams tucked away under my belt in the optimistic hope that they would soon allow me to fly by myself. As my hours gradually increased towards the required number to fly alone, so did the excitement and to be honest, so did the nervousness. At the end of each flight, as we practised take-offs, circuit flying and landings, there was always that anticipation that they would send me off on my first solo flight.

One of the most difficult things about being an instructor, as I would one day find out for myself, is knowing when to allow your student to fly alone. It is easy to be overcautious and wait until your student did everything perfectly. However, very few pilots, regardless of experience, can achieve that standard. If, however, you keep asking your student to fly circuit after circuit, landing after landing, then eventually, they will lose confidence and repeating the same mistakes, they will invent new ones. Send someone into the air without the skill and confidence to make sure they can get safely down again also shortens your career as a flying instructor. The trick is for both student and instructor to feel happy and this is not always a straightforward task. Today was that day, although I had absolutely no idea of what the day had in store for me, when I arrived at the flying club that morning. The plan was for a one-hour flight followed by an afternoon studying for the remaining ground exams.

The first circuit of the day went reasonably well. The take-off was a little untidy, but I climbed straight ahead until I started a gentle turn to the left. The circuit at any airport comprises four segments, starting with the climb out from the runway, then a ninety-degree climbing turn, left or right depending on the direction of the circuit. This is followed by another ninety-degree turn to position the aircraft on the downwind leg levelling off at one thousand feet and flying in the opposite direction to the runway, to allow you to set up for an approach to the runway back in the original direction. Once you have flown a sufficient distance past the runway, another ninety degrees descending turn puts you on a base leg and you fly on the heading until you make a last turn to line up with the runway. Whilst doing all this and watching your height and speed, you tell air traffic control when you are on the downwind leg and turning onto the final approach. You also have to perform the after-take-off checks, the downwind checks, and finally your landing checks. I now understood why it was so important to have all these checklists fully memorised as there was no time to get a checklist out and read it. To get each part of the circuit, with the changing heights, speeds and headings all correct and then carry out a smooth landing, was a little like trying to rub your stomach and pat your head at the same time. You also have to speak to the air traffic controller and carry out all your checks. There were so many things you had to get right at the right time. To bring them all together at the same time and do it consistently was a tough ask. However, I bravely fought my way around three circuits.

After each landing, we performed what is known as a 'touch and go'. Basically, after landing, instead of slowing down and taxying off the runway, you apply full power and take off again. At the point of applying full power to start the next circuit, it was noticeable that the aircraft wanted to turn left as power was increased and at one point, I forgot to allow for this and we headed towards the control tower. The pitch of the controller's voice sounded a little higher when I told him we were flying downwind. Lesson learned and I would make sure I never did that again! After my third landing, I was asked to taxi back to the holding point at the start of the runway. After performing all my pre-take-off checks, my instructor left with the words, "Good luck! Fly one circuit only! Try not to break anything!" How rude, I thought! Maybe, I had upset him with my last landing or maybe he did not fancy another flypast of the control tower or maybe, just maybe, he thought I could fly. So, there I was, two aircraft ahead of me, both patiently awaiting permission to depart. I heard a voice asking for permission to take off; the voice sounded strangely familiar, unsurprisingly really, as I realised that it was my voice. Gosh, I sounded great, I thought, almost as if I knew what I was doing. At least I sounded like a pilot, even if deep down, I knew that I was feeling very nervous and unsure of myself.

"You are cleared for the take-off, report downwind." Were these to be the last words I would ever hear?

One thing about being alone in the aircraft for the first time is that the weight of the aircraft's load has suddenly halved. In my case, the instructor's absence had an even greater effect, as he was, let's say, a man of ample proportions. The aircraft no longer had the extra burden aboard and responded accordingly. I shot along the runway and before I knew what was happening, I was hurled into the air, using about half of the normal runway distance. The nose of the aircraft was pointing skywards at an alarming angle and I fought to bring the aircraft back under control. At what I thought was eight hundred feet, the point at which we normally started out to turn towards the downwind leg, it amazed me to see we were at one thousand two hundred feet and still climbing. This was terrible news. To fly in the circuit, you had to be at one thousand feet as there could easily be another aircraft passing overhead at two thousand feet preparing to descend to join the circuit. Instinctively, I pushed the nose of the aircraft down, forgetting to reduce the power. The aircraft stopped climbing but as the manoeuvre was so extreme, I continued to climb and was only prevented from hitting the roof by my seatbelt. At least I had stopped the climb. However, we were now pointing at the ground and the speed was increasing at an alarming rate. Pulling back as hard as I could, I immediately reduced the power to stop the speed increasing. Suddenly, we were back to the starting point, climbing like mad, but this time with no power, the speed started reducing, again at an alarming rate. The whole affair was like a bucking bronco. All I needed was a cowboy hat to wave about to complete the analogy.

Before it got completely out of hand, I remembered the advice that an airplane likes to fly and it's normally the pilot that impedes this. I set the power at the normal setting and let go of the controls. Slowly, the aircraft, free from my clumsy interference, settled down into a more or less straight-and-level attitude. Phew, thank God for that. During all this excitement, I had completely forgotten to tell air traffic control that I was downwind or as close to it as I could manage. I had forgotten all my checks as I struggled to find the runway which should have been on the left. It was nowhere to be seen. How the hell had that happened? It was then that I noticed I was heading off towards Brighton, a place I am normally pleased to visit. However, today was not the time and I quickly turned back towards where I hoped the airfield was. At precisely this moment, the controller asked for my position as he could no longer see me. Miracle upon miracle, the airfield suddenly reappeared and I found myself in an ideal position to turn onto the final approach. I replied that I was shortly turning finals to land and I was amazed once again, at how calm my voice sounded. The controller confirmed that he now had me in sight and he cleared me to land. Once again, I had forgotten my checks and I hurriedly tried to go through my landing checklist from memory. However, my memory had other ideas and after being so badly frightened over the past few minutes, it had decided it didn't want to play anymore. At this point, the runway was getting close. I had two choices, attempt a missed approach and do it all again or just hope for the best. I opted for the latter choice and closed the throttle and probably my eyes, I couldn't be sure. I put all my trust in the little aeroplane and thankfully, it didn't let me down as eventually, we stopped bouncing enough for me to taxi away from the runway towards the clubhouse. Shutting everything down as quickly as I could, I sat there staring out of the windscreen not quite believing what I had just done. Once my hands had stopped shaking, I thanked my aircraft for bringing me safely back to earth. I strolled back towards the clubhouse, just as my instructor came out to greet me.

"So, how did it go?" he inquired casually.

"Yep, not too bad at all, thank you," I replied, keeping my voice as level as I could. I followed him, as usual, for our debrief. At least, thank God, he had not been there to see my humiliation. Settling down in the briefing room, I was asked to draw a normal circuit on the whiteboard and mark each point where the pitch and power needed to be changed and when we should do our checks and radio calls. Luckily, my memory had returned from wherever it had been hiding and I drew a perfect circuit, complete with all the required information. I sat back down, feeling very pleased with myself.

My instructor then stood up and drew a very different circuit with different heights and speeds, which extended as far as Brighton and back. There were no checks on this circuit and the radio calls were all in the wrong places. He asked me if I recognised this circuit and sheepishly, I had to admit that I had a faint idea of where it had come from.

"Well," he said, "at least we are ahead on one thing: I was going to demonstrate how to land the aircraft without the use of flaps, but I see you have already done that." How the hell did he know all this, I thought to myself. It was a ploy that one day soon, I would use myself. However, for the moment, I was completely in the dark.

Feeling very dejected, I decided that the afternoon ground school could wait, so I went to the pub instead.

Chapter 6

A Pilot at Last - Now for the Difficult Bit

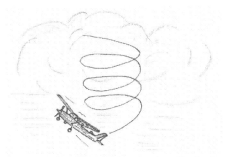

After two pints of beer, things looked a little less depressing. That is the beauty of alcohol. It slowly dawned on me I should celebrate. I had flown solo for the first time. There would never be another time I could say that. The more I drank, the less significant my flying errors became. The take-off was nearly perfect, the climb out was as straight as it was possible to fly. The circuit was maybe a little too wide, but in retrospect, I had really enjoyed the aerial views of Brighton and its beaches. Maybe, I had gone a little too high, but what's a few hundred feet in the greater scheme of things? My checklists? I could not really excuse myself for forgetting those. If I had remembered all I had been taught, I would have put the flaps down for landing, but I consoled myself with the thought I had been fortunate that my aircraft did not have retractable landing gear. Forgetting to put that down would have made the landing much shorter and a lot noisier. Come to think of it, I realised that my landing was good, considering I had no flaps. In fact, I was rather proud of myself for managing such a feat of airmanship. By the time I left the pub, I had convinced myself and anyone who would listen, that I had probably flown as good a first solo as it was possible to fly. With that happy thought in mind, I had just enough common sense to realise that maybe, driving home was pushing my luck just a little too far for one day. The two-mile walk would also, I hoped, clear my head a little, so off I set, a pilot at last.

The thing about leaving your car two miles from where you live is that it's vitally important you remember this before you pass out and allow for the extra time it will take to retrieve it in the morning. I was on the early shift the next day and I found myself at five in the morning staring at the space that should have been occupied by my ancient and battered car. It had been another auction bargain and I really couldn't believe anyone would be bothered to steal such a contraption. Slowly, memories of the previous night's drinking marathon surfaced from the thoughts rushing through my very hungover brain. "Damn, damn, damn," I heard myself saying repeatedly as I set off for a brisk early morning run. I have a personal hatred of being late for anything. I am usually very early for any appointments and I have never been late for work. Today, sadly, would be the first time I had let myself and my workmates down. Breathlessly I rushed into the loading operations room only to be told that my loading team was already at the aircraft's side. Luckily, they were loading a short haul aircraft, which they did without my help. Had this been a larger aircraft, there would have been a lengthy delay and hundreds of people would have been affected by my lateness. I vowed there and then that I would never again allow this to happen and forty years later, I have still kept this promise to myself.

Two days later, I once again presented myself at the flying club, by now, a much humbler student. I even resisted swapping the model aircraft around, something I could never have resisted a few days earlier. I realised that to get through this course, I needed to give it my total concentration and commitment. After a coffee in the reception area, I reported to my assigned briefing room fully ready to apologise for my appalling attempt at solo flying and for not attending the subsequent ground school. As I was a few minutes early, I got my books out and prepared for the next stage of my course. The door suddenly opened and who but the chief flying instructor himself should walk in. I was expecting my normal instructor and had prepared what I considered a near perfect apology for my efforts last week. This new turn of events was very unnerving. More in hope than expectation, I pointed out this was room number five and he may have made a mistake. Sadly, he had not. Once again, I was taken back to my school days as he settled himself at the desk in front of me. My heart sank even more when he produced my training file and slowly digested its contents.

"So, how do you think it's going? "he enquired.

This was definitely a loaded question. Did I admit that I had made a complete mess of my first solo flight and had scared myself, my instructor, the air traffic controller and anyone else who was unlucky enough to be around? Or did I play it cool and hope that my instructor had not been too unkind in his comments and that there were not too many complaints from the other people involved?

"Good, all things considered," I replied, my mouth once again getting way ahead of everything else.

He looked straight at me, his eyes never moving. I wished he would say something and when eventually he did, I wished he had kept quiet.

"Let's go find out, shall we?" he said and with that, he turned around and walked out. I was not sure what to do. We always had a briefing before a flight. I expected a briefing now. I wanted a briefing otherwise how would I know what to expect? I hesitated. Maybe, he had gone to get a coffee, or to find a model aircraft. After a few minutes, I thought I had better find out where he was. To my utter disappointment, I saw him walking towards the aircraft, so gathering my things, I rushed after him. After a very thorough check of everything outside of the aircraft, eventually, we settled into our seats.

"Right, I want you to taxi out and fly three circuits," he informed me. "I want you to call out all of your checks as you complete them and please just forget that I am here," … like that was going to happen!

Since my last flight, I had spent many hours drawing out a perfect circuit and then filling in all the points where checks and radio calls needed to be made. I had also memorised all the power and pitch settings needed to get the correct airspeed and aircraft attitude. On paper, I considered myself a bit of an ace. Could I possibly put this into practise on the actual aircraft? If this was to be the premature end to my flying career, I was determined to go down fighting. We taxied out to the holding point and I performed all my checks, calling each one out loud. I then asked for permission to take off and to fly three circuits. The tower cleared us for take-off after the aircraft that was just landing. I had never felt so nervous in my life. Gone was the cheery instructor who always seemed to be on my side and would help me with little suggestions as the flight progressed. Instead, I had this headmaster type who seemed determined to stop my career before it had really got started. With these thoughts at the forefront of my mind, we slowly taxied into position to await our take-off clearance. No words were spoken between us.

Upon being cleared for take-off, I slowly increased power making sure that we stayed in a straight line. At exactly the correct speed, I gently raised the nose of the aircraft to the correct angle. We were airborne and I felt surprisingly calm. I flew the first circuit more or less at the correct height and heading and remembered all my radio calls and checks. Eventually, we lined up with the runway and this time, I had my flaps exactly where I wanted them. The power was correct; the heading was correct; the attitude was correct. All I had to do now was allow the aircraft to fly itself with only the minimum inputs from me. I had been taught to fly the aircraft towards the runway, until the edges of the runway filled the side windows. At this point, I had to reduce the power to idle and gently raise the nose of the aircraft as it descended the final few feet onto the runway surface. I knew this manoeuvre was known as flaring the aircraft, the most vital part of any landing. Perform this flare too early and the aircraft will climb away again until it runs out of flying speed, known as a stall, definitely not something you wanted to try close to the ground. If you flared the aircraft too late, then the aircraft would fly itself into the ground, again not the best way to return to earth. There are many variants of these two extremes where you flare a little early, the aircraft climbs, but you lower the nose and attempt another flare if there is sufficient runway left. If you flare a little too late, the aircraft will literally bump back into the air and you can either attempt another landing or fly away again for another circuit and landing. I prayed that neither would be required as we crossed over the threshold of the runway and I slowly closed the throttle and raised the nose and waited, waited. Nothing! Where the hell was the runway? I was sure it was just below us last time I looked.

"Very good," I heard a voice say. "Shall we try another one to make sure that was not just luck?" I couldn't believe I had landed without my noticing. Thanking heaven that he hadn't realised, I smoothly increased power and launched us back into the sky. The next circuit was not quite to the same standard, but it seemed to be acceptable as after my next landing, I was instructed to taxi back to the flying club. I was wondering about the third circuit and was just about to shut the engine down when I was told to leave it running. As he unstrapped himself, he left the aircraft with the parting words, "Now see if you can do that without me sitting next to you." Without another word, he walked away. I was never to fly with him again as he left the flying club a few weeks later. I only hoped that it had nothing to do with me.

Over the next few days, I continued to fly more circuits by myself, interspersed with more flights with my friendly instructor. I gained more confidence as we practised leaving the circuit to fly off on short cross-country flights. I learned very basic map reading, which enabled me to find the airfield again. In reality, I was very fortunate to be flying from Shoreham Airport; it was by the sea and only a short distance from a very large power station chimney. It was almost impossible to get lost, although I must admit, occasionally, it was a close call.

We then learned how to re-join the circuit after our local flying. To do this safely, we had to fly overhead the airfield at two thousand feet and descend on the 'dead side' of it to join the other aircraft already in the circuit at one thousand feet. I thought this was a strange way to describe the part of the airfield over which to perform this. However, it seemed to work and if the active circuit was right-handed, then we descended on the left side and vice versa. It took a little getting used to and it quickly became apparent that you really had to know your right hand from your left hand if you wanted to get on in this game. Once I more or less had got the hang of this, they allowed me to fly short local flights by myself.

This was the first time that I really enjoyed myself. Suddenly, I had time to relax and take in the wonderful views. Now, I was not occupied by heights, headings, radio calls and checks. I headed off to the west of Shoreham towards the larger seaside town of Worthing. Here, I performed a series of lazy turns, climbs and descents, always keeping an eye out for other aircraft. The feeling of complete freedom is difficult to overemphasise. It was a heady mixture. After twenty minutes of sheer joy, I decided that I had better return to the airfield. This is where, as I mentioned earlier, Shoreham really comes into its own. I turned eastward and there in the distance, was the chimney of the power station. Head towards it, call the air traffic controller for permission to re-join the circuit and before I knew it, I was safely downwind performing my 'before landing' checks and requesting permission to land. With an enormous smile on my face, I taxied back and shut the aircraft down. Walking back towards the clubhouse I really felt for the first time that I knew what I was doing, it was a feeling that was not to last very long.

At the very start of my training, they had warned me of the fatal consequences of the dreaded stall. Basically, an aircraft has to be moving forward at a certain speed for the wings to generate enough lift to keep the aircraft in the air. This speed varies according to factors such as the weight of the aircraft, and if you have the flaps or landing gear down. My aircraft had its undercarriage permanently down, so the stall speed depended on how much flap or power we had at the time of the stall. Therefore, we had to practise stalls with various settings of both power and flaps.

I was shown a very simple approach to a stall and how to recover from it before they allowed me to fly solo. To do this, we slowly closed the throttle and gently raised the nose of the aircraft. The speed quickly reduced towards our expected stall speed of around fifty knots, or fifty-five miles an hour. As the speed slowed, the air flowing across the wings would break down and I felt this as a vibration throughout the aircraft, a little like driving over a cobbled road at speed. This is the first sign of a stall and it is vital to know how to recover from this potentially deadly situation. The first thing to do is lower the nose of the aircraft, which would allow the airflow to return to a smooth flow over the wings, creating lift once again. The next vital action was to re-apply full power which would prevent the aircraft from losing too much height, something that could save your life if you were at a low altitude. After a demonstration, I had to show that I could recover safely. It was quite a gentle exercise and I felt happy that I knew how to recognise an oncoming stall and how to recover from it.

We now had reached the point in my training where we were required to fully stall the aircraft and learn how to recover. This was very far from being a simple or gentle manoeuvre. In fact, it nearly scared me to death! We taxied out as usual after a long and detailed briefing. Even my instructor seemed a little quieter than usual and I was soon to discover why. We took off and climbed away to find ourselves a quiet piece of sky where, hopefully, we could practise without other aircraft to get in our way.

We climbed higher than I had been before, up to five thousand feet, which was as high as we could ascend without entering the airspace reserved for the large commercial airliners. After a very good look all around and below, I was asked to demonstrate the power-off-flaps-up stall I had practised before. However, this time, I was told to ignore the pre-stall buffet and to continue to raise the nose of the aircraft. I was apprehensive. The poor aircraft did not enjoy being put into this position and was doing its very best to warn me not to be so stupid. The buffet, a sort of vibration, became worse until suddenly, the stall warning horn shouted out to alert me to the impending hazard. I was desperately keen to do as the aircraft wanted and lower the nose and apply power. However, I was told to keep raising the nose, until eventually, we entered the full stall.

Now, the full stall is basically the aircraft giving up its attempts at staying in the air. It has done everything it can to warn you. Probably, you have ignored everything and now, the aircraft can no longer fly. The airflow over the wings has now completely broken down and the wings have lost all of their lifting power. You are stalled! However, the aircraft still has one trick up its sleeve. As you reach the stall, with the nose pointing towards the sky, if you let go of the controls, the nose will drop. This will un-stall the wings. If you apply power, then once again, all is well as long as you have sufficient space below you to recover. Well, I thought, that was not too bad, a little uncomfortable perhaps, but my stomach had stayed where it belonged and I felt pleased with myself. It was job done.

"Right, now let's try a proper stall," were not the words I was expecting to hear. "Let's go back and have a cold beer after scaring ourselves," would have been much more welcome.

Instead, we then went through a series of flaps-down-power-on stalls and after these, my stomach was definitely not where it belonged. The flaps, the part of the wing you see moving up and down at the back of the wing when the aircraft takes off or lands, are designed to allow the aircraft to fly more slowly without stalling. Whereas the stall speed may be fifty-five knots without flaps, once you lower full flaps, this can be reduced to forty-five knots, very useful during take-off and landing. However, the downside to this is that if you stall the aircraft with the flaps out, the warnings are much shorter and the effect much more dramatic. Instead of a gradual buffet and a gentle nose drop, the aircraft almost without warning, flings itself at the ground. Sadly, I had to show two recoveries from these stalls. Just when I thought things couldn't get any worse, they did.

"Right, let's look at the worst type of stall," he said. Surely, I must have misheard? What could be worse than what we had just done? I looked across at my instructor and hoped to see a smile spread across his face with him mouthing the words, "only joking." Instead, I thought I saw a slight frown. This was definitely not a good sign.

"Right, I am going to show a full-flap-full-power stall," he said, a sentence that even to this day, sends a slight shiver down my spine.

The object of the exercise was to show how dangerous it was to stall an aircraft in this configuration. Sadly, this could be and frequently had been done when a pilot had allowed his speed to get dangerously low on take-off or landing.

During previous stalls, the aircraft had behaved in a reasonable and predictable manner. The nose would drop and the wings stayed level. However, we now had the effect of flaps and the fact that the engine was at full power. This meant that the nose was considerably higher when the stall occurred, a very uncomfortable position to be in. We also now had the airflow from the propeller washing air across our wings, which meant that one wing would stall before the other. This resulted in not only the nose dropping at an alarming rate but also the aircraft tipping onto its side as one wing had stalled before the other one. Just to make matters worse, you had no idea which wing was going to drop first.

I sat tight in my seat, desperately wishing I was somewhere, anywhere, else. Slowly, very slowly, the aircraft's nose rose as my instructor showed the full stall. I couldn't believe just how high the nose was. We were pointing at the stars. Well, it was day but where I thought the stars would be.

Suddenly, I felt a very large buffet and heard the stall warning horn, no gentle and prolonged warnings this time. The next moment, the nose dropped as if a giant hand grabbed it and pulled it earthwards. At this precise moment, the giant hand took hold of the left wing and threw that earthwards.

I was shocked. I had no idea of where was up and where was down, which was sky and which was earth.

I heard the words, "And recover." I was not sure if they were aimed at me or the aircraft. Whichever it was, eventually, we returned to something like normal flight. It took me a minute to breathe properly. When asked if I was ready to try the same manoeuvre, I wanted to burst into tears. Instead, I replied, "I would love to try it."

Now, the thing about this type of stall, when you are an instructor, is that you have two unknowns, the student as always, and this time also the aircraft. Normally, an experienced instructor knows exactly how the aircraft will behave. This is not always the case with a student who may suddenly pull instead of push or turn instead of going straight ahead. This can be anticipated and allowed for until a student is proficient enough to be predictable. However, this is the only time that an instructor faces two unpredictable animals at the same time. During the first full stall, the aircraft could flick either way and needs an immediate and correct action to prevent the ultimate out-of-control situation, a spin. The poor instructor does not know which way the aircraft will go and how the student will react. It is not a comfortable position to be in. I was sternly warned to let go of the controls immediately if told to do so. With these words ringing in my ears, I checked the airspace around and below me. Once satisfied that we were alone and with great trepidation, I raised the nose of the aircraft. Higher and higher it rose. The engine, at full power, protested. The propeller strained as it tried to grab at the slowing airflow. The aircraft, the engine, the propeller and I were all unhappy at this treatment. Just when I thought I could not raise the nose any higher, I felt the terrible buffet and noise as the aircraft stalled. Immediately, it flipped to the right this time and threw itself at the ground.

"And recover," came the words from my instructor.

No, let's see how this develops, I thought. It could get interesting. In reality, I tried to lower the nose to un-stall the aircraft, apply the correct rudder to stop the aircraft spinning and lastly, to reduce power as the airspeed increased as we headed earthwards. Although really badly shaken, somehow, I got the aircraft flying again. I had had enough and when asked if I would like to try another stall; it took a lot of willpower not to use physical violence. "Oh well, take me back to the airfield and show me a flapless landing," was his reply and I was sure I detected a sigh of relief. The landing itself was far from my best, the speed was high and the nose was low, but for the moment that's the way I liked my aircraft. The debrief was short and to the point; I think we both had alcohol on our minds.

I had a week before my next flight and my instructor's parting words informing me that we were going to explore what happens when a stall goes wrong, literally had my head spinning. It was going to be a long week. The time quickly passed and I found myself, once again, in what I rightly considered to be the danger zone. We were about to spin the aircraft.

An unintentional spin is basically the result of a stall where the wing has dropped and the pilot fails to recover. I say unintentional as believe it or not, there are pilots who do this for fun. More fool them, I have always thought. Once the aircraft spins earthwards, the rate of turn will quickly increase if the pilot does not follow the correct recovery procedure. It is a most alarming position to find yourself in. You are pointing directly at the ground, which is revolving like mad. In reality, it is you and the aircraft which are spinning but that's just detail when you find yourself in this position. To recover from this, you have to decide which way you are spinning, not always a simple task and then use your foot or rudder pedals to apply full pressure in the opposite direction. Hopefully, this will stop the spinning and then you can gently pull the nose back to where it should be and adjust the power to return to level flight.

At the time I was training, in the late 1970s, it was a legal requirement to enter a spin, allow the speed of rotation to increase with at least three complete turns and then to recover, which I can assure is not a straightforward or easy thing to do. At the time, I was in my early twenties, fit and I thought, brave. Spinning scared the heck out of me. I could only imagine what it could do to someone learning to fly in their retirement years. Luckily, the authorities came to their senses and took spinning out of the curriculum. They realised, too late for me, that pilots were far more likely to kill themselves practising spinning than they were to kill themselves in an unintentional spin. Therefore, they left it to the pilots who enjoyed extreme sports. However, this was a long way in the future and today was the day I was going to have to show that I could spin an aircraft and live to tell the story, something I evidently did.

My instructor met me with the words, "I hope you have not eaten anything today. I do not want to wear your breakfast." I quickly assured him that not only had I forsaken breakfast, but I had also hardly eaten anything for the past day or so. This seemed to reassure him and off we went to find our aircraft after the usual briefing. I declined his offer of a coffee which again seemed to improve his mood. Mine was definitely on the decline.

Once again, there we were, our nose pointing skywards, the engine and propeller screaming their displeasure and myself strapped into my seat, as tightly as I had ever been. "Just follow me through on the controls," were the last words I heard before the aircraft's nose snapped earthwards and the left wing disappeared completely, I prayed that it was still attached to the aircraft. Apparently, we were in a right-hand spin, although for all I could tell, we were upside down and going backwards. The intensity of the spin increased, pushing me deep into my seat. Everything was happening at an incredible speed.

The words, "and recover," were music to my ears as the aircraft gradually slowed its spin rate until we were in just a steep dive. My instructor slowly raised the nose and applied power as we returned to normal flight.

"Right, your turn now," he informed me. "And don't forget, it can spin either way," he emphasised, hardly reassuring words.

I checked we were alone in the sky. Anyone watching must have been convinced we were mad or in deep trouble and to be fair, I would have agreed with them, if asked.

Higher and higher went the nose, the speed came back slowly at first and then, as the wings lost their lift, the speed reduced very quickly. Just as the buffet and stall warning started, I recovered.

"No. No. No," shouted my instructor with a few expletives mixed in. "You have to let it stall. Even then, don't recover, let it spin."

Damn, I thought to myself; I hoped that I might just have got away with that.

Right then, I gritted my teeth and thought just how hard can this be? I held this thought to the point the nose of the aircraft was pointing at the ground and the right wing passed over my head.

"I will tell you when to recover," my instructor informed me in a slightly higher pitch than normal.

The aircraft spun to the left, each rotation noticeably faster and more dynamic than the previous one. By the fourth spin, I had definitely had enough and desperately wanted to be somewhere, anywhere else.

"And recover," he said, finally.

As instructed, I immediately applied a full opposite rudder to stop the spin before I could gently raise the nose, at the same time, reducing the power until we were once again in level flight.

Well, that was the plan. I pushed the right rudder pedal and to my horror, the aircraft increased its rate of spin. Had I made the fatal error of applying the wrong rudder? Just as I was about to swap feet, the aircraft stopped spinning as quickly as it had started. After I had managed to get the aircraft flying straight and level, I asked my instructor, I must admit, in a very high-pitched voice, what the hell had just happened. His reply did not fill me with confidence, "Yep, it sometimes does that, but not very often." I headed back to the airfield before he had the chance to ask me to do another one.

Chapter 7

Getting Lost

I was now at the stage where I could take off, fly about a bit, re-join the circuit, land and stay as far away from a spin as I could, without making a complete fool of myself. So far, so good. I almost felt like a pilot … almost. It was time for me to fly the nest, so to speak. Up to this point, I had no genuine concerns about where I was. I had the English Channel on one side, Brighton and Worthing on two other sides, and the South Downs to the north. As long as I stayed within this bubble, I was safe. It was just about impossible to get lost. I was flying in the aviation equivalent of a fool's paradise. Up and down the coast I flew until it was time to go home, aim for the big chimney, keep close to the coast or the Downs and hey presto, up would pop the airfield. It worked a treat every time and gave me a false sense of security. I was all too soon to find out just how difficult it is to map read from an aircraft.

My ground school instructor, the wonderful Martin Peel, gently led me through the complexities of differing charts, slide rules, wind vectors and all the other skills needed to navigate from one airfield to another without upsetting anyone. There is also a very real danger of wandering into restricted airspace. I was having to share the crowded skies over the UK with all the commercial and military aviation, neither of which take kindly to a tiny two-seater aircraft flown by a pilot with a paper map on his lap, blundering his way through their airspace. Outside of my Shoreham comfort zone, I had two of the busiest airports in the world less than fifteen minutes flying time away and the Royal Air Force was not that far away either. To prevent me from competing with an airliner or a military fighter, they had carved the airspace up into sections. The civilian passenger aircraft flew in controlled airspace, which as the name suggests, is controlled by an air traffic control centre. Military aircraft also had their own slice of airspace. I knew the small amount of sky that was not taken up by these two authorities as uncontrolled airspace and that was my new playground. The major problem was knowing where one section of airspace began and another ended. Also, you needed to know exactly where you were at all times, otherwise you could easily find yourself in huge trouble. Heathrow, Gatwick, or any of the large military airfields nearby took a very dim view of any private pilot ruining their carefully laid out plans.

This was the beginning of the eighties and computers, satellite navigation, mobile phones and all the other technologies we have available to us today, were science fiction. I had to learn to navigate in more or less the same way as all the pilots that had gone before me, and that was known as dead-reckoning navigation. Basically, I had a large map covering the South of England. On this map were marked all the airfields and the airspace around them. The map also showed where the controlled airspace began and at what height. For example, around dear old Shoreham they only controlled the airspace at the airport or a few thousand feet above the ground. As long as I stayed below this height and let the Shoreham controller know when I wanted to land, or overfly his airport, all was well.

If I wanted to fly somewhere else, I had to work out a route that would keep me away from the forbidden, controlled airspace. This is not as easy as it sounds. For a start, sadly, there are no roads or road signs in the sky. To make matters worse, where you point the aircraft is not necessarily the way the aircraft will go. You have to allow for the effect that wind will have on the aircraft's progress along your chosen route. As an example, if you want to fly to an airport directly north of the airport you are at, then taking off and flying north will only work if there is no wind - a very rare thing - once you get airborne. However, if there is a strong wind from, let's say the west, then if you pointed the nose of your aircraft north, it would mean that the wind would push you a long way to the right of where you wanted to go and probably, into the dreaded controlled airspace. To stop getting hopelessly lost, you had to allow for the effect the wind would have on the progress or track of your aircraft along your route. To make matters worse, the effect the wind has will vary each time you change your heading. To make things even more complicated, you had to accurately understand the strength and direction of the wind in the first place to allow for it. I decided that it seemed almost impossible to get anywhere without getting horrendously lost. How right I was to be concerned.

Our task today was to take off, climb directly above the airport with a series of climbing turns and once at two thousand feet, set off to fly to Blackbushe Airport, a journey of around fifty miles which should take about thirty minutes, depending on the wind. If the wind was against us, it would take longer and if it was behind us, it would take less time to get there. The trick of this navigation business, I had been assured, was all in the preparation before take-off. So, there I was in the classroom, my map spread out in front of me, desperately trying to find this Blackbushe Airport they meant me to navigate my way to. If I could not find the airport on a map sitting in a classroom, what chance had I got of finding the real thing? An aviation map is a peculiar beast compared to the ones we would use when driving. There are no simple roads with towns, cities and villages marked along the way. Oh no, that would have been far too easy, so the cartographer who drew my map, put in all those things together with as much detail as he could fit in. The overall effect to the untrained eye was a little like a child had scribbled over the entire map, or a spider had walked into an inkpot and then wandered all over it. In short, it was very difficult to read and that was why I was struggling to find Blackbushe. Seeing my frustration, my instructor wandered over to see how I was getting on. He stood beside me for a few seconds and then without saying a word, he leaned slowly forward and rotated the map until it was the right way up. As he walked away, I distinctly heard a loud sigh. To this day, I am not sure if it was from him, me, or the both of us. One thing I was sure of, it was not a good start.

Eventually, I was ready to put all my calculations to the test. I had drawn my proposed route on the plastic-coated map; I had calculated the effect the wind would have on my progress; I had written a series of checkpoints I could use to chart my progress; I had written the radio frequencies I would need to contact the various air traffic controllers; and finally, I had worked out how much fuel I would need to get there and get back again. Luckily, it had not occurred to me I could have cycled to Blackbushe in the time it had taken me to prepare for the flight. That realisation would have dampened my enthusiasm.

With my map and flight log proudly sitting on my lap and my instructor looking slightly bored, we bumped our way over to the take-off runway. It was a good take-off, well apart from the fact that my map and log fell off my lap and found their way into the back of the aircraft as we climbed away. The plan was to climb directly above the airfield and then set off on the course I had spent so long calculating. I had not planned that my map and flight log would no longer be in a place where I could access them without leaving my seat. With my instructor holding his head in his hands, I thought vacating my seat would probably not go down too well. Rather sheepishly, I asked him if he would mind undoing his straps and retrieve my navigational equipment. Luckily, with only a few shakes of his head, he agreed. I thought his remarks as to what I would do if he had not been there were slightly unfair and I reminded him I would have put them on the seat he was now occupying. A slight victory, I thought, as I prepared to set course on my first ever cross-country flight, map and flight log safely back in place. I felt very confident as I started my stopwatch, settled onto my calculated heading and waited for my first checkpoint to appear on the horizon.

Now reading a map whilst you are walking, cycling or driving is no simple matter. There is a definite skill required to understand all the various lines and squiggles on a road or walking map. To help you along your way, you have road signs, villages, towns and cities have names; no two looks alike. It would be very difficult to arrive in Birmingham and think you were in Manchester. If all else fails, you can usually stop and ask someone where you are. Assuming they are not also map reading, there is a good chance they will know the answer. None of this, however, is available to you once you leave the ground. Whilst even I could differentiate the land from the sea and recognise a seaside town with a pier and marina, this gave me a false sense of competence as I pointed the nose of the aircraft northwards towards unchartered territories.

I had calculated that I should arrive over my first turning point after twelve minutes. The town I was aiming for was a medium size dwelling with several roads and a river to help me identify it. It was also very important as it marked the area where controlled airspace began. I had to stay to the left of this town or I could end up causing havoc with one of the busiest airports in the world. I had noted the exact time I had set course from overhead Shoreham and the tension mounted as the minutes ticked by. As we approached the ten-minute mark, I looked directly ahead and slightly to the left and right just in case the wind was not as I had expected or allowed for. Suddenly, I saw Midhurst more or less exactly where I expected it to be. Relief flooded through me and I relaxed as I altered course to fly directly overhead to confirm my position before setting off on the next stage of my flight. My plan was to fly in a circle over the town and then settle onto my new heading for Guildford and then the last turn which would take me to my destination at Blackbushe.

Aerial map reading has a golden rule when trying to identify where you are and that is to always, always read from the ground to your map. When you try to identify a town, look at what you can see and then check that the town on the map has the same characteristics. For example, you look at a town from two thousand feet above and you see a major road running through it together with a railway line running from east to west. There is also a river and a church. The trick is to note all this and then look at your map to make sure the town on the ground agrees with the town you are looking at on the map. If it does, then great! You know exactly where you are. However, as I was to learn on more than one occasion, the temptation is to do this process in the opposite way. You think you are overhead of a certain town which has, let's say, a road running from north to south and a river from west to east. You look from your map and you become determined to find the road and river you are desperately looking for. You see a road that almost runs from north to south and ah yes, there's the river, not quite running west to east but close. And yes, a church, I'm expecting a church and there is a church. It's not quite where I expected it to be but it's pretty close. Suddenly, you have convinced yourself that the town on your map is the town you are flying over. So, you set off on your new heading waiting for the next turning point. If you have misidentified a town, quickly, you will become more and more desperate that the next town is the one you are expecting to see. Eventually, you become so keen to match up what you are expecting to see with what you actually see that all your map reading skills disappear. You have become totally, utterly and hopelessly lost, not a situation to find yourself in some of the busiest airspace in the world.

By now, as you have probably guessed, I had fallen into this trap. There I was, circling over Petworth, busily convincing myself that it was Midhurst. Just as I was setting a course that would have taken me overhead Gatwick instead of Guildford, my instructor informed me, he had control, then reached over, grabbed my map and flight log and threw them back into the rear of the aircraft. As I looked at him in astonishment and a certain amount of indignation, I asked as politely as I could manage, why he had done that. As he changed our heading by a rather enormous amount to the left, his reply left me rather crestfallen.

"You obviously cannot use either a map or a log, so they are both better off where I found them after take-off," he barked at me. With that rather hurtful remark, he pointed the aircraft back towards Shoreham, handed control back to me with the instructions, "Just fly back to the coast and turn either left or right until you find Shoreham."

Happy that not even I could mess that up, he leaned back in his seat for a well-earned afternoon nap. My first cross-country flight had not gone as well as I had hoped.

Chapter 8

Back on Track

Now, after every flight, we had a debrief, or a post-flight review of what went well and what didn't go so well. To help illustrate this, my instructor drew a vertical line down the middle of the whiteboard and then asked me to fill in both sides of the board, whilst he went to get a well-deserved coffee. Not one to overemphasise my failings, I wrote on the left side, all the things I thought had gone particularly well. Good take off, omitting the loss of my map, good climbing turn. On and on I went until the left side of the whiteboard was full. I now pondered the empty right side. All I could eventually come up with was that I had got slightly lost quite early into the flight. Satisfied that I had pretty well covered all the pertinent points, I settled back to await my instructor's return, only slightly concerned at the muffled laughter coming from the common room next door.

Half-drunk coffee in hand, he returned to the briefing room and with only a moment's hesitation, he erased the entire left side of the whiteboard. He then sat on the edge of his desk and asked me to read out what was left. Maybe, it was time I asked for a new instructor, as this one obviously could only see one side of a situation.

"Let me look at your map and flight plan," he said abruptly.

I had hoped that we might miss this bit out altogether and get onto the part where I could blame the weather forecaster for giving me such an obviously incorrect estimate of the wind at two thousand feet. No such luck. It took him less than ten seconds to understand how I had got so badly lost so quickly and why I was heading towards Gatwick and not Guildford. He tossed my flight plan back to me and asked me if I could work out what had happened. I carefully checked all my calculations based on the forecast wind, required heading and the speed of the aircraft over the ground. They all looked correct. However, as requested, I went over each calculation once again. Everything, again all looked perfectly fine. It then slowly, slowly dawned on me that all was not as it seemed. Surely, surely, I could not have made such a simple, yet potentially serious mistake. Another few minutes of checking everything confirmed that I could and had, made such a fundamental error. Sheepishly, I turned to my instructor but I found it difficult to look him directly in the eye.

"Hmm, I think I may have allowed for the wind", which was true, "but in the wrong direction," which sadly, was also true. This meant that instead of compensating for the wind blowing me off course, I had doubled its effect. Hardly surprising then, that I was pointing one way but flying another. Everything about the flight seemed doomed from the moment we set course from overhead Shoreham. He was waiting to see how far I got before I realised my mistake.

I headed back to my car and another week of loading aircraft, promising myself that I would never make such a stupid mistake again. It was time for some soul searching and maybe, my father had been right and I was not disciplined and organised enough to make a career out of flying. It was a long and hard week before once again, I presented myself for another attempt at a cross-country flight. I promised myself that it was going to be different, this time. Every calculation was checked and then double-checked. Because I had begun to understand myself and my limitations, I checked it all again. Maps and flight logs were safely stowed for take-off. I completed all the preparations before we even approached the aircraft. I felt unusually calm and nervous at the same time. I was going to give this flight my all and at the end of it, I would be the one to decide if I had the aptitude, ability and character to continue my flying training. Despite anything my instructor said, if I was unsure of myself, I would walk away and look for another career. Well, no pressure then as I slowly taxied the aircraft towards the runway.

The take-off was normal with no maps flying around. The climb to two thousand feet above Shoreham went well. I turned the aircraft onto my desired heading, started my stopwatch, and settled down to concentrate on keeping a constant height and heading. Ten minutes later, a small town appeared directly ahead. I looked down and immediately saw the roads, railway lines and rivers were an exact match with my map. Things were looking up, or maybe looking down would be a better description.

A short while later, a large town appeared on the nose with a ridge of high ground on either side. From my map, I was expecting to see Guildford in a gap within a long escarpment known as the Hog's Back. Sure enough, as the large red brick cathedral of Guildford appeared, I was, once again, rewarded for all my hard and diligent work. A last turn towards the northwest and I was expecting to see a large military airfield on the south side of the motorway, followed by a smaller civil airfield on the north side. To my utter delight, out of the haze, both airfields appeared more or less where I expected them and just as importantly, the time I had calculated that I would arrive.

There was no time for reflection as I now had to fly overhead Blackbushe and join their circuit. This was not as easy as it sounded as I had never landed at any airfield other than Shoreham. Fortunately, there is only one runway at Blackbushe. Unfortunately, it is a very long tarmac one, capable of handling large commercial airliners. Joining the circuit from overhead the airfield went well. I let down to one thousand feet on the dead side of the circuit, flew over the runway to join downwind behind two other aircraft. All was well and I completed my downwind checks in preparation to turn onto finals where I would complete my landing checklist. All looked normal until I was on my final approach when I realised that the runway in front of me was huge. I was used to landing on a short grass runway and I had been taught to judge my landing by the perspective of the runway edges as I crossed the threshold. All those usual visual clues were no longer there. Instead, I had this massive, black monstrosity filling the windscreen. I had always been of the persuasion that when in doubt, do nothing. I was in doubt now and so I did nothing. However, flaring an aircraft as you complete a landing as previously explained, is a basic procedure and you just have to do it.

I decided to do nothing, so I did not flare, as I really could not work out when to do so. The aircraft just flew straight into the runway. It decided that it did not like this at all and promptly bounced straight back into the air again. I was determined that I had not come all this way just to bounce down their runway. There was a lot of runway left, so I tried again, followed by another bounce. Finally, on the third attempt, we stayed on the runway and I taxied slowly off towards the parking area. As I shut the aircraft down and walked towards the control tower to register my arrival, or arrivals, I noticed a few heads turn to see who had just performed that interesting landing. Looking towards my instructor and raising my eyes at the same time, I did my best to deflect the blame. I fooled nobody.

After paying my landing fee, I headed for the air traffic controller's office to get my logbook stamped. The officer signed my book with a flourish whilst informing me I had used up more runway than a Boeing 737 that had arrived earlier that day. I was not sure how to take this, so I reminded him that the pilot of the 737 did not have to pay the landing fee out of his own pocket and as I had paid to use his runway, I may as well use all of it. Laughter followed me as I made my way back down the stairs towards my aircraft. It was time to leave the scene of my embarrassment.

The flight back to Shoreham was subdued and I turned onto my pre-calculated heading and noted the towns, motorways and railway lines as they passed under the nose of the aircraft. I was feeling more comfortable in my ability to navigate my way around the skies. In the far distance, I could see smoke from a factory chimney snaking lazily upwards and then drifting to the south as the upper winds took effect. This confirmed that the forecasters had worked their magic and that I had set the nose of my aircraft correctly into the wind to offset the drift. I realised that at last, I was giving myself time to think ahead instead of just reacting to events. One more glance at my map confirmed that I was exactly where I thought and calculated that I should be. Another glance at my flight log and I gently banked the aircraft to the right to settle down on my next heading, which would take me directly home. There was no autopilot to assist me, so at all times, I had to make sure we were flying at the correct height, speed and direction. As we settled onto the new heading, I checked the radio frequency to call ahead to ask for permission to fly over Dunsfold, an active military airfield. They granted this and the next radio call would be to the controller at Shoreham to ask for permission to join the circuit. I relaxed. We were nearly home. And then, the engine stopped.

If you are lucky enough to be flying an aircraft with two, three or four engines, having one of them fail is unfortunate. It can make your day more challenging. However, it is not game over: you can still fly. I was in an aircraft with just the one engine and when that engine stops, it ruins your day very quickly. The aircraft will continue to fly happily as long as you have enough airspeed to allow the wings to create the lift needed to stay in the air. Flying along moments earlier, I had the luxury of an engine pulling me through the sky at around one hundred miles an hour. This speed gave the wings all the lift they could want. Now, with no engine to help me, the only way I could keep the airspeed high enough to create any lift was to lower the nose of the aircraft and begin a glide towards the ground. Like it or not, I would land somewhere within the next four minutes and that somewhere would not be at Shoreham.

One of the earliest exercises I had to learn was what to do in the event of an engine failing while in flight. Many novice and experienced pilots had lost their lives when confronted with this emergency, especially if it happened just after take-off. The overwhelming temptation is to turn back to the runway you have just taken off from. Although this sounds like a great idea, it is, in fact, a terrible idea if you do not have sufficient height. As the engine fails, you must immediately lower the nose of the aircraft to preserve your precious airspeed. This means that instead of climbing or cruising, you are descending. If you now try to turn the aircraft back towards the runway, you are going to lose a lot of that precious height and airspeed. Turning an aircraft requires a lot of energy and with a failed engine, that energy is in very short supply. The safest thing to do if your engine fails on take-off is to lower the nose and land straight ahead wherever that may take you. Far better to perform a controlled landing in someone's back garden than to spin uncontrollably into an airfield behind you.

Luckily, although I must confess, I was not feeling all that lucky, I had two thousand feet of sky below me. Therefore, I had time on my side - not a lot - but enough to give me time to think and assess the situation. Every aircraft has a best glide speed, a speed which gives the pilot the longest time in the air and also allows for the greatest distance before the inevitable landing. This speed was sixty-five knots for my aircraft and we slowed down whilst I trimmed the aircraft to fly at this new speed. We then began the inevitable descent. My training and studying paid dividends. I had successfully made the aircraft as safe as I could; we would not stall. However, we were going to land, or return to the ground within the next few minutes. The only option I had was to decide where that was going to be.

I began looking ahead and to the left and right to find a suitable field to put the aircraft down on. Brown fields usually meant they had been ploughed and that meant deep ruts which could easily flip the aircraft over with all the associated dangers of fire. Green fields were preferable, although they also had many hidden dangers. Roads were a really bad idea, as the probability of collision with traffic was also very high. I quickly decided that I would rather be loading bags into an aircraft than be flying one at this precise moment.

After another good look around and checking that my speed was still sixty-five knots, I spotted what looked like a suitable field to land in. I rechecked every few seconds to make sure there were no better places to land and also, that there were no power lines in my way. Luckily, I had noticed the direction of the wind from the chimney smoke a few minutes earlier and as you normally always land into the wind, it means a lower ground speed and hence, less landing distance required. I adjusted my approach into the field. I now had a few moments to make sure I had not inadvertently turned the engine off or had turned the fuel off. I also checked that ice had not blocked the fuel flow by selecting the carburettor heat on to full. All seemed normal, well apart from having a failed engine, so I committed myself to the landing. As we got lower my perfect green field lost some of its appeal as I noticed a flock of sheep strolling across the middle of it. I was now fully committed to the landing and to try to stretch my glide or turn towards another field would end in disaster. I ran through the last of my landing checks and prepared for my forced landing. Passing through five hundred feet, I seemed to be too high. I needed to land at the beginning of the field not halfway down it. I put the last bit of flap down and at two hundred feet, I was back in the slot to touch down in the correct place.

My instructor then leant across and opened the throttle back to full power and told me to climb back to two thousand feet. It was a simulated or practiced false landing, although that had made no difference to me as I had to assume it was for real after he had called out, "engine failure" and had cut off all power to the engine. As we climbed away, we were close enough to the ground for me to see all the sheep stop and stare at this strange machine interrupting their grazing. I never knew that sheep could give such filthy looks and the farmer did not look very happy either.

"Hmm. Not bad, I suppose," was all the feedback I received for what I thought was a pretty splendid effort. Despite this unenthusiastic response, I was feeling very content with my performance. We climbed back to the exact position I had been given before the engine failure. I was then asked if I would choose the same field again, to which I replied that it seemed a very good choice, so yes, I would do the same again.

"So, you wouldn't choose that big disused airfield with three huge runways right below us then?" he rather sarcastically replied.

I couldn't believe my eyes. I was so busy looking for a green field that I had totally missed this abandoned Second World War airfield. I had to admit that yes, on second thoughts, I might have chosen that instead. However, I did point out that the sheep in my field would have had another boring afternoon had I done so. With his eyes rolling in his head, my instructor told me to take him home, if I could find it, that is. This was another lesson learned, which I suppose, was the purpose of the whole exercise, although I had to admit that I wasn't feeling particularly charitable as we shut the aircraft down and headed for what was to be another full and sobering de-brief. This whole flying business was a lot more difficult than I had imagined.

Chapter 9

End of the Beginning

The next few flights were structured towards getting me prepared for the next and hopefully last stage of my training: the all-important general flying test. Whilst I was brushing up on my flying skills, I also had to complete my ground examinations and prepare for my solo cross-country qualifying flight. I would be very busy over the next few weeks.

The weather governed all my flying. I could only fly if the conditions permitted. My basic flying licence meant that I could not fly in cloud or high winds or basically, any adverse weather. I was most definitely a fair-weather pilot. As the autumn faded into winter, I concentrated on my ground studies until the weather improved. Money was also becoming an issue again and I needed to work even more shifts as a loader. I decided that I could combine these by applying to work more night shifts. At Gatwick, there had to be a twenty-four-hour coverage by the loading teams. Because of noise restrictions, no jet aircraft were allowed to land or take off between eleven in the evening and four in the morning. This left just the night freighter propeller aircraft that needed servicing. These aircraft moved the mail and newspapers around the country and could normally be loaded and unloaded in a relatively short time. Also, a great bonus for me was that I could get to chat to the pilots as we worked on their aircraft. This proved an invaluable source of information and advice once they knew of my ambition to fly. This quiet period also gave me the opportunity to study for my ground examinations. For me, this was a win-win situation and over the next two months, as the winter weather kept me grounded. I managed not only to recharge my bank account but pass all my ground examinations. Every cloud, as they say, has a silver lining and as the weather settled down, I prepared myself for the final two hurdles and hopefully, to complete my Private Pilot Licence before the end of the year.

One downside to working seven days a week and most nights as well, was that I was left with absolutely no social life. My passion for playing rugby on a Saturday afternoon followed by a few hours standing at the bar recounting mostly imagined sporting prowess had to be sacrificed at the altar of aviation. There would be no more lazy afternoons playing my much-loved cricket. I had to sacrifice tennis, cycling and any other recreational pastimes I had previously enjoyed. Aviation had taken all that away from me. I was fast becoming a social outcast and I just prayed that the end would justify the means.

The early winter storms finally exhausted themselves and the weather settled down enough for me to plan for my qualifying cross-country flight. I was excited and nervous in equal measures as I arrived that morning at Shoreham. The weather that early was cold, with low clouds and a stiff wind from the north. However, the forecast was for this to improve by mid to late morning, leaving the cloud base and wind suitable for my flight. My task was to fly a three-legged flight from Shoreham to Blackbushe and then on to Thruxton and finally, back to Shoreham. Once again, I had to report to the control tower at each airfield to get the air traffic controller to sign and stamp my logbook confirming that not only had I landed safely at their airfield, but that I had also conformed to all the rules of the air and had obeyed all the instructions given to me.

After an early morning coffee, I sat down and planned my flight. There was no particular hurry as the weather was not forecast to improve until late morning. I took my time and carefully plotted my course and studied the arrival procedures for each airfield. Time spent preparing for a flight was never wasted. Two hours later, I was ready to go. All my preparations were completed. I had checked all the latest notices and weathers en route. I would have to wait for the weather at Shoreham to improve. More coffee, another snack and still, I could only just about see across the airfield. Low clouds still hid the tops of the distant South Downs.

Lunchtime came and went, yet I was too nervous to eat and the thought of more coffee became less attractive, especially as I hoped to be in the air soon with no prospect of a comfort stop. The more I stared out of the window, the more I feared that the weather forecast had been very optimistic. I still could not see the top of the hills. I had calculated that my entire trip, including the two landings, would take no more than three hours. Nightfall at this time of the year was just before five in the afternoon. Therefore, to give myself a sensible buffer for unforeseen delays, I decided that if I could not be airborne before one o'clock, I would call it a day and try again next week. Oh, how I was to wish later that I had taken that option.

Fortunately, or as I later realised, unfortunately, the weather suddenly cleared. The clouds lifted and the winds dropped. I rang both Blackbushe and Thruxton to check their weather and whilst it was not a beautiful day, the weather was now good enough. I made my decision. Although it was getting late, I still had time to complete my flight.

Maybe, a clue as I taxied out was that I was the only aircraft moving that day. If it was a clue, sadly I missed it. I had planned to fly at two thousand feet on my first leg. This was optimistic as I entered the cloud base approaching my selected altitude. Still, this presented no significant problem as I descended back to one thousand five hundred feet, a perfectly acceptable cruising altitude which allowed me to stay in sight of the ground. Twenty-five minutes later, Blackbushe appeared on the horizon, albeit slightly obscured by a light rain shower. Undeterred, I called ahead and received permission to join the circuit and was cleared to land whilst I was still letting down into the circuit. It looked like I was once again, the only aircraft in the sky. Still, this made for a reasonably straightforward approach and although the wind buffeted my aircraft as we landed, it was still well within my comfort zone. After parking, I climbed the stairs to the tower to thank the controller for all his help and to get his precious signature in my logbook. With all the formalities completed, I made a quick telephone call to the controller at Thruxton to check that the weather there was suitable for my landing. The news was not as good as I had hoped. However, it was still within limits if again, I flew at one thousand five hundred feet. I checked my watch. It was now a little after two o'clock, still three hours before nightfall, so time was on my side, just!

As I called for taxi clearance, mine was the only voice on the frequency. A feeling of loneliness descended on me and I had to physically shake off this unease as I lined up on the runway and applied power for the flight to Thruxton. Almost as soon as we became airborne, the turbulence started. We bumped our way up to the selected cruising height, only this time, the clouds had other ideas and came down to meet me as I reached one thousand feet above the ground, not good. Still, this was acceptable as there was no high ground or buildings between me and Thruxton as long as I kept strictly on track. Again, I called the next controller to announce my intended arrival and as instructed, I informed him that I was on my qualifying cross-country. There was a definite pause and then he asked me to confirm what I had just told him. Again, I repeated that I was on my qualifying cross-country flight. Once again, mine was the only flight he controlled that afternoon as he gave me the latest weather at Thruxton. It was not the weather they had given me on the telephone only a short while ago. However, I was still in clear air and although the wind had picked up, it was still within my limits. As there were no other aircraft around, he cleared me for a straight-in approach and asked me to report the field in sight. Easier said than done, I thought. Rain was now bouncing off my windscreen making visibility more difficult. There were no windshield wipers to aid me as Mr Cessna, in his wisdom, had decided not to include them on his aircraft. Luckily, I picked out the control tower with its very distinctive black and white markings. As well as being an airfield, Thruxton was a famous motor racing circuit. The control tower doubled as the start and finish points. A gentle turn to the left lined me up nicely with the runway and the racetrack acted as a good indicator, confirming that I was in the correct place to make a safe landing. The rain intensified as I crossed over the threshold and made a firm arrival. Again, the rain made it difficult to taxi towards the control tower.

I shut the aircraft down and had to wait for the rain to ease before I made a dash to the control tower. Typically, I had not thought to bring a waterproof jacket. Entering the controller's office, I presented my logbook for his signature. He eyed me with what I thought was an unnecessary amount of suspicion before finally scribbling his name and a few comments. He was a man of few words or maybe, I had just left him speechless with my arrival. I never found out. I looked out at the ever-deteriorating weather and made my last telephone call of the day to check the weather situation at Shoreham. I was not at all optimistic that I would complete my flight and I was already thinking if I had enough money on me to pay for a night's accommodation and a pint at a local pub. All that changed when I was told that the weather was still well within limits at my home airfield and there were other aircraft flying in the circuit.

Overjoyed, I made my way back to the aircraft, checked that I still had enough fuel for the forty-minute flight home. When I was satisfied, I called up for clearance to start my engine.

I was still wet from my dash to and from the control tower and was feeling the cold, so I was very keen to get going as soon as possible. My hopes of an early departure were dashed when the controller informed me that the wind was now outside the crosswind limits for my type of aircraft. This was the worst news possible. Not only was I wet and cold, but I was also running out of time before nightfall would make it impossible for me to continue as I had no Night Rating on my licence. I started the engine to warm myself, probably not the best idea as my fuel was now getting slightly low. As there was nobody else about, I was cleared to taxi out to the runway and wait there to see if the wind died down enough to allow me to take off. Time was ticking away and I needed to be airborne within the next twenty minutes to allow for a safe and legal flight home. As I was the only aircraft around, I was then cleared to line up on the runway to wait for the wind to stop gusting. I sat there with the damp from my wet clothing slowly misting up the windscreen. I had the heaters and blowers set to maximum, yet I still had to lean forward occasionally to wipe away the mist forming on the inside of the windscreen. As the moments ticked by, I worried about how much of the precious fuel I was now using. Before I set off, I had calculated that I could fly all three legs of my journey and still arrive back at Shoreham with forty-five minutes of fuel remaining. I was now using this reserve of fuel at an alarming rate. I was not in a happy place. Still the wind rocked my tiny aircraft and I accepted that a night in a local pub was maybe, not such a terrible option. Decision made, I was about to request permission to taxi back and shutdown when I was given the latest wind and then cleared for an immediate take off. Without thinking it through, I accepted the take-off clearance and began accelerating down the runway.

Aircraft have a crosswind limit for an excellent reason and I realised this as I fought to keep the aircraft straight. As we left the ground, the turbulence returned with a vengeance and I struggled to keep the ground in sight as I levelled at one thousand feet. Despite the turbulence, I set course for home, determined to do all I could to concentrate on my navigation and put the nagging doubts about the weather and the state of my fuel firmly to the back of my mind. Still, the weather continued to deteriorate. I was now at only eight hundred feet but the visibility was good below the clouds and I was relaxing a little as I made my way homewards.

The time was now approaching half past four and dusk was making its presence felt. I had selected a southerly route to avoid the South Downs hills which would now be concealed in cloud. Although this was a very safe decision, it also added nearly ten minutes to my flying time, further reducing my fuel reserves. I was now passing overhead Littlehampton on the Sussex coast, flying at eight hundred feet in moderate rain, wiping away at the inside of my windscreen to give me some forward visibility. As I approached Worthing, I had less than ten minutes to run and fifteen minutes before nightfall. Things were getting tight. I called ahead to let Shoreham know my position and request a left base join to save both time and fuel. I felt strangely calm and fully in control of the situation. I knew exactly where I was and I knew that I had sufficient fuel and that the weather, although now right on limits, was still acceptable for a crosswind landing. The controllers were also helping me with radio bearings and distances from the runway. They had also kindly lit the paraffin lamps along the runway edges to help guide me in. As I turned onto the final approach, I realised that without these lamps I would struggle to see the runway in the heavy rain and low cloud. Relief flooded through me as I made an acceptable landing considering the weather and as I taxied back to the clubhouse, I realised just how close I had been to making a night landing. It was dark as I tied the aircraft down for the night and made my way into the debriefing room, wherein sat a furious instructor. For once, I could only agree with him: I should have stayed at Thruxton and flown back the next morning. It was a very poor decision to carry on. However, I clutched my logbook, secure in the knowledge that I had the two precious signatures confirming that I had completed my qualifying cross-country flight. All I needed now to gain my licence, was to pass the general flying test. How hard could that be? I was about to find out sooner than I thought.

Chapter 10

The Test

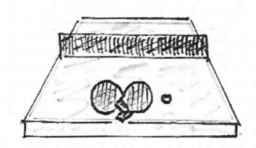

I was coming to the end of my training for the Private Pilot Licence, the first step in the long road to becoming an airline pilot. I had now nearly forty hours of flying behind me, all neatly recorded in my little book.

The only practical test I had taken up to that point in my life had been my driving test and that had not gone well at all. As with my upcoming flying test, I had thoroughly prepared for my driving test. I had diligently learned the highway code; I had mastered the art of driving itself, well maybe not mastered, but I could do a three-point turn without embarrassing myself too much and my gear changes were slick, even if I said so myself. I presented myself at the local driving centre with a brand-new haircut and I had cleaned my car to the best of my ability. I thought I would give a very good first impression. The test itself was going very well. I had performed the emergency stop, the backing into a parking bay and I had completed the verbal exam. We were on our way back to the driving centre to where I assumed, we would complete the formalities before they issued my licence. Driving along the dual carriageway at Worthing's seafront, I was enjoying myself, well up to the point I saw the blue flashing lights of a police car in my rear-view mirror. I slowed down from the forty miles an hour I had been driving at and pulled over to allow the police to race by and catch the villains they were chasing. I was more than a little surprised when they also slowed down and stopped behind me. They really did not need to thank me for such courteous driving.

Whilst one policeman walked around my vehicle checking lights and tyres, the other approached my side window to enquire if I knew what the speed limit was along the seafront. Well, of course I knew that on a suburban dual carriageway, it was forty miles per hour. He could not catch me out that easily. My heart sank when he interrupted me to inform me that if it was a lit carriageway, the limit was thirty miles per hour. Without any further discussion, he issued a speeding ticket and handed it to me. With that, they both returned to their car and set off to ruin someone else's day. I turned to the examiner and asked if this minor episode would have any bearing on my test result. We drove back and parked at the test centre where my father was waiting to greet me. The examiner left the car, to be replaced by my father with an expectant look on his face. This expression rapidly changed when instead of a pass certificate, I showed him my speeding ticket. Hopefully, my flying test would prove to be a little more successful. At least, I couldn't get stopped for speeding in an aircraft.

The day of my flying test finally arrived and as I parked my car, I looked at the low cloud and light rain with a feeling of disappointment. I had arrived very early, as my flight was not due for two hours. I settled myself down with the obligatory cup of coffee and poured over the local weather forecast. It did not look very promising. With two weeks to go until Christmas, we were approaching the shortest day of the year. Looking out at the dark grey low clouds, it was easy to imagine that night-time was about to fall, even though it was still mid-morning. There was an air of gloom both outside and inside the clubhouse. It looked very unlikely that anyone would be flying today.

However, I still had to assume that the skies would clear and in less than two hours' time, I would take the most important flight I had ever undertaken. Therefore, I had my books in front of me for that last-minute refresher.

I knew the basics of the test. I would be expected to demonstrate my ability to perform everything that they had taught me over the last few months. I was comfortable with most of the manoeuvres, although I was still a little apprehensive about stalling and spinning. Would I put in the correct rudder to stop the spin? Would I recover from the full-power-flaps-down stall in time to prevent a spin? I looked once again at the weather outside and realised that with the thick dark clouds barely one thousand feet above the ground, there was absolutely no way we could complete these manoeuvres in this weather. I relaxed, today was obviously not going to be the day I completed my training. I had a stay of execution.

There were several people sitting around the reception area, none of whom looked like they were going anywhere soon. My instructor was about to start a lecture in the ground school classroom and I was tempted to ask if I could join in. My examinations were all completed but any extra tuition was always welcome. I resisted the temptation.

I was due to start my test in less than an hour and I was uncertain how I would be officially notified that it had been cancelled. My examiner was to be a Senior DC10 Training Captain, Chris Yardley, a name I was to remember throughout my career. Up to this point, I had heard of Chris, although I had never met him. He had an excellent reputation and I was lucky to have him as my examiner. Sadly, when today's flight was cancelled, I would be paired with a different and probably, less well-liked individual. My mood darkened once more. Why could things never go according to plan? After the weather I had experienced on my cross-country flight, feelings of self-pity overwhelmed me. Time for more coffee, I thought, as I headed back into the lounge.

One of the best distractions whilst waiting for the weather to clear was table tennis and there in the bar area, stood my salvation. Over the months, many idle hours had been taken up with improving my skills. I now considered myself a bit of an ace. The table was empty as I looked around to see if there were any of my usual partners interested in a quick game. Sadly, there were none of the usual suspects hanging around as I began bouncing the ball up and down on my bat.

"Fancy a game?" came the question, as I searched under the table for the ball I had just failed to keep up in the air. I peered out from my undignified position to see a young chap in jeans and tee shirt holding the ball I had been searching for. I scrambled out and accepted his invitation. However, I felt it only fair to point out that I was quite useful if he wanted to reconsider his offer. Sadly, for me, he declined.

Table tennis may not be classed as a full contact sport but after a bruising fifteen minutes, where I had been hit many times by a small white ball travelling at ridiculous speeds, I had to admit that not only had I met my match, but I had also met someone who played at an entirely different level to the one at which I dabbled at. I thanked him for the game and decided that it was time to settle myself down for the inevitable news that my flying test would be cancelled. I quickly grabbed the coffee that I had intended to drink a while ago and entered my allotted briefing room. I felt no nerves, so sure was I that today's proceedings could not possibly go ahead. As expected, the room was empty, so I made myself comfortable and waited to see if anybody turned up. I would wait for fifteen minutes and then accept the inevitable and go home. Exactly at the appointed hour there was a soft knock on the door and my table tennis conqueror walked in. Before I could explain that now was not a good time for a rematch as I had important things to do, he introduced himself as Chris Yardley. It took a little while for this to sink in. The real Chris Yardley was a senior DC10 training captain, for goodness' sake. He should be, had to be, a slightly portly, older gentleman with thinning grey hair and spectacles hanging around his neck. He should wear grey trousers with a shirt and a sensible cardigan. He should, under no circumstances, be in his early thirties, wearing jeans and a tee shirt and be in far better shape than I was. How could someone so young have so many advantages over me? Life really was not at all fair! All I could think to say was, "Gosh, now I'm glad I let you beat me at table tennis." Happily, he appeared to have a similar sense of humour to my own as he briefed me for the upcoming test. As I sat there listening to his very succinct rundown of what he would expect to see from me, I could not help glancing outside at the persistent low cloud. Maybe, he hadn't noticed, I thought to myself.

Briefing completed, we made our way to the aircraft where I began my normal walk around checking all the control and engine controls systems. I was asked a few relatively simple questions which I had no trouble answering. Once inside the aircraft with all checks completed, I called up to request the latest weather. Surely this would be the point where we decided that the only sensible thing to do was cancel the test. However, Chris was made of sterner stuff and we began to taxi out for take-off. I was trying to fathom out what we could achieve on this gloomy winter's day. Still, all I could do was to follow his instructions and wait and see what happened. I had done my homework on all the runways available today, especially as I expected a simulated engine failure shortly after take-off: I had a plan in my back pocket, which involved a landing in a park where I regularly played tennis, which was perfect for a forced landing. Luckily, the runway we were to use today made this choice even more inspiring, well it would have been, if my examiner had not requested a change of runway to allow me to demonstrate a crosswind take off.

We lined up on this new and unanticipated runway and with my flight controls crossed to allow for the stiff crosswind, I released the brakes and away we went into the unknown, well it was unknown to me. As I had expected, as we climbed away, Chris lent across and slowly closed the throttle at the same time informing me that we had suffered an engine failure. Resisting the temptation to pull his hand away to restore power, I lowered the nose of the aircraft and began looking ahead for a suitable place to put the aircraft down safely. Sadly, my park with acres of open space was nowhere to be seen. However, I had the advantage of being on home turf - I lived less than two miles away. I gently turned the aircraft a few degrees to the left and announced that I would land on a green next to the beach. Maybe not as good as the park, but still perfectly acceptable for a safe arrival. Once I had lined up with my chosen landing area straight ahead, Chris restored the power and we climbed safely away. I was relaxing. This feeling lasted as long as it took Chris to ask me to fly on a westerly heading and climb to four thousand feet. The look on my face must have betrayed my feelings as we entered the forbidden layers of cloud. After reassurances from Chris that he would look after the navigation of the aircraft, I concentrated on making sure that we stayed the right way up as the heavy cloud enveloped us. This was fresh territory for me. I had not been trained to fly in cloud, that would come later. I had also not been taught how to navigate without reference to the ground. Things were starting to become very interesting.

Suddenly, the cloud thinned and then broke up completely and we burst into the most glorious sunshine that I had ever seen, well it certainly felt that way, after weeks of low, overcast weather. It was literally like entering a new world and I was totally entranced. It was beautiful, a transition from darkness to light in a matter of moments. As we climbed away from the flat cloud base, I was captivated to see a perfect halo with the shadow of our aircraft at its centre, dancing along below us. It was without doubt, one of the most amazing sights I had ever seen. With great difficulty, I forced myself to put these thoughts to the back of my mind and concentrate on the matter in hand.

I levelled the aircraft as instructed, at four thousand feet and the test really began. We climbed, we descended and I demonstrated my ability to remain at the correct height whilst performing very steep turns, a difficult manoeuvre requiring almost full power. Inevitably, all too soon we arrived at the section which required me to stall and spin the aircraft. I was enjoying myself so much that at this point, I was feeling more than confident. We stalled at all the various configurations required and each time, I recovered the aircraft well within the expected height loss parameters. Only the dreaded spin remained. Up went the nose, on went the power and we climbed until the point where one wing lost all of its lift and flipped us onto our back. We started spiralling earthwards. I applied the opposite rudder, reduced the power and before I knew it, the wings were level, enabling me to slowly raise the nose and reapply power until we were once again flying straight and level. The upper air work part of the test was now complete. All I had to do was re-join the circuit and fly a normal approach followed by a go-around. After this, a simple circuit followed by a safe landing would see me home and dry. The only problem was that I had absolutely no idea where home was. I was lost, flying above the clouds with absolutely no way of map reading my way back to the airport.

I need not have worried. True to his word, Chris calmly gave me a heading to fly and asked me to descend to one thousand feet. We entered the clouds once again and the bright, beautiful sky was immediately replaced by ever thickening wisps of dark damp clouds as, once again, they enveloped our aircraft. The contrast could not have been more complete as we continued our descent. Eventually, I could see flashes of the sea below as we finally came out of the base of the clouds. I recognised the pier at Worthing and from there, I could make my way back into the circuit at Shoreham. The circuits went as well as I could have hoped for and after landing, we taxied slowly back to the clubhouse and I completed the shutdown checks on the aircraft. It was silent once again, the ticking of the cooling engine the only noticeable interruption to my thoughts. Well, apart from a slap on the back followed by words of congratulations from Chris that I had passed the test. That certainly got my attention.

Yet, my overriding memory, even to this day, was not the test itself, it was that one moment of sheer wonder and awe as we broke out of the all-consuming suffocation of those heavily laden clouds into bright sunshine. I wanted to experience that feeling over and over again. I knew that I could never tire of that feeling of wonder and all these years later, I still have the same emotions as I climb through the clouds. I knew at that moment I really had made the right career choice.

Chapter 11

Easy Part Over - What Next?

Sadly, I was never to have the pleasure of flying with Chris again. Yet all these years later, I still remember his kindness, professionalism and intellect with the greatest of affection. As my career progressed, I realised that there were some incredible people in the aviation world and I have tried to emulate them. Chris Yardley was one of the first of these individuals to influence and shape the way I tried to approach my chosen profession.

I was now the very proud owner of a Private Pilot Licence. The positive side of this was that I could now take friends and family for pleasure flights. The negative side was that I would have to pay for these flights myself as I was prohibited from charging or accepting money for any flights I undertook. This was not sustainable on my loader's salary but it was necessary for me if I was going to take the next step up the ladder and start the long process towards gaining the all-important Commercial Pilot Licence. To put this into perspective, a commercial flight school today would charge upwards of one hundred and twenty thousand pounds just to achieve the basic licence. I calculated that if I tried to save enough money to attend the eighteen months full-time course, I would be at retirement age before I could afford to begin training.

Once again, I returned to the back pages of *Flight International* magazine, only to realise that there were still no sponsorships available, although there were a very small number of pilot vacancies being advertised. At least this gave me some hope it was going to be worthwhile continuing my training. The mountain facing me was that to apply for my commercial licence, I would need to have flown nine hundred hours to be eligible to sit the ground and flying examinations. This put my forty hours flying into perspective, I was heavily in debt paying for those hours and my loading job was very seasonal - busy in the summer but with very little work available in the winter. Something had to change. So, I applied for a more permanent and regular job, hopefully, still within the world of aviation. This new plan brought me in front of a selection board for the exalted position of export clerk in the cargo division of, once again, British Caledonian. Luckily, I convinced them that compiling cargo manifests and then having that manifest cleared by customs was the one career that I had always strived after. I missed out the fact that I only wanted the job to finance my flying and the moment I had completed my pilot licence, I would be gone. I had really enjoyed loading the aircraft and I was slightly dreading the thought of sitting in an office and typing out these manifests. However, it was still shift work, the office was open all day and night to maintain the flow of cargo onto the aircraft and this suited me very well.

I ended up spending two years in that office, working mainly night shifts, as once again, this gave me the freedom to fly during the day. My typing skills were appalling to begin with and I used the entire office supply of Tippex to correct my mistakes. This was long before they computerised the whole process. We had old-fashioned typewriters with carbon paper to create our duplicates. However, I persevered and gave the job the respect it deserved. I also made some excellent friends, two of whom I would end up teaching to fly! It's a funny old world at times. The other major attraction was that I had even more time to visit the flight decks of the aircraft we served. All in all, I enjoyed my time spent in the office.

I now had to sit down and carefully plan the next few steps towards my ultimate goal. My one realistic option was to become a flying instructor and gradually build up my hours whilst being paid to fly rather than paying to fly. This was also going to be a very expensive option. I needed to have flown one hundred and fifty hours before I could even apply to start an instructor course, which was also very costly. On the wages I received, it would be a very long time before I could save up enough money to become an instructor. I needed another job to supplement my income, so I started a one-man aircraft cleaning service back at Shoreham Airport. I approached all the flying clubs and private owners to offer my services at a very competitive rate. There is a lot you can damage on an aircraft if you do not understand how all the bits and pieces work and how delicate they are. Having a pilot licence helped. Not only did I collect several regular customers, but I also hitched a few rides in their aircraft. I now had an alternative plan, an inspired idea and one that would eventually take me to the other side of the world.

My goal now was to reach one hundred and fifty flying hours, which would allow me to attend a course for the Assistant Flying Instructor Licence. Once I had obtained this licence, I could finally apply for a job in a paid flying position. However, that was a long way off. First, I had to reach one hundred and fifty hours of flight time, a very expensive ambition.

I explored alternative ways that I could gain flying experience without the exorbitant costs incurred in the UK. After some research, it became apparent that the cost of flying in the US was less than half of that charged in the UK. Unfortunately, there was a problem. I did not have an American pilot licence and to get an extended visa to stay in the States, I would have to apply for a student visa and these are only issued if you are attending an approved course with a certified flight school. As always, nothing was ever straightforward in aviation.

With this information in mind, I returned to my local newsagent and purchased that week's copy of the infamous *Flight International*. Once again, I immediately turned straight to the back of the magazine and there before me, were pages of advertisements for courses available in America. Had computers and Google been available to me, I would have been able to make a far more informed and sensible choice. With no information other than the advertisements, I had to trust my instincts. I made my choice and applied to a flight school in San Francisco, to study for an American Commercial Pilot Licence. All I had to do now was to save up enough money to pay for the course. Whilst waiting for my adventure to begin, I thought I had better do a small amount of flying, mainly to keep my licence current but also to add to my qualifications. Having nearly been caught out twice by approaching nightfall, I thought it would be a good idea to learn how to fly at night. Therefore, I booked myself onto the five-hour night flying course, expensive but well worth it, I thought, after two of my previous flights had resulted in near night flying.

Shoreham Airport had three grass runways and none of them had any lighting. To solve this problem and allow night training to go ahead every Thursday at sunset, a land rover would place a series of paraffin lanterns down each side of the runway. When everyone was ready and the sun had set, the land rover would race down the runway lighting the lanterns as quickly as possible. The lanterns only lasted about an hour, so the quicker they were lit, the better. It felt surreal as we taxied out over the grass with only one small headlight to guide us towards the runway. There we waited as the lanterns were lit one by one and gradually, the semblance of a runway would appear out of the pitch-black night. Once the task was complete, the clearance was given to take off. With an instructor by my side, we taxied into position. I could feel the heat from the burning paraffin and the smell was also very overpowering. It was like taxiing into a bonfire which, in retrospect it was. Opening up the throttle, these burning lanterns began flashing by slowly at first and then as our speed increased, they blurred into a continuous line. I had never concentrated so much on trying to keep the aircraft straight as hitting one of these monstrosities did not bear thinking about.

As we left the ground, the sights and smells quickly faded and all I could see ahead was a black nothing. On a daylight take off you can judge the angle you are climbing at by the nose of the aircraft position relative to the horizon. Now, of course, there was no horizon and so it became imperative to look inside the aircraft at the artificial horizon in front of you. During my initial training, my instructor had impressed on me not to do this. Night flying had a distinct and different set of rules. Feeling very uncomfortable, I tried to keep the aircraft climbing at the correct angle. My entire world was reduced to the size of a tiny cockpit, a little like driving a car at high speed around narrow country lanes at night and then turning your headlights off, not a good feeling. With a little help, I levelled off at one thousand feet and I turned towards the downwind leg. As there was still no horizon, I found it difficult to judge the turn and we began a steep descent. Realising this, I over-compensated by raising the nose too far and subsequently, the airspeed dropped alarmingly. Immediately, I lowered the nose and the descent continued. This was even worse than my first solo circuit and goodness knows, that had been bad enough. I had lost any previously learned ability to control the aircraft.

With the instructor's help once again, eventually, I settled down into an almost straight-and-level flight. My heart rate slowed, until I realised that I could not see the airfield or the runway. I was flying blind. I did not understand where the runway was and I could not see any landmarks to help me. Eventually, my instructor told me to turn left and begin a shallow descent, which for me, was easier said than done. However, he talked me through the turn and then suddenly ahead and below me, a series of little bonfires appeared. I completed my landing checks and concentrated on keeping the lights in sight. As we came over the runway, the smell of the burning paraffin returned, which at least meant that I was not trying to land on a dual carriageway. I tried to judge the landing in the usual way, which did not work as I could not see the runway edges. However, the lanterns proved to be an acceptable alternative and I was very surprised when we made a reasonable touchdown. Power on and off we set again. We had an hour in which to fly as many circuits as we could. Each time, my flying became a little more accurate and although at no time, did I feel comfortable, I was starting to appreciate that night flying was at least possible. On the final approach, the flares were becoming noticeably dimmer and a few had burned themselves out. I blamed this for my last landing of the night being the worst, by far. Oh well, there was always next Thursday.

Eventually, after another three Thursdays, I was ready for my first night solo. By this time, I had begun to really enjoy the sensation of flying at night, especially on a moonlit one such as it was that night. My only concern was what to do in the case of an engine failure. There could be no gentle glide into a field of my choosing, I would simply drift down into a black void and hit whatever happened to be there. Best not to think of such things, I thought to myself as the flares once again began to rush past and again, I climbed away into the night sky. My solo complete, I presented my licence to have it endorsed for my night rating. I was slowly becoming more qualified.

Chapter 12

America: Into the Unknown

With my application and deposit paid, I settled down to work seven days a week typing and cleaning in equal measure; I had little opportunity to fly for the next eighteen months. Eventually, I had amassed the funds and obtained the American student visa that would allow me to leave both my jobs and set off to begin the next stage of my training. I handed in my notice at Gatwick and let my customers at Shoreham know that from now on they would have to fly dirty aircraft. It was a real wrench to move on: I had made many friends at both airports and I would miss their company. I had booked my flight, withdrawn all my money from the bank and had a start date with my new flight school. I was all set to go.

My flight to San Francisco departed at two-thirty the next afternoon and I spent my last evening in the company of my oldest friend, Pete Brown. We had known each other since early childhood and our paths would continue to intertwine over the coming decades. He had been given the simple tasks of taking me out for a few beers that night and then to drive me to Heathrow Airport the next morning in time for my flight. As I was to be reminded many times, Pete is very good at some things and not so good at others. This time, he was brilliant at finding great pubs to drink at; he was not so good at finding his way to the airport the next day. This was before the orbital M25 motorway had been constructed and we set off from Pete's house a lot later than I was comfortable with. He assured me that he knew a shortcut to Heathrow and we would be there with plenty of time to spare.

Only slightly appeased, once again I began to re-check that I had everything I needed for my adventure. The flight school had insisted that they wanted a very large deposit to be paid in cash on the day of my arrival. They had booked accommodation for the duration of the entire course and the only other expense I could expect was for food and drink. I was slightly concerned that I would have to hand over so much money on trust, but I believed that this was normal practice. Therefore, once again, I checked that the large brown envelope containing my entire savings was safely tucked away in my briefcase. I looked at my watch and saw that time was getting tight. I glanced at Pete as he laughed at another of his own jokes, apparently with not a care in the world. Being ardent rugby fans, as we passed Harlequins' home ground, we both commented how well they had played that season. Now a full thirty minutes later, I was less inclined to comment on Harlequins' season as we passed their ground for a second time. Instead, I enquired again if Pete knew where he was going!

My heart sank as he finally admitted that we were completely lost and no, he never carried a map in his car, as he had never needed one. I felt my hands contract into fists and it took all my self-restraint to prevent myself from engaging in a little physical violence. My check-in time came and went and still we drove around in ever decreasing circles, passing from south of the Thames to the north only to repeat the process in the opposite direction a few minutes later. By this time, I had given up all hope of making my flight and was trying to work out how much money I had just lost. Eventually, by following the line of aircraft approaching Heathrow we arrived at terminal three, only ninety minutes later than expected. We were just in time to see the Boeing 747 Flight BA285 to San Francisco lift gracefully into the sky ... thanks Pete.

We parked and made our way to the check-in desk to enquire what we might salvage from this disaster. I tried my best apologetic expression while pleading for clemency and another chance to fly with British Airways. My efforts were met with a very frosty reaction from the check-in agent, who informed me that I had missed my flight and that the airline would only refund me or issue another ticket under exceptional circumstances. I was stunned! My entire trip was based on a very limited budget and I had blown this before I had even started. I was about to turn away and accept defeat when my soon-to-be ex-best friend intervened. With an approach I could never hope to emulate, he sprang forward and set about using a charm offensive on the agent. Incredibly, her frown was soon replaced with a smile and then a full belly laugh. Then, I heard him explain that I was on my way to learn to become an airline pilot and one day when I returned, I would become a Boeing 747 captain with British Airways, and if she could put me on the next flight, I would repay her with an upgrade to First Class. This time, we all knew that he had gone way beyond the bounds of possibility. However, she relented and I found myself the proud and much relieved holder of a ticket to San Francisco and the flight left in two hours. Only Pete could have possibly achieved such an outcome. I hated him and loved him all at once and quickly disappeared into the security line whilst I was still ahead.

As we taxied out for take-off, I was impressed with the sheer size of the aircraft, another Boeing 747. It seemed to take an age to make my way back to the very last row of seats. I had read somewhere that as a 747 rotates at take-off, because of the size and length of the aircraft, the people in the back go down before they go up. It was a useless piece of information, although it was noticeable, if you looked out for it. With this and other thoughts running through my mind, I made myself as comfortable as possible and slept for a good proportion of the flight. Finally, I was on my way and for the first time in a long time, I could relax, well at least for the next ten hours.

This tranquillity lasted until I reached the immigration queue after landing. After the seemingly obligatory two hour wait, I was finally standing in front of the overworked and short-tempered immigration officer. I handed over my passport with the newly gained student visa printed boldly on the last page. The questions came short and sharp and I felt more like a suspect than a student. After we had established the facts, I was then thoroughly grilled on where I would stay and who would finance everything. I produced the letter of introduction from my flight school, a document he abruptly pushed aside with barely a glance at the contents. Again, he asked where I would stay and how I intended to finance my course. I once again politely explained that all the information he required was in the letter he had just discarded and if he could be bothered to read it, he would get the answers he required. Well, as I immediately found out, you never, never tell an American immigration officer what to do. The next thing I knew, I was being escorted to a room for further interrogation. Welcome to America, I said to myself silently.

A further two hours later, I was standing by the kerbside at the Arrivals hall looking for the promised transport to the flight school. It slowly dawned on me that I was nearly six hours later than expected. There would be no-one to meet me so I would have to find a pay phone and let them know that I had finally arrived. I returned inside and found a public pay phone booth. My next problem was immediately obvious from the name. It was a pay phone and I had no dollars or change to make a call. Off I wandered to find a money-changing kiosk. All my cash was in the large brown envelope at the bottom of my bag for safekeeping. I rummaged around and eventually, produced the envelope. Carefully and doing my best to hide my nest egg from prying eyes, I extracted a few notes to change into dollars. With this transaction completed, I hurriedly made my way back to the phone booth.

I rang the flight school only to get an answer machine message as they were now closed and could anyone calling, please call back the next day. That was not what I was expecting and so, with more hope than expectations, I called again. This time, just as the answer machine was about to kick-in a real live person took over. Before my money ran out, I quickly explained who I was and apologised for being so late. I also enquired how long it would be before my transport would arrive to take me to my hotel. It was now early evening in San Francisco and four in the morning on my body clock. I was abruptly informed that it was far too late for a car to pick me up. They gave me the address of the motel I had been booked into and told me to report to reception at nine o'clock the next morning. So much for a warm Californian welcome, I thought to myself as I made my way to the nearest taxi rank. My now exhausted and muddled brain registered the fact that I would now need to change even more money to pay for the taxi. Back I went to the money changing kiosk and once again, began rummaging for the precious envelope containing my finances. Suddenly, I froze as realisation dawned on me. I had emptied my bag to find a pen and paper to write the address of the motel and I had left the envelope containing my money by the telephone. I turned, and suitcase and bag trailing behind me, I sprinted back to the phone booth I had recently vacated. As I ran, I was haunted by the consequences of losing everything I had worked so hard for over the past two years. I could barely contain my emotion as I realised that my money had most likely gone forever. The phone booth was just a phone on the wall with a plastic dome overhead to reduce background noise. I couldn't imagine that my envelope would have gone unnoticed in the bustling concourse. Someone was going to be very rich and I would be sleeping in the airport tonight before attempting to beg for a ticket home the next morning.

I skidded around the last corner and heart in mouth, looked into the booth. Unbelievably, there was my envelope. I snatched it up and to my everlasting relief there was my money, untouched. I just stood there motionless as relief flooded through me, tinged with anger at my stupidity. After my heart rate slowly returned to normal, I returned and changed more of my newly regained money and hailed a taxi. I was now really struggling to stay awake and thirty minutes later, we pulled up outside what was to be my home for the foreseeable future. Making sure that I had everything with me, I entered the reception area. Until this point, I was so tired that I had not really paid all that much attention to my surroundings. It was only now, as I waited for someone from reception to answer the call bell, that I realised how rundown the whole motel really appeared. I signed in, although fortunately, as it turned out, I insisted on only paying for one night and not a full week, as they asserted was in the contract with the flight school. I picked up my bags and left the reception area to make my way to my room. As this was a motel, each room on the ground floor had a parking space in front. Parked outside most of these rooms were a collection of ancient and very dilapidated pick-up trucks. On further inspection, there appeared to be more activity inside these trucks than there was inside the rooms. It slowly dawned upon me that most of the rooms were being rented not by the week, but by the hour. Had I not been so exhausted, I would have called another taxi and left immediately. I very much doubted that I would get my money back. Resigning myself to a very unpleasant stay, I entered my room. It was even worse than I had imagined. However, after putting on extra clothing to protect myself from the filthy bedclothes, I fell into the deepest of sleeps, hoping that tomorrow would be better than today. It could hardly be worse.

With an eight-hour time change, I was awake by four o'clock the next morning. There was no room service available in my luxury surroundings, so I thought I would take a walk to see if I could find a convenience store. It was still dark as I made my way through the sleazy car park, trying my best to avoid the broken furniture and bedding strewn everywhere. What sort of establishment was this? How could anyone want to stay in such a disgusting place? Having lost my appetite, I returned to my room and sat on the edge of the filthy bed until it was time to get a taxi to the airport where I would spend the next few months. The prospect was definitely losing its appeal.

I checked out as quickly as I could without giving the customary 'have a nice day!'. My destination was the small Hayward Executive Airport, almost directly across the bay from the main San Francisco International Airport and just along the road from the other main international airport in Oakland. It was a little like being back at Shoreham with both Heathrow and Gatwick within a few minutes flying time away. I was soon to find out the similarities stopped there. As we pulled off the highway and drove around the perimeter road, I was impressed by how modern and affluent the airport looked. We passed hangars with gleaming multi-million executive jets awaiting their next flight. I wondered if I had come to the correct place. This looked far too upmarket for someone like me. As we passed the executive section, the aircraft got smaller and the buildings somewhat less impressive. We were entering the flying school section of the airport. Still, we carried on until we reached the maintenance hangars where all pretence of comfort had been replaced by practical structures. They dropped me off outside one of these hangars. The expression on the taxi driver's face should have forewarned me, but I was too keen to fly to worry about anything else.

I entered the hangar and looked around to ask someone where I could find my flight school. Eventually, I found a mechanic with his head deep inside an aircraft's engine bay. I had always found that aircraft engineers were wonderfully informative and helpful and his greetings did not disappoint me. After we completed the normal formalities, I asked if he knew where I could find my flight school. His expression darkened as he asked me why I wanted to know. On hearing my explanation, he called across the hangar to his supervisor, who wandered across to see what all the fuss was about. I repeated my story and he listened without comment. Eventually, he looked directly at me and with a wisdom honed over many years advised me to be very careful dealing with this school. He told me that before parting with any of my money, I should insist on seeing their aircraft and training facilities and meeting their instructors. Then, I should come back and see him. This all seemed very strange. Surely, any flight school must be certified to the same standards as they were in the UK? Pondering these wise words, I set off to find my new school.

I passed the final hangar and there before me was a very shabby Portakabin with a faded sign above the door announcing that this was indeed my school. My heart sank. Still, never judge a book by its cover I thought as I entered the building. The inside made the outside look good. There were empty coffee cups everywhere next to overflowing ashtrays and dirty tables. The reception was just a large table with books and maps strewn around. My flying school at Shoreham was basic although always spotless and tidy, but this was the opposite of that.

The owner suddenly made an appearance and immediately began to complain that I had wasted his time yesterday by not arriving on the correct flight. In the same breath, he enquired if I had the money for my course. This was definitely not the welcome I was expecting or felt I deserved. I was determined not to make any hasty decisions as this school had applied for and obtained my student visa. As politely as I could, I asked if I could get a coffee and some breakfast as I hadn't eaten since arriving the night before. They showed me where the coffee vending machine was as that was the only refreshment available. I sat down and asked if I could look through the training syllabus and I was told I could see those later, when all the paperwork was completed. That I took to mean once I had handed over my money. Undeterred, I asked if they could show me around the school and look at the aircraft. Reluctantly, he agreed and called for one of his employees to conduct a tour. The rest of the building, what there was of it, was much the same as the reception area. There were two briefing rooms, both very basic, with no visible teaching aids. We then went out of the back of the building onto the apron. There sat two ancient and exhausted Cessna 150s. Now, I had flown these before, although I was more used to the updated version of the Cessna 152. I was quite happy to fly this version. I knew very well that this was a cheaper aircraft to rent, and reducing costs was very high on my wish list. My guide then turned around and walked back to the school. I asked if it was possible to have a good look inside the aircraft prior to us going back, only to be told that he did not have the keys. I informed him I had already opened the door, so keys were unnecessary.

During my flying training, I had been taught the importance of the pre-flight external and internal inspection of the aircraft you were about to trust with your life. As I was about to hand over my life savings to fly these aircraft, I felt it was my right to have a very good look around both of them. As I continued my inspection, my guide looked very uncomfortable and asked me to stop, an invitation I declined. He left only to return a few moments later, followed by the very irate owner of the school. I was told in no uncertain terms that until I had paid for my course, I was a trespasser and that I should leave the apron immediately. I had already seen more than enough and quietly followed them back to the reception area.

They placed a flying contract in front of me and they asked me to sign it and to produce the balance owing. Naturally, I declined. I told them I was very concerned about the condition of their aircraft and their facilities. I also expressed my total dissatisfaction with the accommodation provided and explained that I could not possibly live there over the coming months. I expected some disagreement regarding these statements. However, I was unprepared for the torrent of abuse that followed. I was told in no uncertain terms that I had agreed to the contract and they had spent time and money in sponsoring my student visa, securing an instructor and making aircraft available for me. They also informed me they had already paid for my accommodation and therefore, they wanted their money there and then. I began to feel very uncomfortable and I noticed there were now two other men in the room. I stood my ground and refused to pay any more money and said that I would be leaving. Threats followed that they would call the immigration authorities and cancel my visa unless I paid the balance owed. Tension was now at breaking point and an air of violence was permeating through the room. Surely, I would not be physically assaulted and mugged? I was preparing to defend myself when the door suddenly opened and the chief mechanic, with whom I had spoken minutes earlier, walked into the room, followed by two of his colleagues.

He turned to me and very casually asked how things were going and before I could answer, he guided me by the elbow, asking if he could have a quick word with me outside. I was about to protest that my bags were still by the side of my chair when I noticed that his friends had already picked them up and were following us. Rarely have I been so relieved to leave a building and I thanked my new friends. They invited me to have a coffee and informed me that they would call a taxi for me. My relief was only temporary as the realisation dawned that I no longer had a flight school, a student visa or anywhere to stay. This was most definitely not what I had envisaged as my American Dream. I thanked the mechanics and asked them if they had any recommendations for a local flight school. They told me they had no personal experience of training schools but that a company by the name of Hayward Executive Training had some of the newest and best maintained aircraft on the airfield. This organisation sounded very expensive and out of my price bracket, but what did I have to lose, so off I set on the short walk along the perimeter road.

The building appearing in front of me resembled an up-market law office rather than a flight school. I felt rather scruffy as I made my way through sparkling double doors into more of a departure lounge than reception area. The whole place had an air of calm and understated character. The contrast to my previous experience could not have been more complete. I stood there, not sure what to do or where to go. I decided that I had made a mistake and instead of being at a training school, I had made my way into the terminal building for the executive jets sitting outside. As I turned to leave, a very pleasant voice asked if they could be of assistance? I turned to explain my mistake and was met with a wide and welcoming smile. Had the receptionist mistaken me for a wealthy customer, as she was now inviting me to take a seat and asking if I preferred ground or instant coffee. She also offered me continental pastries. Well, for me that was a game changer. I was starving and could have demolished ten cups of coffee, so I thought I would explain my mistake after breakfast. That she was very attractive played absolutely no part in the decision to delay my departure. She left me alone for a few minutes, which was just as well as my mouth was constantly full. Finally, a very smartly dressed chap arrived and asked if he could help me. Damn, I thought, he could have waited a little longer as there were still two pastries to get through and I was only on my third cup of coffee. Wiping crumbs away from the corners of my mouth, I explained that I seemed to have made a mistake and that actually, I was looking for a flight school with a similar name to the one on the outside of his building. With the explanation out of the way, I picked up my bags and prepared to leave.

"Please follow me," was the unexpected reply. "I'm sure that our chief flying instructor is available to answer any questions you may have." With that, we left the main reception and walked the short distance to the classrooms. Here was another, albeit much smaller, reception area with yet again, another very pleasant receptionist who true to form asked me to take a seat and enquired if I would like a coffee and croissant. Well, I thought, why not? I was confident that she would not find out I had already emptied the main reception of their food supply! Making hay while the sun shines was my thought, I deserved a little luck. Once again, before I had finished my feast, they showed me into the chief flying instructor's office. Everything about the man and his surroundings screamed professionalism. It was more like a small airline than a flying school where everyone was in a uniform and polite. Surprised that I had got this far, it was now time to own up to being a complete fraud. There was no way I was ever going to afford to study here.

I explained my predicament and how I had been rescued by a group of mechanics. I further explained that although I was looking for a new flight school, unfortunately my previous school held my student visa authorisation and consequently I may have to return to the UK to reapply for a visa. He asked me if he could have a look at my flying licence and also my passport, and I had no hesitation in handing both over to him. If he had asked, I probably would have handed all my money over, such was the trust this man instilled. I was asked if I would like a tour of the school and aircraft and if I came back to see him in an hour, he would see if he could come up with some answers for me.

I returned to reception, hopefully, to finish my feast, but sadly it had all been cleared away. No sooner had I sat down when a very keen instructor approached me and asked if I was ready to have a look over the facilities. They showed me the classrooms, all wonderfully equipped with the latest teaching aids and I was sure that if you were about to fly a high- or low-wing aircraft, the correct model would be available. It all made poor old Shoreham look very dated. We moved onto the apron and stood in front of sparkling training aircraft parked in rows. He invited me to look over whichever aircraft I chose. They were all painted in the school colours and were immaculate. We made our way back to reception and I waited to be called back into the office. Whilst I was waiting, the receptionist once again came over to see if I needed anything. It was a quiet morning, and we ended up chatting and I explained why I was there and told her about the incident at the other flying school. She was very interested in all things British and seemed to find my accent amusing. Until that point, I had assumed that I had no accent. I was soon enlightened with an accurate impersonation.

Eventually, I was called back into the office. This was where I would be told the cost of the training that I required, so I braced myself and prepared to apologise for wasting their time. The first thing he explained to me was that Jenny, the receptionist I had been talking to, had been on to the immigration services and they had agreed to transfer my student visa to his school as it was fully approved. This was wonderful news and I immediately relaxed a little. He then passed a folder across the table and explained that it contained a detailed breakdown of their charges and the total cost of obtaining my American Commercial Pilot Licence. I took a deep breath and opened the folder. It took a short while for me to absorb the details as each part had been itemised. I turned the page and there at the bottom was the total cost of the course. I was taken aback and shocked at the figure as it was almost within my budget. I could not believe that an establishment such as this would compete financially with the ramshackle school I had recently escaped from.

I was told that there was absolutely no hurry and assured that I could take as much time as I needed to decide. Time, sadly, was something that I did not have as I was homeless and needed to start a course as soon as possible. Once again, I explained my predicament and enquired if this offer included accommodation as that was going to be expensive. He informed me they did not offer accommodation and I would have to pay for that separately. This was why the total cost was so similar to the one I had been previously expecting to pay. The other school had included accommodation in their offer, even if it was in a rundown dump of a motel. This realisation about the price comparison devastated me. For a wonderful moment, I had thought I could afford to study at this amazing school. However, as the cost would leave me with very little money for accommodation and food, it was abundantly clear that it would not be possible for me to study and fly here. I thanked the instructor and returned to reception to collect my bags, which were being cared for by Jenny, the receptionist.

Deciding to sneak in one last coffee and this time, a donut, I asked her if there were any good, cheap motels nearby as I had to have somewhere to stay whilst I tried to find another flying school or failing that, return to the UK. Very kindly, she enquired how my interview had gone and if I were about to start flying with the school. I explained that I would love to study at the school. However, after the cost of the course, I would not have enough money for accommodation. Motels, even the most unpleasant ones, were prohibitively expensive for extended stays. She agreed and told me it was such a shame as their school was by far the best place to fly. Talk about rubbing it in, I thought. With that she disappeared, I presumed to call a taxi for me. I was finishing my second donut when Jenny returned and I stood up to collect my bags and set off. Her next sentence stunned me.

"Please don't take this the wrong way, but I have just called my house mate. We have a spare room and you are very welcome to rent it whilst you are here."

I stopped chewing my donut and just stared at her, unable to say anything. I assumed that I had misheard and that she was suggesting I rent a room somewhere near her. She repeated her offer and looked a little confused by my lack of a response.

"Do you have any donuts at home?" was the first thing that came to mind. I hoped she understood British humour.

We both sat down and I explained to her I had very little money to rent a room, especially in a house. I asked her what sort of rent she and her flatmate wanted. She replied that they had not decided and she asked me how much I could afford. I wished all business deals could be this friendly. I got my files out and made some swift calculations and came up with a monthly budget for rent that was so low, I was embarrassed to tell her. After she insisted on knowing, I told her what I could afford each month. "Wonderful," she replied, "that is more or less exactly what we wanted." It was the only time Jenny ever lied to me, or the only time I was certain that she was not telling the whole truth. She stuck out her hand and declared it a deal. I was totally in shock. I could never have imagined that when I walked in the door less than two hours before, I would have found the perfect place to fly and have found the perfect person to share a house with. Things like this never happened to me; I always tended to walk on the unlucky side of life. I jumped up and after accepting her proposal told her I had better let them know that I would accept their offer before they withdrew it.

"Don't worry," came the reply. "I have already told him you have arranged your accommodation and you will be starting tomorrow." It dawned on me that it was not only her flatmate she had been talking to when she had disappeared. There was one last detail that I had to clarify and that was how far away was her house and how would I commute to the airport each day. Was there a bus service or could I walk, or maybe cycle? Jenny informed me it was a thirty-minute drive and there was no direct bus or train service available. However, as she worked six days a week, I could come in with her each day. This just got better and better and I thought in a moment someone would pinch me and I would wake up back in the previous hell hole of a school. Yet I was very much awake and when Jenny asked if I would like to put my luggage in her car to save me carrying it around for the rest of the day, I replied that it would be a great idea. She handed me her car keys and said it was the first red car just out the back. Thanking her for the umpteenth time that morning, I grabbed my bags and set off to find her car. To this day, I still find it almost impossible to believe, but it is true. I opened the door and there staring back at me was the most perfect red, 1966 Ford Mustang Convertible. Surely, this could not be Jenny's car. However, the keys fitted and I carefully laid my bags on the back seat. Today had just turned out to be beyond my wildest dreams. An American nightmare had turned into the American Dream. I was ready to fly once again. Luck … or maybe, my funny accent, had granted me a new start. It was now up to me to make the most of it.

Chapter 13

A New Way to Fly

We set off at the end of that first day, hood down, driving across the San Mateo-Hayward Bridge. The whole of the San Francisco skyline was set against the backdrop of the Golden Gate Bridge. The sun was setting which bathed the entire scene in a warm light which only added to the mesmerising effect. I could hardly believe that I would make this place my home for the foreseeable future. I looked across at Jenny and then glanced at the long, red bonnet of the mustang as it carved its way through the commuter traffic. I had the most surreal feeling. Could this all really be happening in such a brief space of time? So much had happened in less than the twenty-four hours I had been in San Francisco. I was still lost in thought as we pulled up outside a townhouse in Sausalito. The area looked amazing, very cosmopolitan and laid back. Surely this was not where Jenny lived? I was expecting something far less glamorous. True to form, she had surprised me once again as I grabbed my bags and followed her up the steep steps into the house.

Sausalito today is one of the most prosperous and expensive towns in the Bay Area, home to the rich and famous. Even in the late seventies, it was a very special place which could best be described as shabby chic. The view from the living room down over the town was wonderful and I would spend many hours over the coming months enjoying that view whilst studying for the various tests I had to pass. This first evening, however, was all about making the right impression on both my new housemates. I had asked Jenny if she minded stopping at a local store where I had bought two bottles of their best wine and some snacks. Hopefully, they both enjoyed good wine as much as I did. Introductions completed, we settled down to chat against that amazing backdrop of Sausalito's harbour. Jenny's friend, Michelle, worked for a large advertising agency based in downtown San Francisco and was doing rather well spending many weeks travelling all across the world. During my stay, I was only to meet Michelle on a handful of occasions due to her work commitments. As I sat back with a glass of wine, it was difficult not to feel a certain amount of satisfaction with life. The real work could wait for a while, it was time to relax.

A bright and early start found me, once again, back at Hayward Aviation to complete all the remaining formalities. I held a British Private Pilot Licence, which could be automatically transferred to an American licence after I had passed the American Air Law ground examination, so this had to be my priority. The whole ethos of the British and American attitudes towards flying were diametrically opposed to each other. Back in the UK, the attitude of the CAA seemed to be geared towards how to stop people flying whereas in America, it was how do we get people flying. Obstacles that were put in my way whilst trying to get my British licence had either never existed in the US or had been torn down. For example, when I sat the medical examination back in England, it had taken months before I finally was granted my medical certificate. Here in America, just one visit to the clinic and I walked out with a Federal Aviation Authorities, or FAA, Class 1 Private Pilot medical certificate, contact lens wearing was not a problem here. Most large airfields had an FAA office on-site to facilitate any queries pilots might have. It was in this office I would have to sit my Air Law examination in a few days' time. If successful, I would then immediately be issued with an American licence. In the UK, I would have had to travel to London to get my licence issued and that could take up to two weeks. Life moved at a different pace here and I very much liked it.

I bought a copy of the Airman's Air Law study guide and was amazed at how simple and instructive it was. There were pictures and illustrations explaining not only the law but why the law was there. It made understanding the regulations much easier and also helped me to memorise the details. Compare this to the stuffy and unreadable volumes I had to memorise for my British licence and it felt like a breath of fresh air. I was enjoying a subject that had previously given me many sleepless nights. The other bonus was instead of sitting in a cold, featureless flying clubhouse, I was enjoying world class facilities with endless cups of coffee and donuts. What was not to like? I was more than content to spend my first few days in a classroom learning that my new playground in the sky had many positive differences to the one I had left behind.

Without wishing to go into a detailed explanation of all things American, it was becoming increasingly obvious that as long as you stayed away from the large international airports (known as class A airspace) and you stayed below eighteen thousand feet, then basically, the sky was there for you to explore and enjoy. Well, the chances of the aircraft I was due to fly getting above eight thousand feet would be slim, so the limit of eighteen thousand had no bearing on my intended flights. The classification of various airports was a little more complicated. However, after a few hours of reading, I was comfortable that I understood when and where I could fly. The rest of the Air Law was very similar to that I had studied before and therefore, after just two days, I presented myself at the FAA office to sit my exam. At the back of my airman's manual, I found several practice examinations to help candidates prepare.

Things were not like this when I was studying back at home. If you managed to find a practice exam, it would bear no comparison to the real thing. However, it was the complete opposite here. I opened my examination paper and there before me, were a series of questions taken directly from my manual, or vice versa, it really did not matter which way around it was. Luckily, I had always had an excellent memory for certain things and I glided through the fifty questions in around fifteen minutes. I handed my completed paper to the adjudicator and I walked out less than thirty minutes later, holding an American Private Pilot Licence. Why could things not be this straightforward in England?

Anyway, I had far more important things on my mind as I made my way back to the flight school, where I could now fly legally and I could not wait to explore my new surroundings. I had an introductory flight booked at three o'clock to assess my abilities and knowledge of all things American. Therefore, I had a few hours to spare, time for a walk around the apron and to decide which of the aircraft I would most like to fly. The majority of my flying had been on the trusty Cessna, which was a great training aircraft and the cheapest to fly. I had also been checked out on the Piper 28, a four-seater low-wing aircraft, wonderful to fly and one that felt more like a proper aircraft. It was also ideal and more comfortable for cross-country flying. As I looked out across the Bay towards downtown San Francisco and then further around until I could see the beginnings of the Rocky Mountains, I realised that there was an awful lot of country to cross.

As much as I desperately wanted to fly the Piper, I knew that cost was the most important element in any decisions that I would make. Still, no harm in daydreaming. Also, on the flight-line, were the more advanced aircraft with retractable undercarriages and variable pitch propellers, something I definitely could not afford. Finally, there were the twin-engine aircraft which were expensive and something that one day, I would aspire to fly. However, for now, cost was king and the cheaper the better. The estimate for my American Commercial Pilot Licence had been based on flying the Cessna. So, for now, I resigned myself to that aircraft. The American licence differed from the one in the UK: I needed one hundred and fifty flying hours to qualify which would allow me to do some very basic commercial flying. It was so different from its British counterpart that the UK authorities did not even recognise it. It slowly dawned on me that I would not be able to use my American licence when I got it, as I did not have the green card necessary for me to work in the US. I was about to start a course to gain a licence that I was not allowed to use in the US and which was not valid in the UK. How on earth had I got myself into this situation, I wondered, as I gloomily made my way back to the classroom? I consoled myself with the thought that it was really all about gaining flying hours and experience.

I put my concerns to the head of training as he briefed me for my first flight. He had been so helpful in getting me enrolled into the school and I was now telling him that the course was not what I had originally hoped for. Instead of immediately showing me the front door, he kindly advised me he would consider my problem, but only after he had checked that I could fly at all. After a thorough briefing, including the differences in air traffic control procedures, we finally made our way out onto the flight-line. We passed the row of two-seater Cessna aircraft and stopped at a beautiful Piper 28 four-seater touring aircraft. There, standing next to it, were two rather expectant looking students to whom I was introduced. My instructor informed me they would come along for the ride as they were about to start their private licences and had never flown in the Bay Area before. Well, them and me both, I thought, as all four of us climbed aboard after the usual thorough external checks. As an experienced pilot, well, qualified at least, I was expected to act as pilot in command and the instructor was only there to observe and would only take control if he thought the aircraft was in any danger.

All pre-flight checks completed, I informed him I was ready to taxi out. Astonished, he looked at me and asked me why I had not completed any checklists? Equally astonished, I informed him I had completed all my checklists from memory using mnemonics as I had been taught to do. This really upset him and he let me know, in no uncertain terms, that no aircraft at this school would be permitted to fly unless the pilot had completed all the printed checklists. Anything less was unprofessional and dangerous. He thrust the checklist in front of me and I went through each item, which I had already done using my mnemonic list. Peace restored, albeit temporarily, I called up for taxi clearance. My request produced the most rapid set of instructions I had ever heard, which included five distinct sets of information, none of which I really understood. This was not a good start. How could I ever hope to fly in American airspace if I could understand nothing I was being told on the radio? In my most well-mannered British accent, I asked him if it was not too much trouble, would he mind, most awfully, repeating what he had just said and a little more slowly if that was possible. Well! From his reply, you would have thought I had told him I had just made his daughter pregnant. As I had only been in the country a matter of hours, this was very unlikely. He repeated his instructions, this time even faster and louder than before. I was about to reassure him I had never even met his daughter when my instructor interrupted and calmly repeated back the taxi instructions. He then pointed at a taxiway and told me to head in that direction. We had not even moved an inch and I had already failed mightily to impress him. How could things be so different I thought to myself, as we taxied out, following an executive jet, towards the active runway.

Hayward Executive Airport is a small, local airport, as mentioned, only a few minutes' flying time from two giant international airports. Had this airport been in the UK, it would have been a little like Shoreham, a grass runway, a terminal building and a few hangars. Yet here was an airfield almost as large as Gatwick, with all the facilities found at any large airport. It was truly inspiring to see the size and variety of aircraft that used Hayward and there was I, taxiing along in a queue that included executive jets and airliners. It all felt very grown up and I realised that I was really enjoying myself, despite not understanding the instructions from the controller and being told that I had to use a checklist. This felt like real flying and I imagined myself in one of the large aircraft ahead of us, accepting a coffee from a stewardess as we were about to set off across the continent. I looked back inside my own toy aeroplane and at the instructor sitting beside me and reality quickly returned. I had a very long way to go and my journey started here, well it would have, if only I could understand what the air traffic controllers were saying to me.

Shortly after being cleared for take-off for the second time, I slowly taxied into position. Once cleared for take-off, the controller expects you to expedite your departure as he has usually cleared at least one other aircraft to land on your runway and he also wants to get at least one more aircraft away at the same time. With a verbal reprimand ringing in my ears, I quickly applied full power and set off down the longest runway I had ever seen, and this was only a small provincial airport. Goodness knows what the large ones were like. Climbing away, we gently banked to the left towards the awe-inspiring San Mateo-Hayward Bridge. From here, we turned towards the coast, staying low to fly under the approach path to the runways at San Francisco International Airport. As we reached the coast, the sparkling, blue Pacific Ocean in all its splendour, opened up before us. It was a magnificent and breath-taking sight. I felt a tingling sensation run up my spine as I remembered how much aviation history had been made in this very spot. Howard Hughes had based his aviation companies here and the largest aircraft of its day, the Spruce Goose, had made its one and only flight in the very airspace I was now flying in. What a difference from following the coast of the English Channel to Bognor and back. This was most definitely the real thing.

Following instructions, I turned left and followed the coast towards Monterey. I had begun, before I left home, to study the use of navigation aids to help me along my way. In light aircraft, there were two basic radio aids, the non-directional beacon, known as the NDB and the VHF omnidirectional range beacon, known as the VOR. Luckily, my aircraft was equipped with both these aids and I tuned in the Stockton beacon and turned towards it. On such a beautiful day as this, all I needed to do was follow the coastline and absorb the stunning scenery. From Monterey, we turned inland and climbed over the beautiful Redwood ridge and back towards the San Mateo-Hayward Bridge, which was a great way to find Hayward Airport. I was slowly beginning to understand the rapid-fire speech from the air traffic controller as we lined up with the runway. The warmth of the day produced a few thermals which gently lifted, then lowered the aircraft as I tried to settle myself down for my first landing in America. With a little bit of luck, I landed more or less where I was aiming, without scaring any of my passengers. I was quite pleased with myself. An angry controller quickly dispelled this complacency, asking me to vacate his runway immediately. How rude, I thought as I slowly taxied my way back to the flight-line. As I shut the aircraft down, making sure that I did everything by the printed checklist, the instructor seemed reasonably pleased with my efforts, as did the students in the back of the aircraft. My first American flight was over and apart from struggling with the air traffic controller's instructions

I felt I had made a splendid effort! Time for a coffee and maybe a donut as well.

Chapter 14

Time to Change Course

The one thing I really had to get right was my inability to adapt to how differently the controllers treated pilots in the US. In Britain, everyone was exceedingly polite to each other and neither the controller nor the pilot ever raised their voices. They gave all instructions in a very calm and efficient way, with never more than two instructions in any one transmission. For example, a controller would ask you to turn left onto a heading and climb to a specific height, simple and very difficult to get wrong. In the US, the controller would often give you three, four or even five different instructions in the same breath and at a speed that almost defied belief.

"Piper November 1234, turn left onto zero-nine-zero degrees, climb to six thousand feet on the altimeter setting of three-zero-zero one inches and contact departure control on one-two-four decimal three-five. Oh, and have a good day." Well, after all that he had ensured that my day would be anything but good.

If you asked them to repeat any instructions, you were likely to be rebuked with a loud angry reply which only made matters worse. I was sitting with my coffee in hand, once again, reading my airman's manual, when one of the flight instructors sat next to me and enquired as to how I was getting on. After explaining my concerns, he asked me if I had been in the operations room. I didn't even know there was an operations room! I was not sure if this was something that I was meant to know but had missed. I followed him down a corridor I had not even noticed before and there, at the end, was an office with all the information you could need. Rows and rows of aircraft manuals, a giant whiteboard showing the location of all the aircraft operated by the school and luckily for me, there was a radio tuned into the tower frequency. They invited me to put a headset on and listen to all the live radio communications. I could switch from the tower to ground control, departure and arrivals. Basically, I could listen in to everything said in and around the airport. This was an absolute lifeline for me as I could listen in as long as I liked and I took up the invitation. For the next few days, I sat there, headset clamped firmly on, listening to as many conversations as I could. Slowly, slowly, the mists cleared and I began to understand the way American controllers went about their business. I found that by predicting the format of their instructions, I could insert the details into this framework. I devised this method without the pressure of having to cope with flying the aircraft at the same time. Eventually, I emerged from my lockdown in the operations room with a much clearer understanding of what to say and when to say it and I had also made a new friend. I was keen to take to the skies again and felt a lot more confident, ready to give as good as I got with these controllers.

Before I could fly again, I had to decide how to move forward with my training. I had finally come to realise that pursuing the American Commercial Pilot Licence may not be the best way forward if this licence was not going to be acceptable in the UK. With this thought in mind, I went to find the chief flying instructor once again. I think he was beginning to wish that he had not made me such an excellent offer to join his school. After a long discussion, we came up with a solution to my predicament. I would continue to build my hours up at Hayward but would do so without instructor training for an American licence. Once I had flown the one hundred hours that I required to start my Assistant Flying Instructor Licence, then I would continue my training back in Britain. To stop me from getting into any bad habits, they would check my progress every other week. This would save me a lot of money, which I could then put towards my Instructor Rating. The icing on the cake was when he told me that as I would not enjoy flying the Cessna all over the countryside, I could fly the Piper for the same cost.

I left his office with the prospect of three months of flying whenever and wherever I wished to go and all of this flying would be in the far superior, four-seater Piper. I was in heaven and went to find Jenny to tell her the good news. As I had already had a check ride in the Piper, I would be allowed to fly whenever an aircraft became available. Luckily for me, this worked really well as more often than not, there was always a spare aircraft when I needed one. For my first solo flight from Hayward, I replicated the route I had previously flown. I wanted something that was familiar. Pre-flight checks completed, I called up for taxi instructions and this time, I understood what I was being told. I had been Americanised as far as the radio instructions were concerned. However, I wanted a bit of revenge. Therefore, I used all the correct phrases but spoke in the most British accent I could muster. I may have lost the phraseology war but a brief resistance here and there was no bad thing.

I lined up behind a landing executive jet and started my take-off roll the moment they had cleared me. As I climbed into the morning sun, the unfolding panoramic picture again mesmerised me. The Bay sparkled. I could make out Alcatraz and behind that famous prison, the Golden Gate Bridge proudly displayed its heritage. As I turned towards Monterey, I levelled off as a series of airliners flew overhead to begin their approach into San Francisco. I felt an intense pleasure that I could join this extraordinary aerial ballet and I felt that my future really belonged here. Forty minutes later, I was lining up on my approach and shortly after that, I was sitting in my aircraft as I completed the shutdown checks, feeling utterly at peace with the world. The only thing missing was an attractive friend with a red Mustang convertible to take out for a drink and a meal. Luckily, I knew just where to find one.

One of the many great things about Sausalito was the laid-back promenade with a collection of trendy places to both eat and drink. Jenny and I were sitting on the balcony of one such establishment, watching as the ferry made its way out into the bay for the quick trip to Fisherman's Wharf. In front of me, I had spread out a map of the surrounding area and was proudly showing off the proposed routes that I would fly over the coming days and weeks. Being a usual thoughtless, self-centred twenty-year-old, I had assumed that Jenny would share the excitement I felt now that I had decided not to pursue my American licence in favour of just building my hours. I told her of my plans to return to Britain as soon as I had reached my goal of one hundred and fifty hours to start my instructor course.

In retrospect, my total insensitivity was astonishing. I had given absolutely no thought to the possibility that Jenny enjoyed my company and had hoped that I might be around for a lot longer than I intended to be. Our relationship had been platonic. I was pathetically grateful to Jenny for taking pity on a homeless stranger and I had no intention of taking advantage of her. In fact, I had tried my best to do the opposite. On days when I was not flying, I would endeavour to be as useful as I could be around the house. While I was not great at home improvement, I knew the basics and set about fixing anything that required attention. I also cleared the small backyard and made it into a habitable area. I knew I was paying far too little rent, so by doing tasks like this, I felt I was at least helping to pay my way. I was far too wrapped up in my selfish world to consider anybody or anything else. I was behaving appallingly but sadly did not realise this. Well, I had not realised it until a few days later, when our third housemate returned and made me aware of the problem.

That realisation was still to come and this evening, eventually, I got Jenny to laugh and the rest of the evening glided by as we took in the sights and sounds of the night. We decided that on her next days off we would fly up into the Rocky Mountains to spend the night. Apparently, motels were cheap once you got away from the city so the whole adventure would be well within my new budget. I went to sleep that night still not quite believing that all this was happening to someone who had been cleaning and loading aircraft only a few months ago. All I had to do now was not make any stupid mistakes, as I was intending to fly into some very dangerous and mountainous areas. Maybe, I would live to regret making promises after one too many glasses of wine. With this sobering thought running through my mind, I finally drifted off to sleep.

Chapter 15

Valley Flying

Determined to fulfil my promise, I planned a trip that would allow us to explore the extraordinary beauty that lay just to the north of the Bay Area. Sitting in the briefing room, I unfolded a map of the area I wanted to fly to. I had heard of the Napa Valley and Sonoma and my finger ran over the map in front of me as I tried to locate them. As with most rolled up maps, you let go of one corner and it quickly tries to find its partner on the opposite one. I had temporarily solved this problem with a strategically placed cup of coffee. Eventually, I found what I was looking for and after a few calculations, decided that this would be a great warm-up flight to prepare me for the more difficult flights I intended to undertake in the future. The plan was after take-off, to fly up the Napa Valley, home to the famous wine region and then land at the northern end of the valley at Sonoma. To have lunch, sadly without wine, and then to fly to Santa Rosa for a cup of coffee. My last leg would take me across what I hoped would be beautiful pine forests until I reached the Pacific. I would then turn left and follow the Pacific Highway back towards San Francisco and home. The names of the places I was intending to visit seemed somehow unreal, more familiar in television dramas or films. Was I really going to fly to these places? It made my previous cross-country flight to Blackbushe and Thruxton seem a little tame. Still, no time to ponder such things as I continued to plan. I wanted to get this flight under my belt as soon as possible. I went to the operations room and discovered, to my delight, that there was an aircraft free the next day, after which there would be only limited availability. Well, that concentrated my mind and with the confidence of youth, I booked the aircraft out from eight in the morning until eight at night. I did, after all, have my Night Rating and if I could land on a grass strip illuminated by a few bonfires, then landing at a fully equipped airport should not present too many problems. Oh, the foolishness of youth! I settled myself down to plan my flight in greater detail. I really could not allow any errors to creep into my calculations, I had no intention of repeating past mistakes. I needed to plan for refuelling in both Sonoma and Santa Rosa and I also needed to withdraw enough cash to pay for fuel and landing fees just in case they did not accept my one and only credit card. I had my work set out before me and only a few hours to plan the flight before I went home to get some sleep. It was going to be a long day tomorrow, in actual fact, much longer than I could ever have imagined.

The weather early next morning looked very promising as clear skies were forecast with a gentle breeze off the Pacific. I checked the forecast for Sonoma and Santa Rosa and everywhere was forecasting clear skies. This was going to be a fabulous day to go flying. I rechecked all my calculations from the previous evening and all was good. I also had the added comfort of the VOR navigation beacons dotted along my route which would help guide me towards my destination. I packed all my gear together in my flight bag after filing a flight plan with the air traffic controller at Hayward. Excitedly, I went to find Jenny as she had swapped her day off with a friend and was coming with me. I had even visited the pilot shop in reception and had spent far too much money on a pair of Ray-Ban Aviator sunglasses. I thought they made me look very 'Charlton

Heston,' or even like Tom Cruise in *Top Gun*. In reality, I probably looked like a dodgy porn star. Luckily, or maybe not, everyone was too kind to tell me that.

I wandered into reception, desperately trying to look as cool as possible, only to find Jenny at her desk. Her friend had forgotten she was meant to be working that day and so Jenny could not accompany me on the flight. I was really disappointed and my first thoughts were to postpone the flight until Jenny was free. A quick dash back to the operations room confirmed that the aircraft would not be available for an entire day for at least another ten days. I had booked the aircraft and I would be charged if I cancelled. I went back to tell Jenny the bad news, although I must admit that I kept a keen eye out behind my new sunglasses, just in case there was another beautiful woman who fancied flying with Charlton or Tom. Obviously, there were none, so after my goodbyes, I set off, slightly deflated, towards my aircraft. I even took my sunglasses off. There was nobody to impress and anyway, it had clouded over, which nicely reflected my mood.

As I called for taxi instructions, I looked around at the three empty seats and again reflected that it was such a waste. I had even enquired if anybody at the school would like a day out, but nobody could spare the time or they really didn't want to be seen with someone wearing such ridiculous sunglasses. Whatever the reason, I was on my own. As they cleared me for take-off, the gathering cloud had now shown its true identity. It was a sea mist which was creeping in from the Pacific. The hills to my left were now completely obscured by low clouds. However, a glance to the right, my intended direction, still looked clear, so I accepted my clearance and began the take-off. The sea mist was now sweeping across the bay and the San Mateo-Hayward Bridge disappeared as I began my climb. This was slightly unnerving as I was going to use the bridge as my first turning point towards Sonoma. At two hundred feet, the nose of the aircraft was swallowed up by the ever-advancing mist, whole swathes of countryside were also disappearing as I entered the eerie fog bank. Before I had the chance to become too concerned, I broke out into dazzling bright sunshine and my heart rate slowly returned to normal. To my far left, I could make out the skyscrapers of downtown San Francisco, their noses pushing through the fog into bright clear skies. The tops of the massive Golden Gate Bridge towers stood out, although the actual road and footpaths were hidden by the fog. The entire effect was spellbinding. It looked as though a giant hand had rubbed away complete sections of the Bay Area, leaving just the higher levels visible. I sat alone in my small aircraft and felt a total detachment from the real world. I was quickly brought back to reality as an irate controller gave me a frequency change for the second time. The spell broke and I continued my climb towards the Napa Valley and my first destination of the day.

The sky was now clear and the sun shone without interruption, helping with my limited navigation skills. I turned left as I re-crossed the north bay shoreline and picked up the snaking Highway 121 which, if my calculations were correct, would lead me directly to the Sonoma Valley Airport. Sure enough, less than forty minutes later, a long tarmac runway appeared out of the shimmering morning's haze. There were no other aircraft around and they cleared me for a straight-in approach and landing. The Piper is a wonderful aircraft and if you point it somewhere, it carries on that way, unlike the Cessna which would wander all over the sky. Gently reducing power and extending the flaps, the approach was relaxing and smooth. Before I knew it, the tyres were making a little screeching noise in protest at being put onto a hot piece of tarmac. They soon quietened down as we slowed to a fast-walking pace and taxied towards the terminal building. This was my first taste of a provincial airport, away from the hustle and bustle of the Bay Area and I was impressed. Everything was orderly and well designed, with smart new looking hangars with rows of equally smart aircraft parked outside. They gave me explicit instructions where to park and a very warm welcome as I made my way into the main terminal building. Halfway there, I remembered that I had left my most prized possession in the aircraft. I quickly trotted back, unlocked the door and retrieved my sunglasses. With these now firmly in place, I continued back towards the terminal.

Whilst there were no executive jets, there were several very expensive looking twin-engine turbo propeller aircraft sitting on the apron awaiting their next flights. I walked behind one of these aircraft and then emerged in front of it. Anyone looking from the terminal may well have assumed that the cool dude with the sunglasses had just flown a very cool aircraft, although I very much doubted that I fooled anybody. I went in search of the operations office to pay my landing fee and to file for the next stage of my journey. As I was flying under visual flight rules, I did not have to file a flight plan, unlike the aircraft that were flying under instrument flight rules. I had no Instrument Rating anyway so that was not an option. Good airmanship dictated that it would be an excellent idea to let someone know where I was intending to fly. There was a vast wilderness out there where even to this day, aircraft can and do, disappear without trace. If anything went wrong, I wanted as many people as possible to know where I was or at least where I was intending to be.

Formalities over, I had a look around the airport. I was in no hurry. I did, after all, have the aircraft for the whole day, so might as well use the whole day. I wandered into the first hangar I came upon and there before me were several beautifully maintained vintage aircraft, most of them having been built in the nineteen forties and fifties. It was like being in a sweet shop when you were five years old. My eyes did not know what to look at first and I wanted to touch and feel everything. I was still wearing my sunglasses, so I had to try to maintain some sense of decorum and not run around whooping with delight. An elderly mechanic wandered over, I presumed to throw me out, so I turned to leave.

"Just saw you get out of that real nice King Air," was his opening line, which I had to admit left me a little lost for words.

"You're kinda young to be flying such a sophisticated aircraft," he continued. The penny dropped. My little circle around the back of the executive aircraft to appear once more at the front had fooled him and I felt embarrassed. I quickly explained that my aircraft was the little Piper parked just behind the King Air.

"Hell, I used to do stuff like that when I was your age," he said between racks of laughter. It looked like I may not get thrown out after all. After a quick introduction he informed me that he was not actually a mechanic, he just liked to experiment with his Piper Cub. His proper job was flying a Boeing 737 for United Airlines, this was just a hobby. He invited me into a small office where a continual supply of coffee was available, something I had noticed applied to most offices in America. He chatted about flying and seemed interested in what I was trying to achieve, both in the States and back home. He had come from a military background straight into airline flying after he had left the services. He seemed amused and more than a little sceptical when I revealed my ambitions to fly for the airlines. Still, he was hospitable and we spent a very informative hour together as he showed me around the rest of the aircraft in the hangar. After a last coffee, we said our farewells as I headed back towards my aircraft. A short while later, I taxied into position on the active runway. Checklist complete, I set off into the mid-morning sun to explore the rest of the Napa Valley and to find Santa Rosa. My day was going very well, I thought to myself as I settled onto my next heading and new adventures.

I had read about a wine train that runs along the Napa Valley, taking in most of the more famous vineyards and as luck would have it, there it was directly ahead of me. This was far too good an opportunity to miss. I slowed down, descended to five hundred feet and followed the train; no need to navigate, let the train take the strain, I happily thought to myself. So, off we both set, heading north from Napa itself. The views were simply stunning, hills on both sides and vineyards scattered along the valley floor. I pulled ahead of the train and then turned back with a lazy turn to the left. Climbing and passing overhead enabled me to once again, creep up behind the train. I could happily do this all day. As with all things flying, there is always something or someone waiting to ruin your day, if you are not careful. The valley narrowed and the hills either side towered alarmingly above me. I could also see that the train driver was not impressed with my antics. Time to leave, applying full power, I steadily climbed out of the valley. The day was warm and my rate of climb was not as fast as I had expected as the aircraft struggled through the thin air.

Eventually, I rose free of the valley and the views became even more impressive. I relaxed and once again, enjoyed myself, until I realised that by following the train, I had left my intended flight track. I was now a little unsure of my position, or to put it another way, I was lost. As I'd been taught, when uncertain of your position, the best course of action is to look at the ground, identify some features such as churches, railway lines or towns and then look at your map and try to match what you see. I looked down and there below me was, well nothing really, lots and lots of nothingness. Bare scrubland with no roads, no towns, no anything. I looked at my map and it also showed lots of nothing. Well, this didn't happen in Southern England, there was always something, the trick was working out what that something was. Here, there really was lots of nothing and it was immediately obvious that with lots of nothing, it was going to be very difficult to determine where I was.

My saving grace was the VOR radio beacon that I had only just started to understand and use occasionally. The airfield at Santa Rosa had one of these beacons. I looked at my map, saw the frequency of the beacon and dialled it into my receiver. However, the needle on my instrument stubbornly refused to show any interest in telling me which way to fly. This was not looking good at all until I remembered that the beacon had to be in the line of sight of the aircraft. There were still hills around me which could block the signal, so I began a steady climb. As I passed three thousand feet, relief flooded through me as my needle suddenly burst into life and pointed directly towards Santa Rosa and salvation. I began a gentle turn and my heartbeat slowly returned to normal. Twenty minutes later, I was talking to the control tower at Santa Rosa and they gave me vectors to line me up with their main runway. I felt very important as I was sequenced behind a regional airliner and cleared to land. This was real flying and I could not keep an enormous smile off my face as I settled onto the runway. The day was definitely getting better and better. Time for lunch, I thought to myself, as the engine began cooling down with the usual clicks and I opened the doors to allow some fresh air to waft over me. I realised that I was starving.

As with all the airports I had visited so far, Santa Rosa was more like an international airport in Europe than a small provincial airfield. I wandered into the terminal building to be met with rows of check-in kiosks and car hire desks. This was very much a fully equipped, functional airport. How on earth was I, in my little Piper Warrior, allowed to land at an airport like this? Still, that was a question I would ponder on, once I had demolished the enormous plate of food that had been placed in front of me. This was better than the stale sandwich and lukewarm coffee they had served at Thruxton and Blackbushe.

All I had to do now was to plan the final and longest leg of my journey, towards the Pacific coastline and then south back towards the Bay Area and home. I set off to file my final flight plan of the day. If I could be airborne in thirty minutes, I had calculated that I could be back at Hayward by five o'clock, in time to catch a lift home with Jenny. I checked the weather along my intended route and everything looked good. The only slight concern was the sea mist still drifting in and out of the Bay Area, although it was forecast to clear by the time I arrived. I made the wise decision to fill up with fuel in case there were any delays getting into Hayward. I called the refuelling company and asked them to meet me at my aircraft. I was politely told that I would have to taxi over to their refuelling area. Tankers did not get out of bed for the amount of fuel I required. Suitably chastened, I returned to the Warrior and requested permission to taxi to the pumps. This caused some amusement among the controllers. Apparently, they don't call them pumps as they do at airfields I had visited in England. After I made myself understood, I set off to find the refuelling apron, which was where the pumps were. All this took a lot longer than I had expected, so it was nearly an hour later when I found myself airborne once again.

I climbed over the most beautiful pine forest on the way to my first turning point at Bodega Bay. It never ceased to amaze me how quickly civilisation was left behind and once again, there was nothing but trees below me. As I continued my climb, I could see the Pacific Ocean appear on the horizon, so at least I was heading the right way. Thirty minutes later, I was doing a series of turns over the lovely little coastal town of Bodega Bay before finally turning south to follow the Pacific Highway all the way back to San Francisco. I could now put navigation to the back of my mind and just enjoy the scenery as it unfolded below me. The sun was setting, casting amazing shadows across the many hills which marked the contours of the coastline. My next turning point was the Golden Gate Bridge itself, where I intended to turn overhead Sausalito and then inland towards Oakland and finally on, towards Hayward. This was a little more complicated than following the coastline past San Francisco and turning over the San Mateo-Hayward Bridge, but I thought I had it in me to navigate my way around. The first hint that all was not going to plan was the sight of a few low clouds brushing the tops of some coastal hills below me. I was still flying in bright sunshine. However, I was losing sight of the ground below me. This sent little tingles of apprehension down my spine. I sat up a little straighter, put my sunglasses away and tried to put on my serious pilot's face. This could get interesting.

Another twenty minutes went by and the fog bank below me kept moving on and then offshore. Eventually, I could once again, only see the towers of the Golden Gate Bridge pushing majestically through the cloud. Not a great sign. At this point, I decided that it would be far better and safer to keep to the coastline and fly towards Monterey, where hopefully, I could get around the fog bank and approach Hayward from the opposite direction. As I was now approaching San Francisco, I thought that maybe I had better call them to let them know my change of plan. I contacted the approach frequency and was abruptly told that they were far too busy to help as they were handling traffic unable to land due to fog. They gave me strict instructions to stay well away from controlled airspace and well, nothing else really. How rude, I thought. Well, there goes that plan. I now had to avoid the one piece of airspace I was vaguely familiar with. Trying to keep a stiff upper lip, I briefly considered putting my sunglasses on again. That seemed to work in all the aviation films I had ever seen. Had Jenny been with me, I think I really would have put them back on to hide the apprehension that was etched across my face. What to do now? I could not fly along the coast and my other route was now covered in fog. Added to this, nobody had the time to talk to me as I could hear just how busy the frequency had become, even some airline pilots were sounding a little concerned. What hope did I have with my very limited experience?

When faced with a problem, I have a habit of turning around and going back the way I had come. It had worked in the past, so it was definitely worth a try now. I had liked Sonoma airport and I had made a friend in the hangar, so I pulled the nose of the aircraft around and headed back. The fog had now crept up behind me and was covering all the low ground as far as I could see. The tops of the hills were occasionally poking their heads up as if to look around before being once again swallowed up by the ever-increasing fog bank. I set course for Sonoma, hoping that I could reach it before the weather closed in and shut the airport down. I set maximum cruise power and sped up. I called up their approach frequency and was so relieved that they had time to actually speak to me. This was more like it. The controller asked if I could accept an instrument approach as the weather was rapidly deteriorating and was unlikely to be suitable for a visual approach. I had no Instrument Rating, a qualification that allows a pilot to fly in cloud. Therefore, I could not legally accept this approach. For a fleeting moment, I considered just accepting the very tempting offer. However, I wanted to become a professional pilot and now was not the time to ignore the rules of the air. With a certain resignation, I admitted that I was not qualified to accept an instrument approach, fully expecting to be sent away as I had been from San Francisco.

Much to my surprise, the friendly controller informed me he would offer me a special visual approach and gave me a heading to fly. Relief swept over me and I followed his instructions to the letter. He gave me further headings and asked if I had flown an instrument landing system approach before. I admitted that I had not. I thought I detected a sigh as he informed me that he would hand me over to the next controller for a precision approach radar landing, whatever that might be,

I thought to myself. The next few minutes were exhilarating and terrifying in equal measure. The controller asked me to check if I had three greens. Three green what? I thought but wisely kept it to myself. Quickly looking at my instrument panel, I could see nothing green and told him so. This time, the sigh was noticeable as he asked me if I had my landing gear down and had three green lights to confirm they were down. I informed him that as my landing gear never came up, I assumed that it was still down. The Warrior had a landing gear that did not retract and extend. I was then told not to reply to any of his instructions until he told me to contact the tower. He then continued to talk me down for hopefully, a safe landing.

"Warrior November three four, you are five miles from touchdown. Turn left five degrees and start your descent from one thousand five hundred feet at eight hundred feet a minute. You are now three miles from touchdown. You are left of the centre line. Turn right five degrees. You are fifty feet low. Reduce your rate of descent. You are now on the centre line. Turn left three degrees. You are now fifty feet high. Increase your rate of descent. You are on the centre line. You are on the glide path. You are cleared to land. Contact tower. Good day and good luck."

I was flying in thick fog, three hundred feet from the ground when suddenly, a runway appeared in front and thankfully, below me. I throttled back as I had allowed my speed to increase after being totally absorbed in following all the instructions. Luckily, the speed was not excessive and I gave a small prayer of thanks, my tyres squeaking as they met the runway. I was down. As I taxied back to the spot that I had left only a few hours earlier, I passed on my thanks to the controllers who had brought me safely back to earth. I was deep in their debt. The whole airfield was now enveloped in an eerie grey blanket as the last of the evening's sun was obliterated. As I walked towards the hangar, again, I felt a small shiver run through me, I had definitely got away with something today, another time I might not be so lucky. I went to the small office where I had met the United Airlines captain and to my relief, he was still there, packing up his gear. He turned as I entered the room and gave a knowing smile.

"Hope you learned something today, kid," he said. I looked at him puzzled, until he pointed out the radio on the shelf behind him. "Anyone who does not know what three greens mean has no place to be flying in the conditions out there," he duly informed me. "Still, you didn't kill yourself, so maybe, just maybe, you may make an airline pilot one day."

With those words ringing in my ears, I asked him if he knew of anywhere that I could stay the night as the thought of waiting for the weather to clear and flying back to Hayward filled me with dread. He asked me where I lived and after informing him that I lived in Sausalito, he offered to drop me off as it was only thirty minutes out of his way. Thirty minutes! I refused. I could not possibly expect him to do that for a total stranger. He informed me I was not a total stranger. We had met earlier that day and we were both aviators, so we were anything but strangers. It really impressed me that this man considered me a fellow aviator and so I reluctantly accepted his generous offer. As we were about to leave the office, he asked me if I had forgotten something. Embarrassed, I quickly apologised for not thanking him.

"No, you have already thanked me. Don't you think you should let your school know what you have done with their aircraft? You never know, they may need it again, one day."

Damn, I ran to the phone and called the operations room. The phone rang for an eternity. Eventually, it was answered by a very irate voice, not a good sign, I thought to myself, was I in real trouble for not getting their aircraft back? I told them who and where I was and that I intended to bring their aircraft back tomorrow when the weather cleared. I braced myself for a good telling off but instead, I was thanked for letting them know and congratulated for making a safe and sensible decision to divert rather than attempt a risky approach into Hayward. Apparently, one of the other aircraft in the fleet had attempted to get back and had accepted an instrument approach which had resulted in the aircraft being badly damaged. He was very glad that I had not made the same unfortunate error and not to worry about the aircraft as they would fly me out tomorrow to collect it. As I put the phone down, I wondered how much longer my luck would hold. God, I needed a beer when I got home that night.

Chapter 16

Preparing for Mountain Flying

After my Napa Valley adventure, I thought it was time for some serious local flying, preferably within sight of the airport at all times. This new conservative approach lasted much longer than I had imagined, nearly a whole day. That night I had my maps spread all over Jenny's dining table as I planned a real adventure, hopefully, this time, without the scary bits. I wanted to experience flying into the Rocky Mountains, well hopefully, not literally into them, but to fly to the Rockies promised to be exhilarating. My finger wandered all over the map until I finally decided to fly north as it looked more desolate and interesting. My finger stopped at the town of Red Bluff. I did not understand why I chose that location. I guess I must have liked the name. Anyway, the die was cast. My first leg was to be from San Francisco to Red Bluff, a distance of around two hundred miles, so about two hours' flying time away, perfect. Right, where to go next? My finger began wandering all over the map once again, until it stopped at Reno. This was also a distance of around two hundred miles. My finger was better at navigation than I was. I looked Reno up in my travel book and it appeared to be a poor man's Las Vegas. Well, I was poor so that looked like a good omen. Reno it was then. I sat back, feeling very satisfied with myself. It would be just over four hours' flying time to reach both Red Bluff and Reno, more than enough to have earned a beer or two in Reno where I intended to stay for the night.

Whilst I was busily working away, it suddenly occurred to me that it would be only polite to ask Jenny if there was anywhere that she would like to visit. After all, she was coming with me this time and I owed her so much. After another glass of wine, I discovered that Jenny had friends in Lake Tahoe, which was only a short flight from Reno, a perfect place to visit in late summer, not so good later in the year, when it turned into a winter wonderland. The decision was made. My last choice was Carson City, a real cowboy land where many famous films and television series had been filmed. This was *Bonanza* and *Rawhide* country. I just had to see that, although Jenny was not so enthusiastic. But she admitted that she had never been there, so luckily, I was able to convince her. The final leg back to San Francisco would take in a detour to fly over Yosemite National Park which I calculated would be the longest leg at just over three hundred miles, not a problem for an experienced aviator with sunglasses.

I sat back, feeling pleased with myself. I now had a plan, an excellent plan I thought and although it was going to eat into my budget, I felt that both Jenny and I deserved two days away from the hustle and bustle of San Francisco. I just hoped that this time, there would be no unexpected fog banks to ruin my day. This was the first time Jenny would be flying with me and I was desperate to impress her. We drove into Hayward the next day and I booked an aircraft for the two days that Jenny had off work. There was no going back now. I had a week to prepare for our trip and I passed the time by local flying and improving my navigational skills using radio aids. The more I used them, the more comfortable I felt. I also practised my landings. They seemed to be getting worse, not better, with time. After an afternoon of touch-and-go circuits, I ironed out some of my bad habits and finally taxied back to the flight school with a renewed feeling of competence, hopefully, not misplaced. Feeling rather pleased with myself, I completed my post-landing checks and wandered into the operations room to return the aircraft keys and my headset trying to look as cool as possible. I was about to go in search of a coffee when a voice called me back. They informed me that the chief flying instructor would like to see me in his office as soon as possible. Well, that was the end of my feelings of self-adulation. I must have made a rather large error to be summoned in this fashion. So, it was with some trepidation that I gently knocked on his door. Funny, I remembered, on my first day he had said that should I ever have any problems, his door was always open; it never was. Oh well, here goes, I thought to myself as I obeyed his command to enter.

He came straight to the point informing me he had just been told of my plans to take his receptionist away for two days and that I was intending to fly into some challenging airfields over some equally challenging territory and what did I have to say for myself? Well, that caught me off guard. I had expected to get a dressing down for something I had done and here I was, getting the same treatment for something I had so far only intended to do. Was he going to stop me, or was he going to congratulate me on such a splendid idea? He did neither. Instead, he asked me if I thought the Piper Warrior, with its limited speed and endurance, was a suitable aircraft for this plan of mine. Immediately, I saw he had a very valid point. However, it was the only aircraft I could afford and he already had kindly allowed me to fly the Piper at the cost of the Cessna. In my defence, therefore, I put this point across backing it up with some calculations I had put together about range and endurance. He sat back in his chair and studied me carefully, enough to make me feel slightly uncomfortable. "I also understand that you carried out a full surveillance radar approach into Sonoma last week?" he said. Now, we were getting somewhere. Here comes the telling off. We both knew, I did not hold an Instrument Rating and was, therefore, unqualified to make such an approach. He had put me off balance and was now about to deal the knockout blow. I braced myself and instead of trying to justify my actions, I kept quiet and allowed him to continue.

"I expect you know that another of our aircraft attempted a landing here at Hayward instead of diverting as you did?" I told him that yes, I had heard and I felt sorry for the unfortunate pilot and aircraft and wished them both a speedy return to flying duties.

"Yes, well, that's as maybe, but therein lies the problem. We are now one aircraft short and we cannot allow you to take an aircraft away for two days when we now need all the aircraft for training."

That was a real hammer blow and I felt the air leaking from my lungs as I attempted a reply. How was I going to break this to Jenny, who had been counting the days until we left?

"Therefore, I propose a solution to our mutual problem," he continued, once again pausing and looking at me as if he were deciding as he spoke. My ears pricked up and I waited with bated breath for the next sentence. I could not imagine what he was going to say next. Was he going to loan me his car so I could drive instead? He then continued by asking me if I had ever noticed the stubby aircraft with the funny shaped tail parked in the apron's corner.

I had noticed this aircraft on my first day; I had been told that it was a Beechcraft Bonanza. Although still a single-engine aircraft, the Bonanza was a pure-bred racing car compared to the Warrior. Not only did it have a much larger engine, but it also had a propeller that you could adjust for greater speed and an undercarriage that went up and down again allowing the aircraft to go much faster without the drag from the wheels. Had I been flying this on my radar approach, I could have confirmed that yes, I had three greens, assuming I had remembered to put the landing gear down. I was still busily daydreaming when I was asked again if I had noticed this aircraft.

"Yes, sir, it's a Beechcraft Bonanza, with a variable pitch propeller and retractable landing gear which can cruise at one hundred and sixty miles an hour and climb to eighteen thousand feet, I think."

Again, he stared at me, I suspected I kept surprising him.

"Yes, that's the one. How would you like to take that aircraft instead? We don't use it for basic training."

At first, I was overjoyed until reality raised its ugly head and my euphoria quickly evaporated. To fly such an advanced aircraft, I would have to sit two exams, one for retractable landing gears and one for variable pitch propellers. I would then have to undertake at least three hours of dual instruction before being let loose on such an aircraft. Apart from this, the cost of hiring the Beechcraft was double the cost of the Piper, money I could not afford. I thanked him for his offer but politely declined. My adventure would have to be cancelled.

"I know what you will have to do to be qualified to fly the Beechcraft; I wrote the conversion manual."

I conceded that was an advantage, however, the cost was too great, a fact even the chief instructor could not deny. He then informed me that it was not my fault he was an aircraft short. Indeed, if I had attempted to land at Hayward that night, he may well have been two aircraft short, so he was prepared to let me fly the Beechcraft for the price of the Warrior. I was about to interrupt when he finished by informing me that he personally, would conduct the conversion course to make certain that I could handle such a complicated aircraft. I was in the middle of a heartfelt thank you when he dismissed my gratitude with a sobering remark: "It's not you I am particularly concerned about, it's Jenny. Good receptionists are very hard to find." Uncertain if he was joking or not - I suspected the latter - I left his office in search of the Beechcraft's operating manual. I now had a lot of extra work to do, two ground examinations followed by a three-hour flying test. What had I let myself in for? When in doubt, I did what I had become accustomed to, I went to find Jenny.

After two days of study, once again, I presented myself at the local FAA office to sit my two ground examinations. I just about understood why there was a need for the variable speed propeller exam. If you tried to take off or land with an incorrect setting on the propeller it would most definitely ruin your entire day. There were a series of complex aerodynamic reasons for this. Most passed over my head. I learnt all the answers to the practice examinations and thank goodness, there they were, once again, repeated in the real exam. The only practical thing I had learnt was to always take off with the propeller in fine pitch, as that gave you the greatest power and also, to land with the propeller in fine pitch, just in case you had to perform a go-around or a touch-and-go landing. Everything in between was really a matter of playing with the pitch control until the engine sounded happy. It was a little like trying to get the best gear on a bicycle when you are pedalling up a steep hill, it's not the same gear you would use on a flat road or going downhill. You always went up a steep hill in the lowest gear and experimented with the other gears until you felt comfortable. Lots of theory but in practise, not too complicated, just about worthy of a ground exam.

Why, oh why, did I have to sit an exam about a retractable landing gear? There are two and only two things you can do with a retractable undercarriage, you can put it up after take-off and you can lower it before landing. If you forget the first bit, the flight will take longer and it will be noisier. If you forget the second bit, the landing will be very much shorter and very, very much louder. I grasped these elementary concepts in about thirty seconds. I sat the examination and once again, ticked the correct answers that I had learnt by heart the previous evening. I presented my answer sheets at the front desk and it took the clerk about the same time it had taken me to write my name to inform me I had passed. I handed over my licence and a twenty-dollar note. He kept the money, stamped my licence and sent me on my way. All I had to do now was learn the Beechcraft flying manual and convince the chief flying instructor that not only could I fly his aircraft safely, but I could also take his receptionist into the mountains and bring her back again in one piece, not a straightforward task.

The next day, after an evening spent memorising all the power and pitch settings for the Bonanza, I presented myself for the first of my three conversion flights. After a classroom briefing to check my understanding of variable pitch propellers and the bits that go up and down, we set off to find our aircraft.

The first thing that really impressed me was the size of the Bonanza. It was a six-seater aircraft but looked and felt much larger compared to the Warrior. Sitting at the controls, there were at least twice as many dials and buttons to play with. I also now had two levers to push and pull, one for the engine and one for the propeller. This really felt like a big step up from the basic training aircraft I was used to. After checking everything was where it should be, I was asked to perform a series of touch-only drills, including what and how to use all the additional features that I had not come across before. My instructor seemed satisfied that I would not try to raise the landing gear using the propeller levers and vice versa and eventually, we were ready to start.

Starting the engine on a Cessna or Piper is not that different from starting your car. You put the key in, if it's a wintry day, maybe a bit of choke and away you go. If you try this with the Bonanza, there will be one of two outcomes: either the engine will not start and the battery quickly runs flat; or the engine could misfire, potentially causing a lot of damage. To get the best outcome, you had to carefully prime the engine, then set the dual mixture control to the correct setting and then and only then, attempt a start. I carefully performed these actions and turned the key. The propeller turned slowly and then, bang, the whole aircraft shook as the massive engine roared into life. I was really taken aback and for a second, I thought I had done something wrong and the engine would drop out of the bottom of the aircraft. I looked anxiously across at the instructor who seemed totally at ease. My goodness, I thought, it's meant to do that. As the engine warmed up, the vibrations slowly reduced to where I felt content that the aircraft would not shake itself to pieces. Checklist in hand, I began to slowly and methodically read through all my after-start checks and a few moments later, I was calling up for taxi clearance. Taxiing my previous aircraft required a lot of power to get the aircraft moving. With the Bonanza, I just had to think about applying power before I realised that we were going far too fast and had to brake sharply, not exactly an elegant way to leave the parking area, especially as my instructor informed me that he had seen people perform smoother landings than my taxiing performance. At the holding point, I turned into the wind to perform a full power check on the engine. The whole aircraft shook as the turbo-charged engine reached its limit. The noise also made communications difficult and I had to make sure the headset I was wearing covered both ears - normally, I only had one covered.

All checks completed, we lined up on the runway. Clearances received, once again, I applied full power and away we went. With my previous aircraft, the take-off was reasonably civil, the speed slowly built up and at the correct speed, a gentle pull back on the control column and the aircraft lazily left the runway and climbed steadily away. Now, I was expecting a little more exciting performance from the Bonanza. We were very light, only two people on board and a relatively low fuel load, so there was a lot of performance in hand. As the engine reached full power and the propeller snatched at the air, the aircraft immediately raised its nose and shot off down the runway at an alarming rate of knots. I was so busy concentrating on keeping the aircraft straight with the amount of torque being produced that I had not noticed that we were passing one hundred knots and we were still firmly on the runway. This was twenty knots faster than I had intended, so I gently pulled back on the controls. We shot into the air and I suddenly lost all visual clues as the nose pointed directly towards the stratosphere. From the control tower, this must have looked highly unusual, a small aircraft using a lot of runway and then attempting to climb away like a jet fighter.

Meanwhile, back in the aircraft, I was now trying to lower the nose to reduce my rate of climb and regain the airspeed I had lost in my attempted rocket launch. Eventually, I got the aircraft under a semblance of control and continued to climb away. The rate of climb was now considerably lower than I had expected and the noise level was increasing all the time. I was confused and wondered what I had done wrong. I looked across at my instructor who pointed to a small lever just above his left knee. Ah! I thought to myself, maybe it was a good time to raise the landing gear? So, I did. The rate of climb quickly increased, as did the noise from the engine. I reduced the power. The noise, however, sounded more like a screeching animal than an aircraft. Again, I looked at my instructor, this time with a look of total bewilderment on my face. I looked around for a suitable place for a forced landing as I was convinced that something had gone horribly wrong. However, the instructor looked very relaxed as he pointed, this time, to the new lever next to the throttle, the propellor pitch control. I had also forgotten to reduce the pitch and the poor propeller was spinning around at its maximum rotation speed, something that it could not sustain much longer without permanent damage. By pulling this lever back, the noise reduced to a more normal level and we continued our climb towards the Pacific. At last, I relaxed and started, once again, to enjoy being airborne in this beautiful part of the world.

After we had practised a few climbs and turns, I was beginning to get to grips with the performance of the aircraft and how to handle the pitch control on the propeller. The aircraft handled beautifully and with so much power in reserve, it could climb at an incredible rate, so much fun after the very limited performances of the Cessna and the Piper. He encouraged me to throw the aircraft around the sky to get used to all this extra performance and I did not hold back. Thirty minutes later, we were practising the all-important stalls, no significant problems there. Thankfully, the aircraft was not certified to practise spinning. I pretended to be disappointed whilst at the same time, quietly thanking God that I didn't have to spin the aircraft. The upper air work completed, we returned to the circuit to attempt some landings and also, some very much needed practice at take-off.

Nearly an hour later, we taxied back towards the dispersal area, at a much more sedate pace now that I had almost got used to the power available to me. After a much longer shutdown checklist than I was used to on the other aeroplanes, I felt reasonably happy with my performance and after a thirty minute debrief, my instructor felt the same way. He kindly informed me he was satisfied that I could fly the aircraft safely and if I promised to retract the landing gear on every subsequent departure, at the same time reducing the propeller speed, then as far as he was concerned, my check out was complete and I was qualified to fly the Bonanza. We had been airborne for two hours and I had been expecting another check flight the following day! I was free to continue planning my adventure. Happy days, I thought to myself as I went in search of my co-pilot to give her the good news.

Chapter 17

Avoiding Clouds with a Hard Centre

The day dawned bright and clear. I looked across the bay from my window and the sun shimmered off the mirrored surface of a becalmed bay, not a fog bank in sight, thank goodness. Our first flight to Red Bluff was now going to take twenty minutes less due to the much-increased speed of the Bonanza, so we had decided to leave at a more leisurely pace, in an attempt to avoid the usual morning commuter traffic. My life appeared surreal to me as we folded back the hood of the Mustang and threw a couple of night stop bags onto the back seat. Only a short while ago, I had been an office clerk and baggage loader. Now, here I was, driving in the coolest car I had ever seen and about to embark on a challenging, yet hopefully, spectacular couple of days flying. Also, I had a beautiful companion to share all of this with. I was pinching myself as we drove over the bridge towards the airport.

As promised, the aircraft was awaiting our arrival, fully fuelled, cleaned and prepared. I had my suspicions that the extra service was far more likely to be the result of whom I was flying with rather than anything I had said or done. Still, it made a great start to the day and saved me yet more time. I filed my flight plan after checking all the weather and airfield reports. All looked to be exactly as I had hoped it would be, fine, sunny and clear, just what a fair-weather pilot like myself always hoped for. I was still a little nervous about the Bonanza. It was a big, noisy, complicated machine and this would be the first time that I had flown it since my checkout. I was desperate to impress and looking aimlessly around the cockpit, trying to remember where everything was and what it did, was not likely to instil confidence. I slowly read the checklist and methodically carried out all of my checks. I was concerned that I would either over- or under-prime the engine leading to lots of blue smoke and a very premature end to our journey. Happily, however, I managed to push and pull most of the right buttons and the engine coughed only once and then burst into life. If, like me, until a few days ago, you had never been in a high-powered light aircraft, the sounds and vibrations could be unsettling, to say the least. The look on Jenny's face told me very quickly that she also was new to this type of aircraft. I think she was half expecting me to open the door and run away, calling for her to follow before the whole thing shook itself to pieces. To reassure her, I slowly took the obligatory sunglasses out of my top pocket, put them on and then turned to give her my most reassuring smile. I think it worked up until the point where the vibrations had moved the sunglasses halfway down my nose. I put them back in my pocket.

Eventually, the engine calmed down and we made our way with care towards the runway, whilst I tried not to repeat the kangaroo impersonation that had ruined my first attempt. Soon, it was our turn to line up on the runway. Thinking ahead and trying to get Jenny involved as much as possible, I pointed out the landing gear lever and asked her to select it to the 'up' position when I asked her, after take-off. The noise and vibrations returned as we shot forward and a few moments later, we were roaring into the bluest sky I had ever seen with me trying to keep up with the aircraft, which was easier said than done! As I fought to keep the speed under control and the propeller at the correct angle, I was so grateful when Jenny asked if it was time for her to raise the gear. As we were now passing through two thousand feet, I pretended to think about it for a few seconds before replying that yes, now would be a very good time. My subterfuge fooled neither of us, as finally, we transitioned into a cruising configuration. I gently swung the nose of the aircraft towards the northern horizon and we were finally on our way.

Although the Bonanza was a sophisticated aircraft, it had two very important limitations. It was still a single-engine aircraft and secondly, it was unpressurised. This meant that I had to consider the possibility of an engine failure at all times, especially important as we would be flying over some very hostile terrain. Also, being unpressurised meant that we were also restricted to flying below ten thousand feet. Above this height, the air quickly became very thin which would induce symptoms of hypoxia or lack of oxygen. This could produce symptoms ranging from nausea to unconsciousness, not ideal whilst trying to fly an aircraft. The terrain we were flying towards reached heights above fifteen thousand feet so we would have to fly around rather than over the larger mountains. Still, I tried to put these thoughts to the back of my mind and to enjoy the moment as we steadily made our way northwards. The original plan had been to take a direct route up towards Sacramento and then onwards to Red Bluff. Although this was by far the quickest route, the weather and views were so glorious that between us, we decided to just follow the Pacific Highway along the coastline. I informed air traffic control of our new intentions and continued our climb to nine thousand feet where the views became even more panoramic.

The new plan was to follow the coast until we reached Eureka and then turn inland and fly over the Redwood Forest and approach Red Bluff from the north instead of the south. This would almost double the flying time to four hours and quietly, I thanked the ground crew for filling the tanks to their capacity. I really should have thought more about the aeroplane's endurance before committing myself to the new route. Still, I calculated that we would have at least forty minutes of fuel remaining when we reached our destination, a little less than I would have preferred, but still safe, I hoped. Two hours literally flew past and we made a gentle turn over the town of Eureka and headed inland for the first time. This route would require a little more concentration with the navigation as there was no coastline to follow from now on. As we moved further away from the coastline, the view below soon changed to a featureless canopy of trees with only the occasional river to break up the landscape. Looking at fuel gauges, I calculated that we still had over two hours of flying time remaining with just over an hour left before we arrived at our destination - as long as I made no mistakes, of course.

With more luck than judgement and with a little help from the radio navigation receiver, Red Bluff appeared out of the undulating scenery. The gauges were now showing a lot less fuel than I had estimated, so the relief was palpable as I reached over to pick up the landing checklist. I asked Jenny to please make sure that I remembered to put the wheels down for landing, leaving it late on the take-off was one thing, leaving it just a little late on landing would have a very different outcome. I looked at my landing chart which showed a single runway and a control tower frequency and that was about it. I dialled up the tower frequency and requested permission to join the circuit. There was no answer, so I tried again and again and again. There was no reply. Either I had the wrong frequency or the controller was having his lunch. Still, I could not see any other aircraft around and could see that the runway looked serviceable and clear. I had no fuel to fly elsewhere, so I decided that the only option was to land without clearance and discuss it on the ground later. Between us, we managed to get the aircraft onto the final approach with everything where it should be. If there was no air traffic control at this airfield then each pilot was responsible for ensuring the circuit and runway were clear before joining and landing. This, of course, would be my first solo landing in the Bonanza and also my first landing with Jenny aboard and my first landing without air traffic control. Coupled with an ever-decreasing fuel load, I really wanted to make this a good approach and landing. If I got it wrong and we had to fly a go-around for another attempt, fuel would definitely become an issue. The runway was the shortest I had seen for a long time, even shorter than Shoreham. I decided to make absolutely sure that I put the aircraft down at the beginning of the runway and not float along it trying to get a smooth touchdown. We came over the hedge a lot lower than I had meant to and we thumped down about ten seconds earlier than I wanted. With such a heavy aircraft, I was lucky that it did not bounce right back into the sky; the Cessna or Piper would not have appreciated such treatment. As I had taken away much of the forward momentum with my landing, we stopped only a quarter of the way into the runway, definitely a short-field landing, I thought to myself. As we taxied off the runway, Jenny asked with a concerned expression if all my landings were like that. With a reassuring smile, I informed her that no, they were not all like that, sometimes I got it wrong. My arm was just recovering from her punch, which I thought was delivered with just a little too much enthusiasm, as I switched off the last of the radio controls and prepared to go and get a very well-deserved coffee.

Red Bluff Airport was very different from the other airports I had visited closer to San Francisco. This looked very much like a 'one trick pony' type of town and the airport reflected the general area. There were no flashy private jets here, no King Air executive aircraft, no twin-engine aircraft at all. Instead, there was mostly a collection of old, tired-looking aircraft, some of which were very unlikely to ever fly again. We parked close to the terminal building. I say terminal building but a shed might have been a better description. Jenny and I walked into what we thought was the coffee shop where there was a machine which looked as though it had once delivered coffee. However, as with most of what we had seen, it was well past its best. There was literally nobody around. We looked at each other and wondered what sort of place we had arrived at. There was a great temptation to turn around, walk as quickly as we possibly could without drawing attention to ourselves, back to our aircraft and get out of there before the aliens who had captured the local population made an appearance. I think the only thing that stopped us was that we needed to buy quite a lot of fuel as our tanks were close to empty. So, instead, we set off to find out where the aliens had hidden everyone. There were a couple of cars outside the only hangar so that seemed like a good place to start.

The last time I had ventured into an American hangar, I had been wonderfully impressed at the variety, quality and condition of the aircraft on display. That wasn't the case today. This was more like the place where they try to reconstruct the pieces retrieved from a crashed airliner. Well, maybe not quite as bad as that but there were certainly bits of long-abandoned aircraft filling every corner and cubby hole. The few aircraft still in one piece looked as though they were awaiting the same fate as their predecessors. All that was needed was a Bates Motel sign swinging from a single chain with a haunted house at the top of the hill to complete the illusion. After a few shouted greetings, we noticed movement in the far corner and set off to discover what had caused it. There, in the corner, sat a wingless Cessna with a pair of feet protruding roughly where the undercarriage should have been. As we repeated our greeting, the feet began to extend into legs, slowly revealing more of the person as they slid from beneath the aircraft. I think we were both relieved that the form appearing was not of the extra-terrestrial variety and seemed friendly enough. Wiping the oil from his hands, he looked us up and down, obviously trying to work out how and why we were there. I don't think he got many visitors.

We explained that we had just arrived from San Francisco and were wondering where we could get a coffee and some fuel. He asked why would we leave a lovely place like San Francisco and fly here? He informed us that he had always wanted to go to San Francisco. He really struggled with the fact that we had left somewhere he longed to visit, to fly to a place he obviously longed to leave. Eventually, he gave up trying to understand our motives and plans and asked if there was anything he could do to help. We repeated our requests for coffee and fuel and he told us that there was a coffee machine in the terminal. I mentioned that I had seen a broken vending machine there and he confirmed that was indeed the one he was referring to. When I asked him if it worked, he confirmed that no, it did not. My frustration levels were beginning to rise. However, I could see that he was genuinely trying to help, not hinder. Okay, I thought to myself, let's forget about the coffee and buy some fuel and get out of here before the aliens return.

I asked him very politely in my finest English accent if he would be so kind as to let me know where I could refuel my aircraft. This seemed to catch him on the hop and a genuine look of confusion spread across his face. He then informed me that it was not the weekend, a fact I had already grasped, although its relevance escaped me. I assured him that I was fully aware of the day of the week. He shrugged his shoulders and gave me one of those looks reserved for people who needed pity. Not considering myself to be in this category quite yet, I asked him why did it matter that this was not the weekend?

"Well, the refueller only works weekends as nobody flies during the week and if nobody flies, they don't need fuel," he replied.

Well, that told me. It seemed so obvious now. Weekend fliers only fly at the weekend, silly me. It also explained why there was nobody in the control tower. Of course, why would there be if there was nobody flying? It was beginning to dawn on me why the aliens had left, although they must have left on a weekend, otherwise they would not have been able to refuel their spaceships. I shook my head. I was starting to behave and think like a local.

Today was Thursday. The idea of staying here until Saturday filled me with dread and I was sure that Jenny would not see the funny side of a short break in Hicksville instead of Reno and Lake Tahoe. Why had I chosen this place, I thought to myself, probably out loud, as I received a very hostile stare from the mechanic. I was even more annoyed with myself that I had not checked if fuel would be available, I had made the cardinal error of just assuming that it would be. My memory drifted back to my first days at Shoreham where a very large sign hung over the entrance of the flying school, declaring, 'Thou Shalt Not Assume'.

I had been unsure of its exact relevance right up until this moment. How could I have been so stupid as not to check if I could buy fuel? I had this terrible sinking feeling, one not helped by the fact that Jenny's bottom lip had started to tremble. This is silly, I thought to myself. How could we possibly be held captive for two days waiting for the refueller to arrive. I turned to the mechanic who, by this time, was beginning to lose interest in the whole proceedings. Thinking out loud, intentionally this time, I asked if he had a telephone number for the refueller. Maybe, he could come in and fill us up for a small tip? Obviously, this renewed his interest and he enquired how much the tip would be? I asked him how much he thought would be enough to tempt him to refuel the aircraft? He quickly replied that twenty dollars should be enough. Although this was a good tip, I was not sure that it would be enough to get the man here on his day off, so I asked him if he was certain that this amount would secure the deal? He assured me that it would be sufficient and if we went back to our aircraft, he would make sure that the refueller would be there within thirty minutes. Only half reassured, slowly, we made our way back to the aircraft where I began to plan the next flight to Reno, definitely no diversions en route this time. I had well and truly learned from that mistake. Sure enough, thirty minutes later, we saw a very old refuelling truck making its way towards us, trailing large amounts of black smoke as it weaved through the parked aircraft.

The truck parked in front of us and I opened the fuel caps on both wings, anything to expedite our departure. The truck's front door opened and our not-so-friendly mechanic stepped down and started to unreel the fuel hose. I asked him if the refueller would mind us starting without him and was assured that no, he would not mind. When I asked how he could be so sure, he informed me that he was the refueller. I was now really ready to inflict a small amount of pain on his not-too-attractive face. I asked why he had lied to us about the refueller only working at weekends. He looked me directly in the eye and informed me that he was not lying. He was a mechanic during the week when people needed their aircraft servicing and a refueller at the weekends, when the aircraft needed fuel. He did not swap these roles around just to suit people. Everyone knew the score and what to expect from him. I had to smile as I had been cheated out of twenty dollars. However, the entertainment value had made it worthwhile and the really good news was that we would soon be on our way, never to return. That some people actually had to live here was a very sobering thought as we taxied out for take-off. As our wheels, courtesy of Jenny, tucked themselves into the wings, we both looked back at the strange little airfield with the strange little mechanic-come-refueller and we both burst out laughing. Maybe that was the best twenty dollars I had ever spent, I thought to myself, as we set course for Reno and hopefully, civilization.

We were now many hours behind schedule, the extra flying time to Red Bluff, coupled with the protracted refuelling saga had taken their toll and we were now flying towards a rapidly setting sun. We were also flying directly towards the Rocky Mountains and I had to constantly increase power as we steadily climbed to maintain a safe height above the ground. Passing through eight thousand feet, I began to notice that the engine was starting to misfire and we were struggling to maintain our height, never mind climb any further. I began to check that the wheels were up and that the propeller was at the correct pitch setting. All seemed normal. This was not good news, not good at all. Trying my best not to let my apprehension show, I began to consider my options which, to be honest, were not great. The engine was still producing some power, so an immediate forced landing in the very unfriendly local terrain was not an imminent threat. However, it was now getting darker and darker as the sun continued to set behind the hills. If I was going to have to carry out a forced landing, then I had less than twenty minutes before I would lose any chance of spotting a suitable stretch of open land to set the aircraft down. Still, I was sure that the answer to my problem lay within my grasp, I just had to work out what the problem was.

Looking around the cockpit, everything seemed normal, the fuel had not accidentally been selected off, the gauges all appeared normal and yet we were still steadily losing power as I tried to maintain my height. The speed was now also decreasing and I had no option but to give up any thoughts of a further climb and settled instead for a very gentle descent to preserve my precious airspeed. We had less than thirty minutes flying time to Reno and at this rate, I was not at all optimistic that we would make it. Reno is five and a half thousand feet above sea level. I had never attempted to land at an airport over five hundred feet, let alone five thousand. I knew that aircraft engines did not produce as much power at these high-altitude airfields where the air is much thinner than at sea level. Was there a clue here? This was the first time I had attempted such a landing and the first time I had experienced engine problems. There must be a connection but for the moment, I could not work out what that connection was. Meanwhile, we continued our gradual descent and I was now seriously considering declaring an emergency. I started to look around at the inhospitable terrain hoping to spot a clearing.

Then things changed. Slowly, oh so slowly, the engine began to pick up and run slightly more smoothly. In reply, the aircraft became a little more responsive and I found that I could now maintain my height and speed. I felt relief flooding through me, as although we were not out of danger, at least I had bought myself a little more time to try to work out what the problem was. And then it occurred to me, it was the fuel we had just picked up in Red Bluff. There is always a danger of contaminated fuel, which is why it is mandatory to take a sample of fuel from the aircraft and check it has no water in it. Dirty fuel can easily cause an engine to misfire and lose power. It can also cause a complete engine failure. I had been in such a rush to leave Red Bluff that I had forgotten to test the fuel. I cursed myself and I cursed the refueller or mechanic or whatever he was. If we ended up making a forced landing into a ravine, I was definitely going back to retrieve my twenty dollars.

This solution seemed to explain our problem perfectly. Hopefully, the dirty fuel had gone through the system and all would be well from now on. With this encouraging thought, I started to climb back to our original altitude. Passing eight thousand feet, the problem repeated itself. The engine coughed and the power drained away once more. This was now getting really confusing. Was the fuel contaminated or was there another reason for the engine misfiring as we tried to climb? Gradually, the mists began to clear and I could have kicked myself. What on earth was I thinking? I had completely forgotten to use the mixture control as I had never had to adjust it before. Suddenly, the theory I had learned nearly two years ago started to have real meaning. I recalled that a normally aspirated engine required a set mixture of fuel and air to run smoothly. The higher the aircraft climbs, the less air there is available. To keep the fuel-to-air ratio the same, you had to reduce the amount of fuel to match the reduction in air available. This only becomes noticeable above approximately five thousand feet, a height I had yet to climb above. Before this flight, I had always selected the mixture to full-rich and left it there until I switched the engine off. I now realised that I had to adjust the mixture to compensate for this reduction in air. I was very apprehensive as I slowly wound the mixture control back - the only time I had done this before was to turn the engine off. I was literally starting to starve the engine of fuel. After a couple of turns of the mixture control lever, the engine started to respond. Two more rotations and we were back to full power and climbing rapidly. My stress levels started to return to just plain scared and the reassuring smile aimed at Jenny missed its mark by a mile. She clearly was aware of just how worried I had been.

The sun was now fully set as we continued towards Reno. The cockpit seemed to close in on us as the outside world dissolved into the night sky and the cockpit lights created an eerie glow. We both felt alone and isolated in the empty airspace. The engine, now reassuringly purring happily away, was the only thing that seemed to connect us with the outside world. I shuddered once again at the thought of plunging down into a vast blackness full of mountains and valleys after an engine failure. I was more than ready to land.

I called a Reno approach and was surprised at just how busy the frequency was. There were, after all, other aircraft sharing our sky. It was the strangest of things when I heard just how reassuringly calm and confident my own voice sounded on the airways. Maybe, I really did have a clue what was going on after all. We were given headings and heights as we started our initial approach. It was vital to remember that the airport was over five thousand feet high. Everything would happen a lot more quickly in the thin air at this height. For example, the aircraft's ground speed would be a lot higher in this environment. I now had three things to get right before we landed: propellor, landing gear and now mixture. This increased my workload. By now, I was feeling very tired. It had been a long day with quite a few unwelcome surprises. However, there was no room for excuses and with Jenny's help going through the checklist, we finally lined up with our runway, the bright lights of downtown Reno twinkling in the distance. Luckily, the landing was passable this time despite this being my first night land in the Bonanza and it was also my first high altitude landing. I felt a certain amount of pride and was indulging in a little self-congratulation when a very irate voice informed me that I had missed my taxiway. Not a great way to finish the day's flying and the look on Jenny's face told me that I would not be allowed to forget this mistake for a while. Still, we were in Reno, America's second gambling capital. Time for some serious relaxation and recuperation. I couldn't wait!

Chapter 18

A Tight Fit

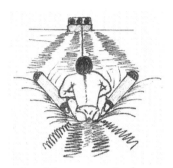

The next morning arrived far too early for my liking. It had been a long night and we took in as many sights as we could fit in. In America, you have to be twenty-one to buy a beer. Luckily, I had just achieved that landmark a few months earlier although my throbbing head didn't feel particularly lucky as I hauled myself out of bed and into a cold shower. I had a busy and difficult day ahead and as the cold water did its best to revive me, I reflected on the lack of judgement I had shown the night before. I should have stopped drinking and gone to bed at least three hours before I finally had. My co-pilot looked in even worse shape as we hailed a taxi and set off for the airport. This was not at all how I had planned the second day of our adventure. My spirits fell even further as I looked at the grey skies and low clouds. A fine drizzle had also started to further dampen my spirits. It looked the perfect day to go back to bed, close the curtains and wait until we were feeling more human and the skies more friendly. Unfortunately, that option was not open to us as we had to return the aircraft that night and Jenny had to be back at work the next morning. Trying to clear my thoughts, I began to study the weather forecasts for Tahoe and Carson City, our proposed stopover points on the way back to San Francisco. This was not looking at all good. There was a front moving in from the north bringing unseasonably cool weather, drizzle and a low cloud base, very unusual for late summer in California. Originally, the plan had been to land at Carson City for a late breakfast; it was only a short thirty-minute flight. Then, we would fly on to Lake Tahoe for lunch with Jenny's friends. Sensibly, we decided not to land at Carson City but to have breakfast where we were, in Reno. Hopefully, this would allow the weather time to improve and the painkillers to get to work on both our headaches. Sadly, the wait was in vain on both counts.

An hour later and we were walking towards our aircraft trying to avoid the worst of the puddles and keeping dry as best we could. We had not brought any wet weather clothing along with us. The flight time to Tahoe was fifty minutes and on a good day, would have provided some spectacular views of the Rocky Mountains and Lake Tahoe itself. Regrettably, today was not a good day and looking around me, all I could see were very ominous lumps of rock rising up into an overcast sky which was grey and forbidding. We were already over five thousand feet above sea level and the mountains reached up to fifteen thousand feet in the surrounding area. Watching the commercial aircraft appear out of the gloom just before they landed, I calculated that the base of the cloud was just over one thousand five hundred feet, which would be sufficient for our short flight to Tahoe. With a confidence I did not really feel, I decided we could make the flight safely. The alternative was to fly directly home, climbing to a safe height and heading west towards lower terrain and then turning south towards Hayward. Had my brain been a little less muddled, I am sure that I would have chosen that option. Unfortunately, today I was not thinking as clearly as I should have done and I really did not want to disappoint Jenny who had been so looking forward to flying into Tahoe for lunch with her friends.

Decision made, we refuelled the aircraft and called for taxi instructions. As we approached the runway, the air traffic controller asked if we were ready to copy our instrument flight details. Of course, as I did not have an Instrument Flight Rating, I could not accept this clearance and informed him that we were on a visual flight plan. He immediately asked me to confirm that I intended to fly a visual route to Tahoe. The incredulous tone of his voice did nothing to put me at ease. Once I had confirmed that this indeed was my plan, he cleared me for take-off with a final instruction to remain clear of the cloud after take-off.

The rain was now steadily getting worse as we lined up on the runway. This was the last opportunity to back out and return to the parking bay. Instead, I applied full power and we accelerated into the deteriorating weather. As soon as we became airborne, the low clouds began snapping at the wings and windscreen. My estimated cloud base of one thousand five hundred feet now seemed wildly optimistic. We were barely airborne and the clouds began to swallow us whole. My headache very quickly became the least of my problems as all my concentration was diverted towards making sure that none of the clouds we were flying through contained parts of the Rocky Mountains. We levelled off at eight thousand feet with the hills around us still reaching over seven thousand feet higher. I was using a radio beacon to guide me away from these obstructions. However, I would soon need to alter course back towards the hills if we were to make an approach into Lake Tahoe. I decided to descend to try to get clear of this blanket of cloud before we got too close to the hills. As we descended, the dread of not knowing exactly where the sky ended and the hills began became even more acute. Slowly, very slowly, the clouds became less dense and we caught occasional glimpses of the ground below us. Although this was encouraging, it still meant that there was the possibility of unseen obstacles hidden in the clouds ahead. The altimeter was now showing that we were one thousand feet above the ground.

Then, suddenly the lake appeared directly below us. Rarely have I been so glad to see a water feature. We now just had to keep this in sight and approach the airport from the lake, where we were certain to be clear of the mountains. We radioed ahead for clearance to make our approach and once again, we were met with an astonished controller asking us to confirm our position and that we were attempting a visual approach in the current conditions. Again, in the poshest English accent, I confirmed that we did indeed intend to make such an approach. We did, after all, have an important lunch date. Luckily, the controller had a sense of humour and he took us under his wing and guided us carefully onto a five-mile final approach before handing over to the control tower for our final landing clearance. My thanks to him were very genuine as our landing gear, kindly lowered by Jenny, touched down on the runway. As we taxied to the parking area, we could see Jenny's friends jumping up and down waving at us. It had been a real risk making this flight and something I would be very reluctant to do again but to see Jenny's face as she leapt down and ran to meet them, I thought that maybe this time it had been worth it. Also, I realised that after all the concentration and adrenaline, my hangover had finally gone. Another very important lesson learned. I would never again overindulge before I was due to fly the next day. Maybe, just maybe, I was growing up a little bit. It was certainly time.

When we had accepted the invitation for lunch, I had, once again, assumed that we would be having a leisurely meal in the airport terminal. How wrong I was! The six of us made our way out of the airport towards the car park where sat a very old and battered van. We all piled in and with a loud bang from the engine and a cloud of blue smoke from the rear, we set off. This was going to be interesting! The weather, in the meantime, had made a dramatic improvement. The early morning low cloud and rain had been replaced by a beautifully clear and sunny day. I was beginning to wish that we had delayed our departure from Reno. It would have been a much less stressful flight in these conditions.

Thirty minutes later, we pulled up alongside a wooden jetty on what I assumed was Lake Tahoe. The lake was completely flat, not a breath of air moved its mirror surface and the early afternoon sun shimmied off the water creating a mesmerising and beautiful effect. With the mountains in the background framing the whole picture, I felt an intense pleasure and sense of peace. What a lovely spot to have lunch.

The back door of the van was pulled open and a variety of objects were unceremoniously dumped on the ground, many of which, I recognised. However, I was struggling to understand what use we could possibly have for a large can of petrol and a number of ropes and other paraphernalia. Maybe, we were going to have an explosive barbecue. A large cool box, stuffed with food and beer, was then produced and everyone grabbed something and set off towards the lake. I was given a pile of towels and other swimming gear and I followed everyone else. We walked along the wooden jetty until we stopped at a large, rather scruffy, power boat. All the luggage was tipped into the boat and before long, we were off at an alarming rate towards the centre of the lake. If I was expecting a leisurely lunch on the boat before being driven back to the airport in the late afternoon in time for the two-hour flight home, I was about to be disappointed. The first clue that this was not going to be just a lunch was when ropes and skis were produced from beneath one of the front seats, followed by spare swimming trunks for those that needed them. Well, that would be me then. Unlike the rest of the party, I had never tried water skiing. I was the only first-time skier. Always willing to give anything a go, I accepted the challenge and was handed a spare pair of swimming trunks.

Well, I say trunks. In reality, I held in my hand the smallest, whitest, pair of trunks I had ever seen. This had to be a joke and as I looked expectantly around waiting to be handed more appropriate swimming attire, it slowly dawned on me that there were no other trunks available. So, feeling utterly embarrassed, I wrapped a towel around my waist and with all the dignity I could manage, I squeezed myself into my costume and dived into the lake before my humiliation became too unbearable. The next twenty minutes basically involved me failing to stand up on the skis and being dragged along on my backside. Not only was this incredibly frustrating, but it also resulted in me receiving a twenty-knot cold water enema with predictable results. Why, oh why, had I agreed to this torture and equally, why had I accepted these white trunks? The rest of the afternoon passed by with copious eating and drinking by all around me whilst I sat feeling completely embarrassed and miserable. I just wanted to get back on dry land and forget the whole afternoon.

Eventually, we were dropped off at the airport in the early evening and said our goodbyes at the side of the aircraft. I tried to get as comfortable as possible as I slid into my seat after all the pre-departure tasks were completed. My backside felt incredibly sore and I was feeling totally miserable as I started the engine. We taxied slowly towards the runway. Jenny sat very quietly next to me. I think she realised that I was not in the mood for idle chat. I had hoped to be landing back at Hayward in daylight but instead, we were taxiing out in semi darkness with the two-hour flight looming ahead of us in total darkness, far from ideal. Fortunately, we were now flying away from the Rocky Mountains and all the hazards associated with them.

As we climbed away from Lake Tahoe, we started to follow the last of the sunset. Twenty minutes later, we were cruising at eight thousand feet in total darkness. I looked across at Jenny, who was fast asleep, exhausted by her impressive performance mono skiing all afternoon, her face gently illuminated by the glow from the instrument panel. I felt a surge of pride that she trusted my flying to the extent that she felt comfortable enough to sleep. Then again, maybe she was just too tired to care? I settled down, adjusted the power for a comfortable cruising speed and we droned steadily through the night sky. I had chosen a route that kept us away from the busy commercial airways and we were effectively alone in the vast Californian sky. My aches and pains slowly subsided and I began to see the funny side of the soiled swimming trunks. Had anyone been able to look into our aircraft they would have been confused to see a beautiful girl asleep next to a quietly laughing pilot. Luckily, there was no one around as we continued on our way.

Two hours later, Jenny woke up as I lowered the landing gear on our final approach into Hayward. I received a gentle punch on my arm as she reminded me that was her job and what was I thinking, doing it myself. After a very soft landing, (which my backside was very grateful for), we finally parked and as the engine died, I realised just how tired I was. On the drive home, the roles were reversed as apparently, I snored all the way back to Sausalito. The adventure was over. We had had some close calls, made some very good and a few poor decisions. Most importantly, I had learned from my mistakes and I had also learned from my successes. Jenny and I decided to have a nightcap before retiring. I suddenly felt a huge sense of loss as I realised that my time in America and my time with Jenny would soon be coming to an end. My visa and my money were running out and I would have to face a new future, earn more money and plan the next stage of my career journey. There was a large part of me that regretted that I could not pursue my dream with Jenny in Sausalito. However, we were both too young to consider such a path. Instead, I went to bed feeling elated at what I had just achieved and sad at what I was about to lose. I almost immediately fell into a deep sleep. Tomorrow could wait a little longer.

Chapter 19

My Final Days in America

Autumnal colours confirmed that I had now been in San Francisco for just over five months. I had arrived as a wide-eyed, naïve, twenty-one-year-old, with a Private Pilot Licence and just over sixty hours flying experience. In the ensuing months, I had trebled my flying hours, flown aircraft and routes that I could only have dreamed of in the UK and lived in a beautiful apartment. I had made friendships that I hoped would last a long time and I'd made a very special friend who, in other circumstances, might have become something even more special. I now had to face the fact that my hours were approaching one hundred and fifty, the minimum that I would need to start an assistant flying instructor course back in England. Although this was an expensive and arduous course, if I passed it, it would mean that I could finally stop paying for my flying and instead be paid to fly. It was with a heavy heart that I made the decision to book my return flight for two weeks' time.

I still had another twenty flying hours to complete before I returned home and as I had enjoyed the night flight home from Tahoe so much, I decided to plan a few more similar flights, this time southwards towards Los Angeles. Unfortunately, Jenny was unable to get any more time off work and I resigned myself to solo flights from now on. My heart was not into carrying out any complicated flight planning and I had had my fill of mountain flying. Also, I was back in my Piper now which seemed so slow and basic in comparison to the Bonanza. Therefore, I had to find something to amuse myself on these long, lonely night flights.

Map on my lap, coffee in my hand, I settled down to plan my last long flight. I quickly discounted flying all the way to Los Angeles and back. It would take me nearly seven hours. Instead, I decided Santa Maria would be a good destination for no other reason than, as with Red Bluff, I liked the name. It should take me two hours and thirty minutes to fly there and roughly the same amount of time to fly back. The wind would be from the west and therefore, would give me the same ground speed on both legs. I wanted as easy a flight as I could possibly imagine and following the coast all the way there and back seemed to fit the bill nicely. Also, I decided that it would be more fun to fly there in daylight and fly back at night, giving me the best of both worlds. Decision made, I attempted once more to persuade Jenny to accompany me. However, after telling her of my plans to return to England, her enthusiasm for flying with me had dramatically reduced and she showed little interest in my flight. I resigned myself to flying alone. At least skimpy swimming trunks would no longer be required!

The following afternoon, I was taxiing out. The fuel tanks were full, my map sat on the empty seat next to me and I had nearly six hours of flying time ahead of me. I should have felt exhilarated. The weather was perfect, the aircraft was perfect, the flight planning had gone perfectly, yet I kept looking at the empty seat next to me and I felt hollow. I had to get a grip and concentrate. Flying was very unforgiving to those that allowed distractions to get in the way. Shaking my head, I applied full power as I was given my take off clearance and I was off into the bright Californian sky. The flight down went as smoothly as I had hoped and once again, seeing the incredible Pacific Highway helped steal any thoughts of Jenny from my mind as I marvelled at its beauty from barely one thousand feet above it. This was pure scenic paradise and all other thoughts were banished as I climbed, turned and rolled the aircraft all over the sky. There was no one to tell me to behave myself and I took full advantage of my freedom. Two and a half hours later, I was on my approach into Santa Barbara, feeling a sense of fun and achievement as I made a very passable landing. It was such a shame there was no one with me to witness it.

It was now late afternoon and I went in search of some refreshments before organising, refuelling and filing my return flight plan. An hour after nightfall, I was taxiing out for one of my last flights before returning home to the UK. I had very mixed feelings. As I reached my cruising height of three thousand feet, I settled back to enjoy the flight. There was no scenery this time and after an hour, I began to feel a little bored. I wanted to have a little fun. I looked at my charts and noticed that the air traffic control on the smaller airfields closed after eight o'clock and if you wanted to use the runway after that time, you simply selected the tower frequency and clicked the microphone three times. Well, this seemed like fun and so I started to select as many frequencies as I could and delighted myself as runways illuminated all around me. Who would have thought that there were so many airfields so close? This was a great sport. I would have continued my new game all the way home, but on hearing a very angry voice on the emergency frequency asking which aircraft was abusing the system, I turned away, descended to a lower altitude and scurried back to Hayward as quickly as I could. Maybe, it was the right time to go home after all, hopefully before they found out who was responsible for the night sky being lit up by runway lights. As I made my way back into the flight school, trying to look as innocent as possible, I noticed that for the first time Jenny's desk was empty. She had not waited for me. It would have to be a bus ride home.

My final day arrived far too quickly. Where had the past few months gone? As my flight back to London was not until later that evening, I had decided to have a late morning with a leisurely breakfast. Jenny had left for Hayward at the normal time and I planned to take her out for lunch and then finally, head off for San Francisco International Airport for my flight back to London. With my bags finally beaten into submission with all my extra clothing packed inside, I treated myself to a taxi to go and meet Jenny. I arrived just before lunchtime and stowed my bags behind her reception area, exactly as I had done all those months ago. I went to say goodbye to all the great people who had helped me since I arrived. Life here would have been much more difficult and much less fun without their help and guidance. With my goodbyes finally over, I went in search of the one person who really had helped me to live, work and play in such a wonderfully caring way. I owed her so much and knew that I could never repay her kindness.

She was not at her desk and so I set off to find her. I knew she could not be far. Twenty minutes later, I was still searching when the operations officer asked me who I was looking for. When I told him, he casually remarked that she was flying with one of the new students. I asked how long they would be. It was like being slapped in the face when he informed me that she would be back tomorrow as she had gone to Lake Tahoe with the newly arrived Australian pilot. My face must have gone a bright red! I felt the heat rising from my neck up. I turned quickly away before my emotions became too obvious. With probably unjustified anger, I guessed he would have a ride back to his new apartment in a red Mustang tomorrow. Suddenly, I could not wait to get out of the building and on my way home. I felt such a fool.

Chapter 20

Back to Life; Back to Reality

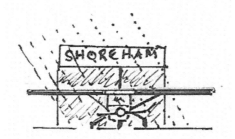

The flight home had none of the drama and excitement of my outbound flight. The driver, unlike my best friend Pete, who had got us lost on the way to Heathrow, knew exactly where the airport was. Also, I had no bag full of cash to leave in a telephone booth. Whilst both factors were a relief, a little distraction may not have been a bad thing as I reflected on my time in the US. It was with a distinctly heavy heart that I made my way across a cold and wet apron towards the Arrivals hall at Heathrow. At least, I was home and that was a thought I tried to comfort myself with, a burning jealousy deep in my veins. Although Jenny and I were never officially a couple, I had grown incredibly fond of her and thought she had felt the same. However, that was now another time and another place. I began to feel excited at being met by my family. Luckily, both my bags had made the same flight as me and I grabbed them as quickly as I could and headed towards the baggage hall exit and into the arms of my waiting family and friends. Well, that was my idea anyway. Sadly, it soon became increasingly obvious that nobody else had shared this plan as I scanned the sea of faces in front of me. This was decades before anyone except Captain Kirk in Star Trek had envisaged having a hand-held device into which you could both talk to and see other people. With this

Twentieth Century limitation, my only alternative was to find a telephone booth and call home. Maybe, they had got the dates mixed up. My mother answered and at first, struggled to recognise my voice. Apparently, I had picked up an accent. She then informed me that she and my father were busy and had friends staying for the weekend. She wished me well and let me know that they were looking forward to seeing me next week. Did that conversation really happen, I asked myself? I dialled my friend Pete's number and there was no answer. I struggled to think of anyone else who would be pleased to see me and who had a comfortable spare bed. The list was very short, so short in fact, that I decided to purchase a rail ticket and set off for home anyway. Surely, they wouldn't turn their son away in his hour of need. I would find out two hours later as I dejectedly pulled my bags along a wet and flooded road towards my parents' house. I had been up now for nearly thirty hours and was feeling very sorry for myself.

My reception was as unwelcoming as I had feared. The house was indeed full, it had only one spare bedroom and that was being occupied by the visitors. I was scolded for not informing them that I was expecting to stay after my return. After a change of clothes and a few phone calls, I managed to find a friend who could offer me a settee to sleep on until I found myself somewhere to stay. Of course, I had previously sold my car, so it was back on the train for the relatively short journey to Worthing and finally, the chance to sleep. As I closed the curtains on a bleak, cold and wet day, my mind could not help returning to the wonderful view from Jenny's house across the bay. Someone else would now be enjoying that view and I sincerely hoped that he had been given an even smaller and whiter pair of swimming trunks. Knowing my luck, the Australian was probably a champion skier and was impressing everyone with his jumps and tricks. Sleep finally saved me from any further feelings of self-pity.

I was awake very early the next day, the eight-hour time change was having an unexpected effect. However, now awake, the morning was the perfect time for planning the next stage of my flying career. This was still well before morning television arrived in the UK, although I must admit that I had become quite used to watching the early morning news programmes - cup of freshly brewed coffee in hand - looking out over the water. I shook my head and rebuked myself for allowing memories of my previous life to interrupt my thought process.

My first priority was to book myself onto an assistant flying instructor course. My second priority was to work out how I was going to find the two-thousand five-hundred pounds to pay for the course - or should they be the other way around? My third priority was to find somewhere to live or should that be the first priority? I decided that probably, having a roof over my head came above everything else. As I was now twenty-one years old and I really did not want to have to ask my parents if I could return to live at home. I had left, or more accurately, been asked to leave, the day I set off for university. I was always welcome to stay for a few days, yesterday being an exception. However, it had been made very clear to me by my father that he expected me to make my own way in the world as he had done. Therefore, all I had to do was find a beautiful woman with a beautiful house who drove a Mustang convertible and all would be well.

Instead, I found a copy of a local newspaper and began scouring the back pages for accommodation. I had returned with enough money to see me through the first month, so I could just about manage to rent a bed-sit and feed myself. Another very pressing problem was transport, or lack of it. I could not rely on buses and trains to get me where I needed to be as they were both far too infrequent and unreliable. No, I had to buy myself a car and that was now my first priority. If the worst came to the worst, at least I could sleep in it. Therefore, I started to study the 'cars for sale' section of the newspaper. It quickly became apparent that I could not afford any of the vehicles on offer. I checked which day of the week it was and discovered that there happened to be a car auction that very evening. I was confident that my old car dealer skills had not faded and I could find something in my price bracket. I was mulling this over when my friend Chris made an entrance scratching parts of his anatomy that I had no wish to see scratched.

I had known Chris since we were at school together and since then, he had done very well for himself. After studying Aeronautical Engineering, he had become a flight simulator engineer, working only a few miles away, in Lancing. Maybe, he had made the better choice, as he had a very well-paid, secure job, a nice flat and a good car, basically everything I did not have. I was beginning to envy him when I realised that being in a simulator, you do not actually go anywhere. It's basically all just make believe. I knew that I wanted to go somewhere in the real world. After a catch-up chat, I mentioned to Chris that I was thinking of going to the car auction that night and would he like to come. He immediately replied that his father had recently given up driving and his car was just sitting on his driveway, doing nothing. Would he like me to ask his father if he wanted to sell it? He was sure that he would not want very much for it. It was quite old but it started and drove well. Of course, I was interested and I implored Chris to call him right away and ask if I could come over to see the car.

Two hours later, I was standing on a driveway looking at what was definitely the ugliest car I had ever seen. It was a bright and I mean bright, yellow Skoda. Now, this cannot be compared to today's Skoda cars which are basically Volkswagens with a Skoda badge. No, this was a 1972 Skoda made by Skoda in communist Czechoslovakia. It was basically a square box with a wheel at each corner and an engine and a steering wheel. After test-driving it, I realised that the brakes were an afterthought and not even a good afterthought at that! The steering wheel did not seem to be connected to the wheels. The whole thing was basically bits of metal and rubber held together by God knows what, all travelling in roughly the same direction. No wonder poor Chris' dad was giving up driving! So would Sterling Moss if he had owned this abomination. I had managed to drive this thing around the block and park it back on the driveway. I thanked Chris' father for showing me the car and told him that I had to go now as my bus left in ten minutes. He replied that I could have it for thirty pounds. I stopped in my tracks, turned around, stuck my hand out, shook his and heard myself saying the magic words, "It's a deal."

This was most definitely automotive rock bottom, the equivalent of an alcoholic licking the last few drops of methylated spirits from an empty bottle. I was laughed at wherever I went and the jokes came thick and fast. How could I double the value of my car? Put petrol in it! How do you know when it's time to scrap a Skoda? When the ashtrays are full. The more people ridiculed my car, the more I grew attached to it. By pulling a handle between the front seats, the little engine gave a cough, made a funny whirring sound for thirty seconds and then it just started, every time. The majority of the cars on the roads in those days were made by a British motor industry destroyed by militant trade unions in the late seventies. Very few of them started the first time; I rest my case. This car was to last me three years and cost almost nothing in repairs. In a funny way, I came to miss that Skoda. We were both down on our luck and on hard times. We looked after each other, although I have to admit, it really was an awful car.

I was now mobile which had been my first priority. Now, it was time to find somewhere to live. After a few viewings, I settled on a holiday home that was let out during the winter months for a very reasonable rent. The whole place was damp and dreary and the idea of actually spending a holiday in it seemed outrageous. However, it was close to the sea, so I suppose that's all some people wanted. For me, it was now my home until next Easter. Happy days! I now had a car and a home so all I needed now was a job to help me save up for my Instructor Licence. Surely, that was not going to be too difficult to find. Sadly, it was.

England in the late seventies and early eighties was not the most thriving economy in the world. The three-day-week and the Winter of Discontent were fresh in the minds of employers and employees, interest rates were sky high and unemployment was at record levels. All in all, it was not a great time to be looking for work. After a very depressing few days looking for any suitable or even unsuitable employment, I decided that if there really were no jobs available, then I wouldn't waste my time looking for one. Instead, I decided that the best course of action was to start my Instructor Licence as soon as possible and become qualified over the winter and ready for when the economy and weather picked up in the spring. Therefore, I decided to ask my parents to loan me the money for the course and I would repay them over the coming year when I finally earned a living, teaching people to fly. I wrote down all the costs involved and the expected income when I qualified. I also included a generous interest rate to make the loan more attractive, especially to my father who had always been very careful with his finances.

Feeling quite hopeful that they would see what an excellent investment this would be, I sat down with both of them and spread my master plan out in front of them. My mother always deferred to my father in just about everything and money was no exception. I realised that I had only to convince my father and all would be well. The simple phrase, "Absolutely not," came as a shock. Rejection can be painful, especially from family, and painful it most certainly was. My only other hope of getting finance was from the banks and if my own father had turned me down, there seemed little prospect of success from that angle. Still, nothing ventured, nothing gained, so I presented myself in front of my bank manager.

In those days, you did actually get to see a real person, not speak to an advisor on the opposite side of the world. I adjusted my tie. My collar was too tight and I had trouble breathing properly. Beads of sweat ran down my back and armpits. I must have looked a real sight in my borrowed suit, complete with flared trousers and wide lapels. After two failed starts, due to my nerves, I finally managed to convey why I was taking up his valuable time with a request for a sizable loan which I had no immediate and obvious chance of repaying. The more I talked, the more the pitch of my voice rose. At the point where I sounded like a twelve-year old girl, I decided that the time had come to stop speaking. I leaned back in my chair and for the first time, really looked at my bank manager. I had held an account since I was seventeen years old, our family having banked with this branch for the past thirty years. The manager, I guessed, was in his early fifties and displayed all the signs of having spent the majority of his working life sitting behind a desk. There was absolutely no way he would consider lending the money to a young man with no security and few prospects. I continued fiddling with my collar and tie to allow more air to enter my lungs. Being a man, I can only do one thing at a time and listening to the manager at the same time as adjusting my attire was way beyond me. I just managed to hear the words, "Will that be all?" as I rose from my chair. I was not surprised at being turned down and I thanked him for his time and apologised for wasting it. His parting words stopped me in my tracks as he announced that the funds would be in my account by the end of the week. I turned and spluttered a thank you, undoing another button on my shirt as I did so. Years later, I found out quite by accident, that my father had guaranteed the loan a few days before my appointment. An act of kindness from my father was indeed rare, so it was unsurprising that at the time, I had never guessed this had been the case.

Chapter 21

Compton Abbas, Wherefore Art Thou?

I had a car, somewhere to live, and the money to pay for my instructor course. Things were definitely looking up and I had actually stopped thinking about Jenny! Well, I had at least stopped thinking about her constantly, which was progress of sorts. I scoured a copy of *Flight International* magazine once again and found a number of schools offering the flying instructor course. Without the slightest knowledge of any of the schools who were advertising, I settled on a lovely sounding airfield called Compton Abbas. The airfield was in Dorset, only a two-hour drive from where I now lived and they were offering very cheap accommodation from Monday to Friday as part of the package. I rang them immediately and due to a cancellation, I was able to book myself onto the next course starting in three days' time. Things were now moving very quickly. I had even managed to get my old job back as a weekend barman at my previous flying club at Shoreham. I made a number of purchases and spent the few remaining days devouring every book I had about the flying instructor course as there was a lot to learn.

The course was due to start at nine o'clock on Monday morning. Not wanting to be late, I packed everything I would need into the Yellow Peril, as I now affectionately referred to my

Skoda and set off at six o'clock in the morning. My car had a top speed of about fifty miles an hour going downhill with the wind behind it. True to form, the little car struggled along the motorway, around country lanes and just about managed it, smoke trailing behind. I had time for a quick coffee in a delightful reception area before my course started. The airfield was tiny, much smaller than Shoreham and was basically a grass field stuck on the side of a hill. Whoever built an airfield in such a location must have had a great sense of humour. The surrounding countryside was beautiful and the views were spectacular. However, if I had been flying overhead this airfield and had suffered an engine failure, this is the last place I would have landed. It was British eccentricity at its finest, find a sloping field on the side of a hill and build an airfield, genius!

As I finished my drink, I heard a voice asking if I was starting an instructor course that morning. I stood up and met one of the greatest characters it was my pleasure to encounter in my aviation career, Ian Mackay. Ian was in his early thirties, tall with a mop of hair swept back from his face. He had a very relaxed manner and from the mischievous look on his face, I knew straight away that I was going to have a lot of fun learning how to teach people to fly with Ian as my mentor. The first two days were all theory and it did not take me long to realise just how little I knew. All the examinations I had passed so far only touched the surface of each subject and they made it very clear to me that to teach, you must know everything and they did mean everything, about the subject. It is no good knowing seventy percent of a subject if you are going to teach your pupil properly. You must know one hundred percent. It is the student that only needs to know the seventy percent to pass the examination. Ian's enthusiasm for the subject was infectious and studying became a pleasure rather than a chore. I was studying twelve hours each day. He was a hard taskmaster and yet the feeling of satisfaction became addictive and I was transformed into a very willing student. I would arrive at the airfield every day at seven in the morning and would still be there at eight or nine in the evening. This probably was also due to the fact that my accommodation was very basic, to put it mildly and the less time spent there, the better. I had been allocated a tiny room in a very rundown old house that had very few basic amenities. Hot water was infrequent enough to make a warm shower a thing to be cherished. I had a room at the top of the house three floors from the nearest bathroom. There was a sink and a tap in my room and that often served as my bathroom. At least I made sure it was clean which is more than could be said of the communal bathroom. On my first day at Compton, I had checked out the receptionist. Sadly, she was old enough to be my grandmother and she drove an old Austin. I realised my good fortune in that department has come to an end. Still, I was only here during the week and I always drove back home late on a Friday night, so I could easily put up with such discomfort. In reality, I spent most of my time at the airfield. I settled in quickly and enjoyed myself immensely.

The course was scheduled to last three weeks, weather permitting. My first flight with Ian came late on the third day. Ian asked me to demonstrate my flying abilities. We were flying an ancient Cessna 150. However, it was the aerobatic model and had a glass roof to allow for inverted flying. The runway at Compton Abbas, as I have already mentioned, was on an appreciable slope. It was also impossible to see from one end of the runway to the other because of a large bump in the middle of the runway. Over the following weeks, I would do my best to flatten this bump with my heavy landings. Unsurprisingly, I achieved no success. I had not flown a Cessna for over a year and I had forgotten just how basic the aircraft was, especially the older model which we were flying that day. We bumped and rattled our way along the rough grass strip and drunkenly climbed away. Everything was shaking, including my teeth.

Once airborne, Ian asked me to carry out a few basic manoeuvres and talk him through what I was doing. After a series of climbs, descents, steep turns and stalls, I felt reasonably pleased with my performance. Well, I did, until Ian took control and showed me exactly how rusty I had actually become.

It is always a pleasure to see someone do something incredibly well. The greatest sportsmen and women always made their sport look effortless and Ian had this gift in abundance. He was not showing off. Instead, he merely made everything look straightforward. The aircraft did everything he asked of it and I sat back in admiration. We then practised some aerobatics. Ian could fly as accurately inverted as he could the right way up. My efforts were a lot clumsier. However, I managed not to stall or lose control, a feat I was proud of. After an hour of throwing the aircraft all over the sky, Ian handed control back to me and asked me to return to Compton for some landing practice. This is where it all went horribly wrong.

I had been concentrating so hard on trying to accurately fly the aircraft, I had completely lost track of where we were. I had been briefed before we took off that I would be fully responsible for making sure we stayed clear of the surrounding military airfields and other controlled airspace. The nearest town was Shaftesbury and I had made sure I knew where that was. Unfortunately, that was over thirty minutes ago and I had forgotten to keep track of our position since that time. Boscombe Down, a front line major military airfield and Empire Test Pilot School was only a short distance to the north of us and there were also several smaller civilian airfields close by. To stray into military airspace could easily result in us being escorted by military fighters. This was, after all, still very close to the ending of the Cold War. About to panic, I frantically began looking around for a recognisable landmark. I had not flown in this part of the country before and I quickly realised that I was completely lost. I looked across at Ian for guidance and received a shrug of the shoulders as a reply. How could I hope to teach other people to fly and navigate when I could not manage it myself?

I tried to slow my breathing and clear my head of all the negative thoughts running through it. Time enough for that when we were safely back on the ground. I was used to the wide-open skies of California where you could fly for hours without the need to check in with anyone. Back here in Britain, someone or other owned every bit of the sky and you had to be continually on the radio asking them if you could borrow a corner of it for a few minutes. I circled. At least if I stayed roughly where I was, I could limit the number of people I was going to annoy.

Suddenly, I remembered that I could use a radio beacon to discover where I was. I looked at the instrument panel to tune into the local beacon. I looked again and just to be sure, I checked a third time. There were no navigational aids on the aircraft. Joking, I immediately asked Ian for my money back. What was he thinking, allowing me to fly an aircraft without the proper instrumentation? He merely smiled and continued to look out of the window. What could I possibly do now, I thought to myself as I continued circling, feeling more desperate each time I went around. I then thought back to my flying in San Francisco when I had also become slightly unsure of my position. Why not call up air traffic control and ask them if they could identify where I was? I knew I was near Boscombe Down, hopefully, not too near and so, I called them up.

I tried to sound as casual as I could and asked them if they could be so kind as to let me know where I was. The controller was talking to two Lightning fighter aircraft and he sounded a little put out to be interrupted by a lowly Cessna 150. He asked me to select a radio identification code to aid him in identifying me. I had no such instrument on my aircraft and felt very embarrassed to admit it. In the meantime, the two Lightning jet fighters were heading off to fly somewhere, probably faster than the speed of sound; the contrast could not be more complete. The controller then informed me he had a radar return which indicated an aircraft flying around in circles. Could that possibly be me? My spirits lifted as I hurriedly confirmed that indeed it was me flying around in that manner. To confirm that I was the correct aircraft, they asked me to fly around in the opposite direction. As soon as I banked away to comply with his request, the controller confirmed that he had identified me and that my position was two miles south of the small village of Tisbury. Kindly, he then gave me a heading, distance and time for me to return to Compton Abbas. How I wished that I could have bought that man a beer.

As promised, ten minutes later, I spotted the little airfield sitting precariously on the side of the hill. I made a few attempts on the sloping runway before I finally managed a passable landing. We taxied back to the clubhouse in silence and I felt drained both mentally and physically. As I completed my shutdown checks, Ian leapt out of the aircraft and headed towards the refreshment area with the parting words for me to tie the aircraft down for the night. I had already nearly lost it once and he did not want me to complete the task on the ground. Apparently, it often became very windy on the top of the hill and aircraft not tied down could be blown away. What had I let myself in for, I thought, as I trudged my way to the clubhouse for the debrief?

I found my way to the briefing room. To be fair, it was the only thing I had found by myself all day. There was no sign of Ian, so I sat down to wait for the barrage of criticism to come my way. It was just after six in the evening and I wondered if Ian had been so upset by my performance that he had gone home. So, I went in search of him. The clubhouse was small and it did not take me long to find Ian sitting at the members' bar with pint in hand, laughing merrily with a group of other members.

Surely, he was not relaying what I had just done? That would be too humiliating. Spotting me, he called over for me to join the group, ordering me a pint at the same time. He then introduced me to everyone and loudly announced that I was proving to be the best student he had ever had the pleasure to teach. Well, this was the most unusual debriefing I had ever had. The beer was a local brew and delicious. A little while later, Ian leaned over and whispered in my ear that he was pleased with my flying and as long as I didn't get lost again, he had high hopes for me. Five pints later, I decided that a taxi would be by far the safest way to get back to my room and I left them all still sitting there ordering more beer. I liked it here; I liked it a lot.

Over the next few weeks, the flying got harder and the theory more detailed. Becoming an instructor, albeit an assistant one that could teach but not send anyone solo, was harder than I had imagined. The course progressed steadily, each day began with me giving a lecture on a selected subject and then going out in the aircraft to teach that subject in the air. Ian would roleplay the common and not so common mistakes a typical student would make and I would have to recover the aircraft to a safe altitude and go through the explanation as to why we had ended up inverted, spinning earthwards and how to avoid making a similar mistake in the future. It was full-on hard work, yet I was enjoying myself immensely and learning so much myself from teaching others. Each weekend, I returned home and met up with friends I had not seen since my school days. One of these friends was Avril, my first girlfriend. We had stayed in touch since I left school but had drifted apart once I departed for university. After a night out and a few too many beers, I asked Avril if she fancied flying with me in a week's time which she happily accepted. I had my instructor flying test booked at Cardiff Airport the following week and I would fly solo from Compton to Cardiff and back again later that day, a perfect opportunity to show off my new skills.

The day of my flying and ground tests arrived and Avril and I set off in the Yellow Peril early in the morning. This was the day that my ugly little car almost let me down. To get to the airfield, the last mile was uphill and parts of the road were very steep. The Skoda had always struggled to get to the top of the hill. I usually had to change down the gears until we ended up in first or second gear at around ten miles an hour but we always made it, that is, until today. It was probably because there were two of us in the car for the first time. We started our climb in reasonably good shape. As the incline increased, the speed fell away and I found myself in first gear before we were halfway up. The clutch was screaming, the engine was protesting and I was swearing. This was the most important test of my flying career to date. How could this be happening to me? I had, after all, invested a lot of money in this car. Eventually, we came to a stop and then gravity took over and despite the engine being at full power, the clutch had had enough and we went backwards. I managed to stop the car at the side of the road, obviously not using the hand brake - that had packed up months ago! By putting the car in gear and lodging a rock under a rear wheel I was able to prevent the car disappearing back from where it had begun. The clutch pedal seemed to be bent into a strange position, could this be the problem? The only thing I could find was a tree branch to bend the clutch pedal back into place and unbelievably, we were on our way again. Avril just stared at me obviously wondering just what she was letting herself in for. Had she known what was to come, I think she would have got out and walked back down the hill. Finally, we coughed and sputtered our way into the car park. Relief flooded through me. Hopefully, that was the end of the drama for today.

My test was with a retired British Airways captain who was based at Cardiff Airport. The plan was to fly to Cardiff, which would take about forty-five minutes, have breakfast there and arrive fresh for my test at midday. Cardiff is an international airport and a major local airport for mainly holiday flights to Europe. It has a control zone surrounding the airport and you have to file a flight plan for permission to enter the zone and land at the airport. It was a Bank Holiday Monday and I expected the airfield to be busy as I filed the required flight plan. It might have been a good idea to leave a little extra time for any delays into Cardiff. With this in mind, I hurried Avril along and with wishes of good luck from Ian and other club members, we climbed into the little Cessna and taxied out for take-off.

Avril had never flown in a light aircraft before and she showed signs of nerves as we bumped over the rough grass surface. Maybe, asking her along had been a mistake and I asked if she would like to wait for me here in Compton but Avril was made of much sterner stuff and she laughed off my suggestion. The weather was not ideal, but not bad enough to consider cancelling the test. We took off, turned gently towards the north and climbed to the base of the clouds at two thousand feet. I said farewell to the control tower at Compton and in reply, they wished me good luck. I had planned to fly northwest until I reached Weston-Super-Mare and then cross the River Severn before making my approach on the westerly runway at Cardiff. Navigation should not have been a problem as I could hardly miss the Severn and there were no major airfields on my route. Avril was enjoying herself and spent her time asking me which town we were flying over. It was embarrassing to admit that sometimes, I was not completely sure.

Eventually, the wide mouth of the river presented itself on the horizon and I prepared myself to call Cardiff's approach for permission to enter their zone. My first two calls went unanswered but I was not too concerned. We were still a long way out and at a low altitude. By the time we were approaching Weston-Super-Mare, I still could not contact Cardiff approach and I tried another couple of frequencies, all to no avail. I could not enter Cardiff's control zone without permission and so I selected the emergency frequency used throughout the world when an aircraft needed help. There was no answer. I now realised that I had suffered a complete radio failure and with only one radio in the aircraft I was now all alone. I could not land at Cardiff and therefore, I made the tough decision to return to Compton. On the return journey I worked out that I could land, change aircraft, refuel and fill in a new flight plan and still get to Cardiff in time for my test. It would be tight but I could do it. Firstly, I needed to find my way back to Compton and land without a radio. Meanwhile, Avril was in her own world thoroughly enjoying the views. Forty-five minutes later, I was circling overhead Compton awaiting a green flare which would show that they cleared me to land. Ten minutes later, I was shutting the aircraft down when I saw Ian running to meet me.

Ian pulled the door open saying he realised I was in trouble when I failed to land at Cardiff and he had been trying to work out where I had got to. I was surprised at the relief on his face. Didn't he trust me? Anyway, he helped me change aircraft and within twenty minutes, we were on our way again, in a new aircraft with a working radio. I followed the same route and this time, when I approached Weston, I heard a friendly Welsh voice clearing me into the zone and giving me a heading for a straight-in approach and landing. Twenty minutes later, I was shutting the aircraft down with less than ten minutes to spare before the start of my test. So much for a leisurely breakfast.

The examiner was a short, grumpy man with a large frame and bald head. The contrast between him and Ian could not have been more stark and I felt uncomfortable. There was no social chat to put me at my ease. Instead, he informed me I would deliver a lecture on the Theory of Flight, stalling and circuit flying, all of which I would then demonstrate in the aircraft. With that, he walked out of the reception area and told me to be in Room Six in five minutes' time. As I stared at his retreating back, part of me was tempted to get back in my aircraft and fly straight back to Compton. There was no way I was going to come out of today with an Instructor Rating on my licence. Making sure Avril was comfortable and knew where the canteen was, I scurried off after my examiner who I must say felt more like an executioner. As I entered Room Six, the examiner was seated next to two young men whom I assumed I would deliver my lecture to. Trying to take the initiative and getting these guys on side, I walked over and introduced myself, a fixed smile on my face. I asked them their names and then asked each how many flying hours they had. There was an awkward silence broken by the examiner, who turned to his sons and told them he would see them later, telling them that he didn't think that he would be very long. They both left quickly me leaving me facing my executioner alone. I delivered my briefings as succinctly as I could.

Over briefing a student is as bad as under preparing them. As I was finishing my Theory of Flight lecture, covering the art of spinning, the examiner just stood and walked towards the door. "I've heard enough. Let's go flying," were his departing words as I collected my notes together and followed him as quickly as I could. As I conducted my walk-around, he asked me to describe just what I was looking for. The same request was true of all my pre-flight checks and it took a lot longer than usual before we were ready to taxi out. Everything I said and did seemed to be examined in the greatest detail and he brought any ambiguity to my attention immediately. He asked me to show all the manoeuvres I had attempted to brief on and then a few more, just for luck. He then took control of the aircraft and he asked me to point out any errors in his flying and how to correct them. This I did, trying to help rather than criticise but my feedback did not seem to please him. We then flew several circuits with me showing what to do and then supplying help when he took over. Two hours later, we were on our last approach when he informed me that he would do the landing. We hit the runway hard enough to propel us back into the air. Immediately realising that he expected me to recover the attempted landing, I announced loudly that I had control. I took over and as there was plenty of runway remaining, I performed a second landing which luckily was one of the smoothest I had done for quite a while. We taxied in without a word spoken between us and I felt that a knife could cut the atmosphere. After all the shutdown procedures were complete, I was told to report back to Room Six in ten minutes' time. Feeling very dejected, I went in search of Avril. I needed to see a friendly face. After a quick coffee, I entered the classroom to discover my fate. There followed a series of questions on every subject I would teach students. Forty minutes later, during which, I was made to stand, I was finally asked to take a seat. There followed ten minutes of complete silence whilst the examiner filled in my scores for each section of the exam. Finally, he put his pen down, pushed his chair back and asked me how I thought I had done. I hated open questions like this. Do I say I was useless or do I try to convince him he was in the presence of aviation royalty? I did neither, instead informing him I thought I had done a reasonable job, especially recovering the aircraft on that landing. This last remark got me a long hard stare and then he drew a breath and announced my fate.

I had passed! Just! He informed me that he liked my briefings although they were a little on the short side. My flying still needed work but that would come with experience. My overall knowledge was above average and that had helped me to achieve an overall pass. He stood up and offered me his hand to shake. There were no congratulations, just two simple pieces of advice. First, he would prefer me not to teach in Welsh airspace as his sons were thinking of a career in aviation and secondly, he informed me that the last landing was not an attempt to get me to intervene, he was genuinely trying to land the aircraft! I felt my jaw drop and finally he smiled. "One day, you will fly an airliner and only then, will you realise just how difficult it is to adapt to a light aircraft." I closed the door behind me and made as quick an exit as I could manage.

The whole examination had taken nearly four hours, much longer than I had expected. It was now late afternoon and if we wanted to get back to Compton that day, we needed to get going. Grabbing Avril by the hand, I hurried back to our Cessna and after requesting a visual-flight-rules departure, we took off without filing a flight plan which was acceptable as long as we remained clear of busy airspace. As time was short, I flew a much more direct route back to Compton, not following the Severn this time. The cloud base was still acceptable although the sun was now slowly setting. Compton had no night facilities. We had to land before it got too dark to see the airfield. Sunset was still over an hour away and I calculated that we had only thirty minutes flying time left until we arrived at Compton.

I felt uneasy just a short while later, when I had trouble recognising a town that was passing below us. It quickly dawned on me that in my euphoria of passing the exam, I had allowed myself to become distracted from the basics of flying. Firstly, I had not filed or even considered my route home. I had then compounded that error by not checking how much fuel remained in the tanks. The test flight had been an hour longer than I had expected. Thirdly, I had not considered when night would fall. I had jumped into the aircraft with the overconfidence of someone caught up in their own success. I looked across at Avril who was oblivious to my concerns. At least one of us was enjoying themselves. I stared at my map and then back down at the countryside below me. At last, I made a connection between the two. Relief flooded through me as I recognised Shaftesbury. We were nearly home, which was just as well as the light was fading, as was the remaining fuel.

Overhead Shaftesbury, I turned south and headed towards Compton. We would land in ten minutes and I could not wait. It had been a long hard day and I was exhausted.

Ten minutes later, I was still searching for the hill with a runway on it. The light was definitely fading fast and looking at my fuel gauge did nothing to reassure me. I must have flown past Compton. I turned the aircraft around and headed north. At this point, I was considering my options. We were lost, we were low on fuel and it was getting dark. How on earth had I allowed this to happen? Only a few hours ago, I was celebrating my achievement and it now looked as though I would have the shortest instructing career on record. I looked across at Avril who was still enjoying the views. I would soon have to tell her I had got us both lost and there was a very good chance that we would have to land in a field at night which was not the way to a long and happy life. I considered calling up Boscombe Down as I had before, for a position check and a heading for Compton. Sadly, today was a Bank Holiday and the military does not work on Bank Holidays. I just hoped that our enemies did not know that. I tried calling on the civilian emergency frequency. However, we were now so low, they could not hear us. I considered climbing higher, but we were so low on fuel that I was not sure if we had enough to climb. We were now five hundred feet above the ground and I began searching for a field to land in. I turned to Avril to break the terrible news.

As a child, I often visited my grandmother who lived in Salisbury, not too far from the area I was now flying over. We were often bundled into the back of the car and driven to the local beauty spots and places of interest to improve our education, although I would have much rather sat by the river fishing. We visited Stonehenge, Old Sarum and the ancient carving of a horse on a chalk hill. I had taken Avril past this carving on the way to Compton that morning. It was a spectacular sight. Just as I was about to tell Avril how much danger we were in, I spotted the most beautiful sight I had ever seen, a white horse carved on a hill. Suddenly, I knew exactly where I was and I knew where to go.

All I had to do was follow the road beneath us and it would take me to Compton. Staying very low, I followed the road I knew so well and saw the road sign for the airfield. It was the same road that I had so nearly broken down on that morning. Turning right, we were at the bottom of the hill and I kept the road in sight and started to climb up to the level of the airfield. There was no time to call the tower controller. I popped up over the boundary hedge, cut the power and landed on the grass runway. Luckily, no one noticed due to the semi-darkness. The tower controller was packing up for the day, assuming that I was night stopping in Cardiff. I taxied back to the dispersal area and ran into the clubhouse to ring the controller and apologise for landing without permission. At first, he was unimpressed that I had broken this very important rule. Thinking quickly, I explained that I tried calling, but my radio must have been playing up again. This explanation seemed to appease him. I just hoped that he had forgotten that I had changed aircraft earlier and the chances of two radio sets failing on the same day were very remote. I'd got away with several things that day and I knew I had definitely pushed my luck. However, fortune was smiling on me. I was now a flying instructor and as such, I could apply for my first flying job. I lost the rest of the evening in far too much alcohol and fond farewells to Ian and all the friends I had made during my time at Compton. Luckily for me, Avril had offered to drive us both home to Worthing that night. I finally left with promises to keep in touch and a solemn oath to return to Compton soon. Sadly, I have seen none of them since that day.

Chapter 22

My First Flying Job

A week later, my flying licence bore the proud endorsement of 'Assistant Flying Instructor Single-Engine Aircraft'. I kept looking at it, turning it over and then looking once again. I had never been so proud of any achievement until now. I had the ability to go out and earn myself a living doing what I loved best. No more loading aircraft, cleaning aircraft, documenting aircraft, I could now get paid for flying aircraft. The world was my oyster. I was still a very long way from becoming a proper commercial pilot. I would need to fly another six hundred hours before I could even sit the flying and ground examinations. However, that was for the future. Today, I could start looking for a job. This was now the beginning of the eighties. Margaret Thatcher had been in power for just over a year and was set to challenge all the industrial unrest caused by the trade union stranglehold on industry. The Falklands War would start in less than two years' time and rumblings, which would eventually lead to the miners' strike, were already being felt throughout the economy. Britain was beginning a transitional period which would completely reshape the country and the lives of everyone in it would also change beyond recognition. Into this brave new world stepped a newly qualified assistant flying instructor ready to do the same to the world of aviation. Well, if there had been any job vacancies, he would have given it a go! The economy was flatlining, the average working man's wage was six thousand pounds a year and very few people had enough spare money to splash out on flying lessons.

Undeterred, I returned to the shelves of my local newsagent to invest in another copy of *Flight International* magazine. As always, I read it backwards, sadly noting the almost complete lack of flying jobs. The very few that were advertised required experience levels that I could only dream of. It was once again a catch twenty-two situation; you had to have experience to apply for a job and you had to get a job to get the required experience. Maybe, I had been a little hasty in deciding that I no longer needed to clean aircraft. I did, after all, have rent to pay and a loan to service. The euphoria of the previous week was rapidly dwindling. I decided that if there were no flying vacancies then the next best thing was to be around an airfield where a vacancy might occur. So, back to Shoreham I went, cap in hand, washing materials at the ready, willing to do any task I could find for gainful employment. I got a part-time position as a barman at my old flying club, Mercury. I also got a few customers who wanted their aircraft kept clean. At least, I was back at Shoreham and talking to people who might be able to help me.

Being a barman, you hear many conversations, most of them were alcoholic-induced nonsense. Occasionally, however, you can hear something of great interest. There were several aircraft owners who kept their aircraft with the flying school to help pay the running costs. From time to time, they also needed someone to move their aircraft to a different airfield where they would pick them up later, or the reverse, they would fly somewhere, have a few drinks and get a taxi back. They needed someone to collect their aircraft the next day and bring it back to Shoreham. I informed them I knew just the man for the job and when I revealed who it was, after a few splutters of their beer, I was in business. As I had no commercial licence, I could not officially charge for this service but they allowed me to claim for expenses which covered my costs nicely. The most important thing was that I was once again flying and building up my hours towards gaining my commercial licence.

Whilst these various jobs kept my head just above water, I was still committed to securing a position as a flying instructor. Every day, I turned up at the flying club and asked to sit in on ground school lectures. Mercury Flying Club was fortunate enough to have one of the most experienced ground school instructors in the country, Martin Peel. Martin had been a flying instructor until the day he was flying aerobatics and perforated an ear drum. The air's loss was the ground's great good fortune and I sat in awe as Martin gave some of the best lectures it has ever been my privilege to witness. I must confess that I based all my future lectures on Martin's style. At least, I was keeping my flying and theory skills up to date. I just needed an opportunity to put them into practice. Fate or Lady Luck, whichever you prefer, can reach out and grab you when you least expect it. They can both make or break you in a single moment and usually, you are powerless to stop either of them, the outcome is not in your hands. One of the flying instructors at Mercury ran into one of these destinies and in a terrible moment of misfortune he lost his medical certificate. No warnings, no hints that all was not well. He went for his annual medical. The doctor found something not to his liking and that was the end of a promising flying career. Just like that, misfortune had robbed him of everything he had ever worked for, my heart went out to him. One day, he was sitting at the bar as I served him a drink, the next day he was gone, never to be seen again.

There was now a vacancy for a flying instructor and Mercury had a reputation for recruiting in-house. They preferred to employ someone they had trained themselves. In a way, this made sense. If you had been trained the Mercury way, then that is how you would teach. This was excellent news for me, not such good news for the unfortunate pilots who had been trained elsewhere. I immediately applied for the job. However, I had absolutely no experience in instructing and I knew there were some very experienced instructors looking for work, so I held out little hope of success. I was lucky enough to get an interview with Captain Ken Honey and his wife, Beryl, who owned and ran the club. Also, sitting in on the interview was Martin Peel and it fell to him to ask me all the technical questions. This question-and-answer session went on for at least thirty minutes and at the end of the interview, I could see that I had made a good impression, especially with Ken and Beryl. Two days later, I was called into Ken's office for the result of my interview. He had my entire training file in front of him, from my very first flight until the last flight a week ago. He looked up from the file and asked me how much studying I had done for the interview. Answering honestly, I told him I had glanced at my books the night before but that was about it. He closed the file, pushed it across the desk and asked me to put it back in the instructor's room. This room was always kept locked as the personal details of all the students were kept there and they were strictly private. They only allowed the instructors access. I reminded him of this and nodding, he replied that I would need this from now on as he slid a key across the desk. I guess I had a new job.

That evening was my last as a barman. The next day, I would start as a flying instructor, but whether this was a promotion or a demotion, I wasn't yet sure. When I found out how much I would be paid as an instructor, I was even more unsure. Martin, the chief ground school instructor, who had grilled me during my interview, sat nursing his customary half pint of bitter shandy before he drove home. He looked up at me, a smile slowly spreading across his face. "I'm glad those interview notes I gave you last week came in handy. Luck must have been on your side as all the questions and answers came up in the interview. Who would have thought it?" With that, he drained his glass and set off on his long drive home. I almost felt sorry for the other applicants for the job. I just needed to live up to the expectations placed in me.

The next day, I arrived in plenty of time for my induction course at Mercury. I had been out and bought the required grey trousers and blue jacket and had even sewn the Mercury Flying Club insignia on my breast pocket, as required. I looked like a schoolboy on his first day at big school. I just hoped that somebody would talk to me at playtime. It was during this first morning that I had to sign my employment contract, which turned out to be a real eye-opener. I had not asked what the salary for an assistant flying instructor would be. To be fair, I would have probably done the job for nothing and that's almost what they intended to pay me. The average wage in 1980 was six thousand pounds a year and I was going to be paid two thousand pounds. I was earning three times that as a loader at Gatwick. I was even taking a pay cut from being a barman-come-aircraft-cleaner. I was shocked at how little my salary would be. Stupidly, I had just assumed that I would get around the national average or maybe, even slightly above it. After all, I was a professional now. My dreams of a smart flat and a new car slowly evaporated in front of my eyes which were inevitably drawn towards a bright yellow Skoda sitting in the car park just outside the office window. The Yellow Peril and I were destined to spend a lot more time together than I had hoped.

I left the induction session feeling slightly deflated. It very much looked like I would have to find a second job to earn enough money to live on, definitely not what I had been expecting. Shaking off these feelings of disappointment, I looked at the positive side of things. I had a job, a real job, and I was going to make sure I gave it my very best. I walked into the instructor's room and an unfriendly face turned to inspect me.

It looked like I would spend playtime alone. I was replacing a long-standing and very popular instructor whom I had met during my own time as a student. There were two types of instructor: the career instructor who enjoyed the job and stayed instructing and then there was the Self-Improver who was using the instructor job as a means to an end and would move on as soon as they had sufficient hours to sit their commercial licences. The two types of instructors rarely got on very well and I was immediately placed into the Self-Improver category which was fair enough. My fellow instructor was definitely a career instructor and had little time for me. I went in search of more friendly faces. I was to quickly learn that the most important person by far in any flying club was the receptionist. It was she or he who would take the telephone calls from prospective students and allocate an instructor to that student. Fall out with the receptionist at your peril as you would find yourself with no students and no extra flying pay. I went on a charm offensive, which, as the lady in question was akin to a strict headmistress with no sense of humour, did little to help my prospects.

Still undeterred, I went in search of anyone who could give me any advice and help and that led me to the maintenance hangar. The flying club was attached to a large aircraft maintenance and sales company, Southern Air. This was aviation on a different scale, more California than Sussex. Southern Air were the major distributors for the Enstrom Helicopter in Europe and selling and servicing other types of fixed and rotary-wing aircraft. There were helicopters everywhere, interspersed with a few executive aircraft, a true Aladdin's cave for someone like me. Having no students to teach, I asked the chief mechanic if I could look at the various machines on the shop floor. Luckily for me, he agreed. In the years that followed, he and I would strike up a good working relationship. For now, however, I was definitely the new kid on the block. I spent that first morning introducing myself to the most important people in aviation, the mechanics who worked tirelessly to make sure I would have a safe aircraft to fly. I asked as many relevant questions as I could think of and in reply, received an avalanche of information that had previously eluded me. I watched engines being dismantled, instruments being recalibrated and avionics being tested. At the end of the morning, I had learned a lot and just as importantly started new friendships which would prove invaluable in the coming years.

I made my way back to the flying club to see if they had allocated any students to fly with me in the afternoon and unsurprisingly, the line next to my name remained blank. There were three other instructors on duty and their rosters were all full. Only mine remained empty. Still, it was my first day, so I was not expecting a stampede of students desperate to fly with me, although just one would have been nice. Halfway through the afternoon, one instructor approached me and explained that he was running late and would I take his next student? I jumped at the chance and readily agreed. Thanking me, he handed over the student's training file and made what I considered to be a very hasty retreat. I opened the file which was much thicker than the other files I had seen and I read the comments. My student was a retired doctor now in his early seventies who was learning to fly as a hobby. He had yet to fly solo, even though he had amassed over fifty hours of flight instruction. As a pilot typically went solo after twelve to fifteen hours' instruction, this seemed very unusual. I read the notes his previous instructors had written and I realised that he had a change of instructor every few sessions. Again, this seemed odd. The remarks regarding his flying skills were not complimentary and some even bordered on rudeness. I closed the file, determined not to prejudge the man before I had flown with him.

Exactly on time, my first ever student arrived and I introduced myself. He seemed a little confused and asked where his previous instructor was as he had specifically requested that he flew with that instructor. I explained the reason for the last-minute swap, whereupon he stood up and politely told me he had had enough of being pushed from one instructor to another. He wanted continuity and I could hardly blame him. He felt that he was being passed around because of his age and moderate ability. Quietly, I had to agree with him. Asking him to sit down and at least have a coffee with me, he accepted. After some polite small talk, during which I discovered that he had been a surgeon and had travelled extensively, often to war-torn corners of the earth. I was fascinated and listened intently. I was in the presence of a real-life hero. Eventually, we returned to his flying training and I asked why he wanted to learn to fly and what he intended to do once he had his licence. This seemed to take him aback a little and he looked at me with renewed interest. "Do you know, nobody has ever asked me that before." I admitted that I had asked every single one of my students that exact question before we started the course. He seemed very impressed until I admitted that he was my first student. I put it to him that as he had had far more instructors than I had had students why didn't we just fly together this once and see if we couldn't help each other. This seemed to appeal to him and so began a long association, even friendship. He never flew with another instructor again and after going solo just the once, we both decided that it would be better if we just flew together whenever he wanted to fly.

He never got his flying licence, although that was not his goal. He had never intended to fly anywhere by himself. He was a widower and lonely and he had wanted a challenge and the company of someone when he went flying. We flew together to Le Touquet in France, the Channel Islands, Devon and Cornwall. He definitely had the ability to achieve his licence, he just lacked the desire. He was happy just to fly the airplane and leave everything else to me. As he once put it, "When someone is firing shells at the hospital you are working in, excitement is something you consciously try to avoid."

We had a flight planned to Dieppe, which was delayed frequently because of the poor winter weather. The flight was finally booked on a crisp clear spring morning. I was looking forward to catching up with him as we had not flown together since the autumn. The day before the flight, I received a telephone call from a member of his family. The doctor had taken a much longer flight, alone this time. Hopefully, he would now be reunited with his wife. I had lost a student and a friend and it hurt. I still miss our flights together.

Slowly I built up a student base and my diary gradually became fuller with each day that passed. Instructors came and went and within months, there were only two of us left from when I had originally started, although the chief flying instructor was still in place. Much younger and more convivial characters had replaced the departing instructors. The workplace was becoming more fun.

My private life was not so much fun and although I had moved out of my holiday home and into a small flat, I was lonely. I worked just about every day that the weather allowed and that left very little time to meet a partner. I was sitting in the flying club one rainy afternoon pondering this problem when I came across the commercial section of the local newspaper. An advertisement immediately caught my eye and made me realise that this could be the answer to my problem. As there was no chance of flying that day because of the awful weather, I got permission to take a few hours off. I rang the telephone number in the advertisement; I was lucky I could meet up that very afternoon. I set off for the short drive to Brighton and rang the doorbell, feeling very nervous. What if I was not liked?

A very attractive lady answered the door and I immediately knew that I had found genuine love. Standing just behind her was the most adorable Golden Retriever puppy that

I had ever seen. I crouched down and he literally flew into my arms. I was smitten and luckily, he seemed to be too. Roffey was twelve weeks old and had been with his new owners for just over a week. Unluckily, or luckily, in my case, their dog refused to accept Roffey and would attack him given any opportunity. Roffey had to go and he went with me. He sat on my lap as I drove back to the airport, licking my face at regular intervals. He jumped out of the car and dutifully followed me into the flying club where he was smothered in affection. I had arrived at work that morning a single man and now here I was, the proud parent of a puppy. I really had not thought this through. What on earth was I going to do with him when the weather improved and I had to fly again? Fate was going to give me the opportunity to find out as the clouds cleared and my next student arrived. I looked around at everyone who had been playing with Roffey to ask them if they could look after him for an hour. Unfortunately, Roffey's new friends had all melted away and he stood by himself in the room looking up at me.

There was no way I could leave him in the car and so I approached my student to ask if he would mind having a passenger. We had flown together many times before and today's flight was a short cross-country practise one. He readily agreed and the three of us set off for the aircraft. Roffey was looking thrilled. At least, there was no dog trying to attack him. I put my new puppy in the back of the aircraft and told him to sit and stay. That worked very well for nearly two seconds, after which he was back on my lap licking my face. Fending off his advances, we made our way to the runway. I had no idea how Roffey would react inflight but I was about to find out. As we bumped over the grass, Roffey peered over the instrument panel and remained quiet. He stayed that way for the entire flight. He was very calm, silent and just looked out of the window and then back at me. He was the perfect passenger and he was either too terrified to move or he loved to fly. In the coming weeks, months and years I knew it was the latter.

As I became more experienced, I took the examination to become a full rather than assistant flying instructor. This enabled me to send students on their first solo flights as well as signing them off as being competent to take their final flying test. This was a much more satisfying job. I quickly learnt to differentiate between a student who wanted to get his Private Pilot Licence for recreational purposes and those who wanted to pursue a career in aviation. Rightly or not, I set much higher standards for the career pilot, although both had to meet the minimum standards. My good friend, who had done his best to get us lost on the way to Heathrow, was one such example.

Pete Brown wanted to fly. However, his career of choice was the Royal Air Force. Personally, I would rather not be shot at, but each to their own. I think Pete finally came around to my way of thinking and left the Royal Air Force to pursue a civilian flying career and it fell upon me to get him through his Private Pilot Licence. I had only just qualified as a full instructor and had not had a lot of experience in sending someone off into the bright blue yonder for the first time. The trick was not to let the student know in advance that you were about to send them solo as if they had this knowledge then nerves could get the better of them. Teaching someone you have known since you were both two years old is never easy and this seemed especially true of Pete and me, as when we were together, we spent most of our time laughing. Despite this, I had managed to get Pete up to speed for his first solo. Until this point, Pete had performed well. Our last lesson had gone particularly well and if the crosswinds had been within limits, I would have sent him solo. Today, however, a different Pete had taken to the skies, everything he had previously done so well now seemed out of his reach. The first take-off was interesting and we pointed skywards at an alarming angle. The circuit that followed left a lot to be desired and the landing was just dreadful, so off we went for another try. Thirty minutes later and Pete was still inventing novel ways to surprise me. This was incredibly frustrating, as I knew he had the ability to perform to a much higher standard. I had to make a quick decision; do I send Pete solo hoping that he could resume his old standard or do I call a halt to the lesson and try another day. Both had their merits and drawbacks. Cancel and Pete's confidence would be badly shaken, send him solo and on today's performance, I would be looking for a new best friend.

As we taxied back to the holding point for another take off, I had to make my decision. Realising that if the worst came to the worst, Roffey could replace Pete as my best friend and with that thought in mind, I told Pete he had better make the next circuit the best he had ever flown. When he asked why, I told him it was because I would not be there to help. With that, I opened the door of the aircraft, stepped out and without a backwards glance, walked away.

It was a long and lonely walk back to the clubhouse and I couldn't resist turning to watch Pete's take off. He lifted off and flew a perfect climb out, turning at eight hundred feet towards the downwind leg. I lost sight of him for a few minutes until I caught the sun glinting off his wings as he turned onto finals. I couldn't help myself stopping and watching his approach. Had anyone been close enough to hear me, they would have thought I had gone mad. I was literally talking Pete through the approach, commenting on his power and height, which all looked perfect from where I was standing. As he came over the hedge at the beginning of the runway, I told him to gently raise the nose and reduce the power. I told him to hold it there and just wait for the aircraft to touchdown, that's it, just nicely on the centre line, hold the nose wheel off a little longer and there we are, finally down, a perfect landing. Well done, mate. I turned with a tremendous sigh of relief and continued walking back towards the clubhouse. I had got out of the aircraft at the farthest point because the runway in use was at the opposite side of the airfield to the clubhouse.

A few moments later, I heard an aircraft approaching from behind me. As I turned to look, I heard a voice asking me if I wanted a lift. Pete had decided not to follow the normal taxi route and much to the air traffic controller's amazement, picked me up. As I climbed aboard, I was very tempted to tell him off for breaking this regulation. However, as we both looked at each other, we just burst out laughing. That's what best friends are for, I suppose. We had both learned a lot from that morning's flying. I had learned that to expect perfection from a student before sending him solo was a mistake, as long as they were safe, then let a student be free to learn from his own mistakes. You cannot always be there. Pete admitted that he had been trying far too hard to please me and had let his flying suffer. Pete went through the rest of his course without a hitch and passed all his examinations and tests with very high marks. We both felt a great satisfaction when he gained his wings.

Winter was now making itself felt and flying days became fewer and fewer, as a cold easterly wind gripped the country. There were still ground lectures to perform and in the run-up to the last Christmas of the decade, I idly looked out of the window onto a bleak and deserted airfield. Our little Cessna aircraft were all tied down in straight lines to prevent damage from the high winds. Everything, except for the weather, was going into winter hibernation and I very much doubted that I would fly again until the New Year. I looked, once again, across the airfield as I thought I had heard an approaching aircraft. Just to be sure, I went outside to investigate.

Sure enough, I could hear what I thought by the level of noise must be a twin-engine aircraft performing a missed approach from a low height. The active runway was the easterly one, which ran directly in front of the control tower and our clubhouse. I stood listening to the fading sound of the engines.

Obviously, the pilot had rightly concluded that the weather made landing at Shoreham out of the question and he had flown elsewhere. I turned to go back inside and out of the cold blustery wind. I stopped once more and strained to identify an increasing noise, I could not believe what I was hearing. Our sensible pilot had returned for another go at landing, not such a sensible pilot after all. I turned back and walked towards our line of aircraft. The landing aircraft would make his approach directly towards me. I stared up at the low clouds waiting for the aircraft, a Piper Aztec, to appear. Suddenly, it broke through the cloud halfway down the runway and well to the right of the centre line. I was urging the pilot to apply full power and abandon this ill-fated attempt at a landing. However, our previously sensible pilot had other ideas and he pushed the nose of the aircraft down as his first bounce resulted in him becoming airborne again. This was a terrible mistake and I watched in horror as the results of his actions followed a sadly predictable sequence.

The Aztec hit the ground once more on its nose wheel, which was not designed for such rough treatment. The nose wheel collapsed and the aircraft swung violently to the right. With the nose of the aircraft now digging a large trench in the waterlogged grass, the Aztec was coming straight towards me, still at an alarming rate. I did what any sensible instructor would do. I turned and ran away as fast as I could. Once out of the path of the runaway aircraft, I turned and watched in morbid fascination as the Aztec, by this time, totally out of the pilot's control, headed straight for our line of aircraft. This would not be pretty. Everything seemed to happen in slow motion as the right wing of the Aztec sliced into our aircraft at the end of the first line. This momentum then swung the Aztec towards the second line of aircraft and the Aztec did the same thing with another of our aircraft. By this time, the momentum of the Aztec was exhausted and it came to an inglorious stop, with its nose buried in mud and its tail sticking into the sky from whence it came. The propellers had also buried themselves into the mud and the engines had stopped. After a cacophony of grinding metal and screeching engines, it became deathly quiet. I was only fifty feet away from the wrecked aircraft and for a moment I hesitated, expecting an explosion and fire. Luckily, neither occurred. I ran to the Aztec as I heard the fire engines starting to race towards us. I jumped up onto the wing and pulled the door open. Sitting there calmly and unhurt sat the pilot, the only occupant of the aircraft. He looked at me, saw my uniform and then apologised for writing off two of our aircraft. I assured him that as long as he was unharmed that was all that mattered and would he care for a coffee or something much stronger. By this time, the emergency services had arrived and they took over. I returned to the clubhouse. The pilot may not have wanted a drink, but I did.

This left the flying club with a big problem. Three of our aircraft had been damaged, and the first aircraft the Aztec had hit was a total write off. We needed a replacement, and the sooner the better. I was called into the office a few days later and was informed that a new aircraft had been located and purchased and would I care to collect it. There were, however, two slight problems. Firstly, the aircraft would need a test flight to make sure it was fully airworthy and secondly, the aircraft was in Stornoway, an island off the north coast of Scotland. One of the bonuses of becoming involved with the maintenance staff at Southern Air was that they had sponsored me to become a CAA check pilot, enabling me to sign an aircraft off after it had undergone major maintenance. The course had been great fun and they had taught me to fly an aircraft to its limits to make sure that everything was working as it should be. This was a hugely satisfying task and I enjoyed every test flight. I was, therefore, the ideal person to travel to Stornoway to check on and then deliver the aircraft. I asked who would accompany me and I was met with blank faces in reply. I informed them I was happy to test fly the aircraft and then fly it back, but I would not do it alone. After an hour's test flight, I would have a seven-hundred-mile trip to make it back to Shoreham and at approximately one-hundred miles an hour that would equate to eight hours flying without an autopilot. With two pilots, this would be a challenge, with just one it would be dangerous to the point of stupidity. I left them to think about it and made up my mind that I would not reconsider. Christmas was now approaching and so the entire project was put on hold.

Chapter 23

Happy New Year's Eve

The weather continued to be very unsettled and I held out little hope of collecting the aircraft before the New Year. My request for a co-pilot had finally been approved and I had asked Pete to help me deliver the replacement aircraft. Christmas came and went. The weather forecast still ruled out any chance of the operation going ahead. I had planned a large party at my house on New Year's Eve to celebrate the start of the eighties. I had everything planned; invites were sent out, catering ordered and alcoholic refreshments delivered. It was going to be a great night. Then suddenly the weather changed. On the twenty-ninth of December, I was told that Pete and I had been booked seats on the British Airways flight to Glasgow the next day. We were then to stay in an airport hotel and catch the first flight to Stornoway very early the next morning. The owner of the aircraft, the island's vet, would meet us at the airport at seven o'clock in the morning. The plan was to complete the test flight and then phone the company to confirm that all was well. Once the call had been completed, the money for the aircraft would be released and we could fly it back to Shoreham. We hoped to be airborne by ten o'clock. Shoreham was conducting night flying that day and closed at eight o'clock in the evening. That would give Pete and I ten hours to get the aircraft back before

Shoreham closed. That should not be a problem, or so we thought.

The next day, we were on our way to Glasgow. It seemed very odd that the flight took just over an hour, the same flight the next day was going to take us over six times longer. Arriving in Glasgow, we checked into the hotel and enjoyed a meal and a beer. We even got to chat to Alex 'Hurricane' Higgins, a world-famous snooker player who also happened to be staying there. The next morning saw us walking towards the Viscount for our relatively short flight to Stornoway. The Viscount was a turbo propeller aircraft from the fifties and it was a great pleasure to fly in it before it was retired not long afterwards. We landed on time and made our way to meet the flying vet, as agreed.

There, sitting outside a hangar sat a beautiful, blue and white Cessna 152, our aircraft. There was nobody about and so to save time, I began a very detailed inspection of the aircraft. The doors were unlocked; crime, I imagined would be a very rare thing here. A good hour later, I was satisfied that the aircraft was in excellent condition with no signs of any previous damage or corrosion. There was still no one to meet us and so we set off into the hangar to see if we could find anybody but it was deserted. I had a contact number for the vet, so we made our way back into the terminal building to call him. Breakfast also beckoned. Pete went to order a full Scottish breakfast whilst I dialled the number I had been give. Eventually, a very sleepy female voice answered my call. Introducing myself, I enquired where the vet was, as we had an appointment to meet him over an hour ago. She apologised and informed me that someone had called him out on an emergency and he would not be back until ten o'clock at the earliest. This was bad news, terrible news. If I could not conduct the test flight until ten o'clock, then we could not possibly set off until at least midday. This would not leave us enough time to fly to Shoreham before it closed. If this was the case, we would not be home in time for my own New Year's

Eve party that very night. Fate had dealt me a cruel blow and I regretted agreeing to the whole thing. Pete meanwhile was finishing the last of his black pudding and I didn't like the way he was eyeing up my breakfast. Rescuing my meal, Pete and I tried to work out a new plan. Our intentions had been to fly from Stornoway to Glasgow, where we would refuel. Luckily, our new aircraft was fitted with long range fuel tanks and we could stay airborne for five hours. The next sector was from Glasgow to East Midlands Airport, with the last flight originally planned to end at Shoreham. Each sector was roughly three hours in duration. Obviously, reaching Shoreham was now out of the question. However, we agreed that if we could get away by lunchtime, we could still make it back to Gatwick Airport, which was open all night. This was not ideal and undertaking a long night flight in a very basic single-engine aircraft was a questionable decision. However, if we wanted to get home, we had little choice.

Eventually, our absent vet arrived and offered profuse apologies, handing over the aircraft keys. As we had completed all our ground checks, we jumped into the aircraft and set off for the trial flight with great haste. Whilst I performed all the required flight manoeuvres, Pete filled out the results on the clipboard on his lap. This was a very nice aircraft and it behaved itself beautifully. It had been very well looked after and passed the test without any areas of concern. In a little over an hour, we were back on the ground and arranging for the funds to be released to allow us to get under way. Formalities finally over, we said our goodbyes and literally ran back to the aircraft. We taxied out at a rather sporting pace and finally, we were cleared for an immediate take-off. Nearly four hours later than scheduled, we were on our way.

Daylight in the far north of Scotland was a rare commodity at this time of the year and although it was only just after midday, the sun was already beginning to set. The weather was beautiful, freezing but visibility was unlimited in a cloudless sky. We climbed slowly to eight thousand feet. There was a lot of high terrain on our route and the higher above the mountains we were, the better we felt. The aircraft had very basic radio navigation equipment and we tuned into beacon after beacon as we slowly made our way southwards. We were flying away from the setting sun and the daylight slowly faded, leaving just a trace of the last day of the seventies on the horizon. As night-time finally enveloped us, I leant forward to turn the instrument panel lights up. We were having difficulty in reading our instruments. I turned the lights up to their maximum settings but nothing happened. We still couldn't see our instruments. This was a serious problem. Flying at night without instruments was dangerous and apart from the fact that we could no longer navigate, there was now a very good chance that if we entered any cloud, we could become disorientated and lose control of the aircraft with fatal consequences. Luckily, every responsible pilot who flies at night carries a torch and I was no exception. With Pete concentrating on keeping us straight and level, I leaned into the back to retrieve my torch. We spent the next two hours with Pete flying whilst I shone the torch light between the map and the instrument panel. It was hard work and required total concentration. I had to anticipate which instrument Pete required and illuminate it accordingly. The only refreshments we had with us were a packet of polo mints and some water. Pete kept muttering that the whole thing was too risky and to ease tension every twenty minutes, he would ask me to break out the polos. This had the desired effect and we both laughed every time we attacked the little mints with a hole in them.

Now, although I had carried my torch, which was literally proving to be a lifesaver, I had failed to include spare batteries in my flight bag. This could have proved a fatal mistake as two hours later, the beam from the torch was beginning to fade and we were both struggling to read the instruments. I was furious with myself for not noticing that the panel lights did not work when I conducted the flight test. However, in bright daylight, the failure of the lights would have been very difficult to spot. I just hoped that there was nothing else I had missed. We had been in such a rush to get away, another mistake was not beyond the bounds of possibility. I tried to push these apprehensive thoughts to the back of my mind as we still had to nurse the aircraft into a safe landing without lights. One single mistake could still prove to be one too many. Fate was on our side once again, as the weather remained benign. The clouds kept their distance as our little aircraft navigated its way towards Glasgow by moonlight alone. Below us was blackness, no lights anywhere. We were over high ground with very little to guide us except our radio. The cockpit was now in total darkness and we could not see to change radio or navigation frequencies. Pete was thinking ahead and had asked me to select the tower frequency half an hour ago whilst we could still see the radio panel. That simple request probably saved us that night. Finally, we could see the bright lights of Glasgow in the far distance. Our spirits rose even further as we finally spoke to the tower controller. Under his instruction, we positioned for a very long, straight-in approach. Any turns could prove fatal with no instruments. Pete flew a perfect approach and landing. Laughingly, I told him that he flew better when he couldn't see what he was doing. As we taxied in, we both let out an enormous sigh of relief as the propeller finally came to a stop. We realised that we had used up at least one of our lives on that flight. Hopefully, the next two sectors would prove less exciting. Before we could even consider taking off again, we had to get the panel lights working. Neither of us wanted to go through that again.

It was now four o'clock in the afternoon. The darkness was complete and Hogmanay was in the air. The whole of Scotland was gearing up for a night of special celebration. The terminal was eerily quiet and to our great dismay all the shops were closed. After checking all the circuit breakers and fuses in the aircraft, we had concluded that the problem with the panel lights was beyond our repair capabilities. We could either stay here in Glasgow or buy a back-up torch with plenty of batteries to get us home. The latter prospect now seemed very remote as we were faced with an empty terminal in which none of the shops were open.

Pete spotted a policeman - someone had to work on New Year's Eve - and asked him if there was anywhere that we could buy a torch and batteries. We explained our predicament and he listened to our tale with increasing concentration. We were not surprised when he informed us that there were no shops open and no prospect of us buying what we required. Both of us felt a great sense of frustration and anti-climax. We had come so far and a lack of a torch was going to prove our downfall. Our newfound friend could see our disappointment and asked us to follow him. We did as we were told and after taking three flights of stairs, found ourselves inside the police station attached to the terminal. Drawers were opened and ransacked. No cupboard was left unopened until two large black police torches were placed in front of us together with an ample supply of batteries. We were stunned. Our prayers had been answered and we offered our deepest thanks, trying to hand over payment. We were rebuked for trying to bribe an officer of the law and were instructed to leave immediately. Besides, he had a crime to solve - two of his colleagues would be missing their torches when they next reported for work.

As quickly as we could, we made our way to the control tower to arrange refuelling, check the weather and file our new flight plan for East Midlands Airport. All looked good and the refuelling bowser was awaiting us on our return to the aircraft. Tanks full, we requested start-up clearance. The skies were still clear, although there was a cloud layer over the Pennines. We should be above the cloud at eight thousand feet. The weather at East Midlands was forecast to be clear also. We hoped our troubles were now behind us and with a favourable tailwind, we should land in just under three hours, nicely in time for a quick refuelling and away on our last leg to Gatwick and to our party. We were both smiling as our little aircraft climbed away from Glasgow, leaving a nation to celebrate New Year's Eve as only the Scots can do. Hopefully, we would join them in spirit well before midnight.

We climbed slowly, following the course of the M6 motorway southwards. The weather was still crystal clear and we could make out the coastline to our left as we made our way past Prestwick and prepared to change radio frequency as we crossed the border into England. Wishing our Scottish friends good luck for the new decade, we spoke to our new controller and asked for a further climb. We were just starting to fly into the top of the forecast cloud layers. As it was mid-winter, there was always the real possibility of encountering ice if we flew into the clouds. Commercial aircraft have systems that can cope with ice by melting or breaking the ice away from the flying surfaces. They also have heated windscreens and ice protection for the vital parts of the aircraft that measure the height and speed. Even with all these devices, a commercial airliner will do everything it can to avoid icing conditions. We had nothing, not a heated window or anti-ice protection anywhere. If we encountered icing conditions, we would have to exit as soon as possible before the ice accumulation affected our flying surfaces and instruments. Stay in icing conditions for more than a few minutes with no protection and the aircraft could quickly become unflyable and plummet earthwards. We were acutely aware of the dangers. However, according to the weather forecast, we should have been safely above the clouds, assuming that forecasters had got it right, which unfortunately for us, they had not. As the cloud thickened, we were alone in an eerily silent world, all-encompassing clouds muffled even the reassuring sound of the engine. It was also dark and except for the light of our torch, we were entering a black void of nothingness.

Whilst Pete concentrated on the flying, I tried to get clearance to climb out of the icing layer into the clear air above us. As this would take us into restricted airspace, I was told to stand by and they would get back to me. I looked across at Pete and could see the concern on his face. He was struggling to keep the aircraft flying level. The tension was obvious, both of us acutely aware of the danger we were in. Pete looked across at me and in the understatement of the year, announced, "This is a bit risky, let's break out the polos." No sooner had the words left his mouth than the aircraft finally gave up any pretence of being able to fly anymore. The nose dropped, the wings stalled and we headed earthwards towards the deadly Pennine Hills. Maybe we would not be celebrating the new decade after all. Everything began to happen at once, Pete started the stall recovery, air traffic cleared us to climb and I dropped the torch. We were now in a most unfortunate position, unable to see anything, heading earthwards in an ice cube. This was not one of my better days. Struggling to get hold of the torch, I just prayed that Pete would avoid a spin. We were unlikely to ever recover before we said hello to the ground below. Retrieving our light, I shone it at the instruments. Thankfully, we were still the right way up, although we were descending at an alarming rate. All the time, I could hear the air traffic controller asking us why we were descending when he had cleared us to climb? Why indeed, I thought to myself. He was the last thing I was worried about at this moment in time. Firstly, we had to regain control of the aircraft and then make sure we did not hit any hills. Then and only then, would we have time to reply to his questions.

The engine was at full power and we were still descending. We were now passing through five thousand feet and the terrain was at two thousand. We were getting too close for comfort. The only positive thing was that Pete now had the aircraft under control, although to maintain a safe airspeed, he had to lower the aircraft's nose, which meant that we had to continue our descent. Taking the torch beam off the instruments for a moment, I shone the light out onto the wings above us, I instantly wished that I hadn't. There was ice everywhere. Instead of a nice clean leading edge of the wing, there was an opaque layer of ice building up literally, as I looked. The fact we were still airborne was amazing. The aircraft was carrying the weight of all this ice on wings that had lost most of their lift. This situation could not go on for much longer. Either we needed to exit the icing conditions in the next few minutes or we needed to lose weight from the aircraft. I looked again at Pete and noticed for the first time that he had put on a few pounds recently. Maybe, I could reduce the aircraft's overall weight with just a little push in his direction. Realising that it would be difficult to explain how there were two of us at take-off and only one of us on landing, I rejected the idea and besides, best friends are hard to find. With a shudder, I noticed Pete looking at my expanding waistline. We were both entertaining similar thoughts, when all of a sudden, we dropped out of the base of the clouds. It looked as though neither of us would have to lose their best friend, well not quite yet at least.

Looking at the instruments, we were now just under two thousand feet above the hills. As the ice accumulation reduced, the aircraft was able to maintain its current height and we could safely lock each other's doors again. The propellor now began shedding the layers of ice that had been reducing its ability to keep us airborne. The noise that the lumps of ice were making hitting the aircraft fuselage was at first, deeply concerning. It sounded as if parts of the aircraft were being shaken loose but eventually, we understood what was happening and once again, we began to concentrate on more pressing matters.

Our problems were still not over as there remained a lot of ice on the aircraft that would not melt as the outside air temperature was minus one. To add to our problems, the windscreen was opaque being also covered in a sheet of ice. Think of your car's windscreen in the morning after a frosty night and you will understand our problem. Unfortunately, we had no means of clearing the ice until we landed and landing without being able to see outside was going to be difficult. It was time for another polo mint. We still had ninety minutes until we arrived at East Midlands so that problem could wait its turn. In the meantime, I had to explain to the controller why we had been descending instead of climbing. He was very understanding and wished us good luck and a Happy New Year as he handed us over to the next controller. By this time, our heartbeats were returning to something approaching normal. Apart from not being able to see ahead, we were now in a more or less reasonable state. Our little aircraft continued on its way in clear air and we could see for miles out of the side windows. It was a beautiful moonlit night with a cascade of stars as far as the eye could see. Just stunning.

With less than an hour until we had to attempt a blind landing, Pete and I discussed just how we were going to attempt a landing without being able to see the runway. As I was the more experienced out of the two of us, I immediately delegated this task to Pete, who wisely refused. We needed to come up with a plan on how to fly the approach, which in fact, should pose no significant problems with the help of the radar controller. Our greatest threat was the actual lining up with the runway centre line and then flaring the aircraft at the correct height. If we made it safely onto the runway, we decided that we could open the door windows to see ahead. Eventually, we came up with an idea that might just work. It would require very accurate flying and more than a dose of very good luck.

On a hot summer's day, I would often leave my aircraft door open until we lined up on the runway. There was no air conditioning and the cool flow of air from the open door allowed the temperature to remain bearable. I was, therefore, used to looking out of an open door as we taxied out to the runway. As we were in a high-wing aircraft, I could see the ground below us. Thus, the plan was to fly an instrument approach until we were over the runway. Pete would look out of his window to judge where the runway edge was and advise me to go left or right to keep us on the centre line, or as close to it as we could manage. Once we were low enough to see the runway edge lights, I would open my door far enough to enable me to judge our height and when to flare and close the throttle to land the aircraft.

With our plan now firmly in place, we asked for the longest, straight-in approach I have ever flown. We were just passing Manchester and already, we were firmly in the slot. Unbelievably, everything went exactly as we had planned and hoped for. The controller did a wonderful job in placing us over the threshold of the runway. Pete took over with a few commands, "left a bit, right a bit" and at the last moment, I inched my door open to see the runway coming up to meet us, just in time to flare the aircraft down into an acceptable landing. We were finally down on the ground. With both doors now open, we braved the bitter wind and slowly made our way to the refuelling ramp. With the park brake set, I switched off the engine and as the propeller finally stopped turning, we both looked at each other, this time, saying nothing. Once again, we both realised just how close we had come to not being around, to welcome in the new decade.

Time was now absolutely of the essence if we wanted to make it back to Gatwick to celebrate the New Year. First, we had to take all the accumulated ice off our aircraft, not a straightforward task as we looked at the layers that were attached to the flying surfaces. East Midlands Airport in those far-off days was more of a freighter than a passenger hub. Parked next to us were a variety of small, medium and large, freighter aircraft, either loading or unloading their cargoes. Several larger aircraft were being de-iced by specialist vehicles. I went to investigate and enquire if they could spray our aircraft. The reply was that yes, they could and the wait would be about three hours. Well, obviously, that would not work for us and I went in search of an alternative means to get us on our way.

I noticed a King Air turboprop, similar to the one I had seen in Sonoma. One pilot was walking around his aircraft spraying everything with what looked like a garden weed-killer container. I approached him, fascinated at how well the process was going. He explained that it was, indeed, a garden spray filled with de-icing fluid and this method was much quicker and a lot cheaper than waiting for the de-icing truck to arrive. After I recounted our plight, he kindly lent me his home-made spraying kit. Ten minutes later, we were clear of ice, the tanks were again full and Pete was completing his pre-flight walk-around. It was now approaching eight in the evening. With a two-hour flight time, we would still be home in time for a rendition of Auld Lang Syne. I hurried off to file our last flight plan, check the weather and pay our landing fees. The en route weather was clear all the way to the south coast, all the airports were clear, except for Gatwick. Having been built on the site of an old swamp, drained to become a horse racing track and finally, converted into an airfield, Gatwick had its own microclimate which could cause localised fog. However, aircraft were still landing and so I filed for Gatwick with Stansted as our alternative.

I had asked Pete to get the aircraft started before I returned, mainly to get the very inadequate heater to warm up the cockpit. Approaching the aircraft, I could see Pete sitting there. The aircraft was dark and the engine silent. Opening my door and sliding into my seat, I enquired why we were not ready to set off. Pete turned and looking directly at me handed me the aircraft's ignition key, well to be more precise, he handed me half of it. Looking at the object in my hand, it took me a moment to understand what I was looking at. Realisation came slowly. The key had snapped in half. Happily, we were in luck as I magically produced the spare key that had fortuitously been given me in Stornoway. Handing the key to Pete, I urged him to get going as we needed to be airborne as soon as possible. He handed the new key back, informing me that it was useless as the other half of his key was actually stuck in the ignition switch. We had come so far, been through so much and now it all looked to have been in vain due to a broken cheap key. I could not believe that our journey was going to end here, awaiting a new ignition key barrel, which there was no hope of getting until the New Year. There had to be a way of bypassing the ignition switch. This was a very basic aircraft, not dissimilar to the cars I used to buy at auction. Several cars I had bought had suffered from faulty ignition switches and the only way to start the car was to disconnect the wires at the back of the unit and to reconnect the correct wires together. Could this work on the aircraft? Well, there was only one way to find out. Upside down with my head under the instrument panel, I located the back of the ignition switch and disconnected the three wires. With Pete shining the torch down on me, I connected two of the wires but nothing happened. I tried again with a different combination of wires, still nothing. On the third attempt, the propeller turned over and the engine coughed itself into life. Making sure that this connection was secure, we returned to our seats and not quite believing that we had hot-wired an aircraft, we set off before anything else could happen.

Climbing away from East Midlands Airport, we made out the lights of London on the horizon. It was now a perfect moonlit night. The visibility was unlimited and the moonlight so strong that we could turn the torch off and read our instruments with no problems. It was probably one of the most magical scenes I have ever witnessed. We were approaching London. On our right, we could see as far as Bristol and to our left, East Anglia was laid out in the distance, both awaiting the arrival of the new decade. There were few other aircraft in the sky; most people had got to where they were going. There was now less than three hours until Big Ben would ring in the New Year and a new decade. We gained permission to fly directly over London at two thousand feet. We had the best view in town and could see the crowds beginning to form alongside the South Bank and Parliament Square. The entire scene was surreal. It made up for all the trials and tribulations we had experienced since leaving Stornoway that morning. Had that really only been today? It seemed like another lifetime ago.

As we left London behind, they handed us over to the approach controller at Gatwick. With a cheery voice, I bade him a very good evening and asked would he be so kind as to position us for a short final, as we had a party to attend. The reply was very curt and to the point. "Do not enter Gatwick's control zone, take up a hold in your current position and await further instructions," came the orders. Well, that was rude, I thought to myself and besides, we did not have enough instruments to take up a hold. Instead, I spotted the Crystal Palace mast lit up on our left, so I flew around that instead. We listened, feeling crushing disappointment as one aircraft after another attempted to land, only to have to go-around at the last moment due to the fog bank sitting right on the threshold of the runway. These aircraft then had to divert to their alternates until there was only one aircraft left and that was us.

The controller asked us our intentions as all the other traffic had diverted. From our circling position, I could see the runway at Gatwick and had watched as one aircraft after another made their approach in clear skies until at two hundred feet, they entered the fog and had to abandon their approaches. Although I could not see the beginning of the runway, the middle and the stop end of the runway were crystal clear. Whilst an airliner has to follow a glide path onto the beginning of a runway, we were not restricted by such constraints. We were working to visual-flight-rules and I could see more than enough of the runway to land on it. Therefore, I asked to make a visual approach. It is rare that an air traffic controller is lost for words, which is normally a good thing, as words are the tools of their trade. Tonight, the situation was different and there was a long pause before they asked me to repeat my request. I duly obliged. I was then asked to confirm my aircraft type, which again, I did. There was an even longer pause before I was asked to confirm that I really was a Cessna 152 and that I intended to make a visual approach at their airfield. After convincing him that I was sane and this was not a New Year's Eve prank, he cleared us to make an approach and land if we could.

We stopped circling the Crystal Palace mast and headed directly towards the visible portion of Gatwick's runway. We descended to the top of the fog bank, which was at two hundred feet. Levelling off just as our wheels were becoming enveloped, we waited until we cleared the edge of the fog bank. From there, it was a simple matter of closing the throttle and continuing the descent onto the portion of the runway that was clear. We still had a mile of runway left as we came to a slow taxi speed and as we were being given our taxi instructions, we could hear clapping and laughter in the background. The controllers no doubt heard our relieved laughter as well. We taxied onto the General Aviation ramp and for the last time that decade, we shut the aircraft down. It was ten minutes past eleven in the evening. I had called home before taking off from East Midlands and now waiting for us was my girlfriend, Melanie. Holding a beer in each hand, she gestured for us to get into the car. We arrived at the party as the bells were ringing in the new decade. After a very late breakfast in the morning, we both realised just how lucky we had been to have made it into the eighties.

Chapter 24

A New Decade, A New Adventure

We finally collected the aircraft from Gatwick a few days later. Heavy rain at Shoreham had flooded the grass runways rendering them unusable, which was just as well as it took me a long time to recover from the party. As I delivered the aircraft for a thorough maintenance check, I asked the engineers to check the interior lighting and the wiring at the back of the ignition switch. In return, there were a few raised eyebrows at the twisted wires but luckily for me, nothing else was said. That Cessna turned out to be one of the best aircraft on the fleet and became my aircraft of choice to fly in. We had been through a lot together and had secrets only a few knew about.

I continued to instruct. However, I knew that I was becoming restless. I needed new challenges and desperately wanted to fly more advanced aircraft. I had passed my Twin-Engine Instructor Rating, which satisfied me for a while. On one memorable occasion, I was asked to fly a Piper Seneca 1 down to Farranfore in south west Ireland and spend two weeks there teaching the new owner to fly the aircraft. This sounded great fun and without reading the pilot's manual in too much detail (I could do that when I got there), I set off alone for the three-hour flight. As soon as I became airborne, I knew that I was in deep trouble. As I moved the ailerons to turn the aircraft, the rudder pedals beneath my feet also moved. The controls had been inadvertently cross connected. Immediately, I declared an emergency and nursed the aircraft around the circuit for an immediate landing, careful not to touch the rudders and ailerons at the same time. This thankfully seemed to work satisfactorily and I landed safely and taxied back to the maintenance hangar. I was furious that they had handed the aircraft over in this condition and went to find the chief engineer on whom to vent my anger. Sometimes in your life it is better to think and not speak. This was one of those times. After quietly hearing me out, he asked me if I had read the pilot's notes. Admitting that maybe, I had missed out a few pages, he leaned forward and opened the manual at the section dealing with flight controls. Piper, in their wisdom, had connected the ailerons to the rudder pedals to help an inexperienced pilot to deal with an engine failure. It was a ridiculous idea and Piper had changed it when the new Seneca came out. However, it was standard on this model and he pointed out to me that had I bothered to read the notes, I would have been well aware of this. Feeling very sheepish, I climbed back into the aircraft and with a flurry of apologies, once again, I set off for Ireland. I spent two weeks teaching the new owner to fly the aircraft, making sure that he had read and understood the pilot notes. The weather was perfect the whole time I was there and when I was not flying, I spent my time walking along some of the most spectacular beaches outside of the Caribbean that I had ever seen. Add in a few pints of Guinness and it was with a heavy heart that I finally had to sign the new owner off as a competent pilot. I could no longer justify staying on.

So, it was back to instructing at Shoreham. There were highlights. Seeing new students' progress and improve was always a source of great pride. My greatest pleasure came from teaching pilots who had the desire to become commercial pilots.

The fundamental difference from training a private pilot and a prospective commercial one was that the latter was usually prepared to put in the hours studying and back this up with regular flying lessons. This continuity allowed both the instructor and pupil to progress at a greater rate than someone who only had the occasional lesson.

My life changed one sunny morning in the early Spring of 1980. The day had started as normal. I had just returned from a spinning detail, not my favourite way to pass an hour. Sipping a hot drink, I was trying to explain to my student that throwing up in the aircraft was not all that unusual and it did not mean the end of his ambition to fly. There was a knock on the door and a secretary from Southern Air put her head around and informed me that the managing director wanted to see me straight away. Well, this was unusual. Although I worked for the Mercury Flying Club, Southern Air owned the building and the two companies had a close working relationship. Why the head of Southern Air wanted to see a lowly flying instructor was beyond me. Maybe, someone had mentioned the hot wiring of the Cessna.

My debriefing was coming to a natural end and once again, my student had started to turn a strange shade of green, so making my excuses, I turned on my heel and exited as I felt I had seen enough of his breakfast already. Following the secretary, I made my way up the flight of stairs into the plush world of the Southern Air offices. After a knock and a curt instruction to enter, I stood in front of the great man himself. I was told to sit down and was offered a coffee. Maybe, I was not in trouble after all? For the next twenty minutes, I was asked a series of questions about my reasons for wanting to fly and what my plans were for the future. I felt like I was being interviewed for a job. In retrospect, that is exactly what was happening. My answers seemed to please him. I had not yet been asked to leave so I assumed that so far, I had supplied the right answers to his questions. Finally, he stopped talking, pushed his chair back and began studying me intently. This was unnerving and I was not sure whether I should stare back or begin studying the pictures on the wall behind him, so I chose the latter. Suddenly, without warning, he stood up and instructed me to follow him. We descended into the main hangar floor and made our way between the executive aircraft until we were standing in front of a new Piper Warrior. He asked me if I had ever flown a Warrior and luckily for me, I could confirm that I had flown the same model in the US. He asked me several technical questions and satisfied, he turned on his heel, beckoning me to follow him. We returned to his sumptuous office. He then informed me he had a proposition to make. He wanted me to take time off from Mercury and teach one of his customers. This would be a temporary contract and would end once his customer had got his Private Pilot Licence, together with a Twin-engine Rating. My confusion must have been obvious as he relaxed his officious manner and filled me in on the background to his unusual request.

Southern Air, being the major distributor of helicopters, also sold fixed-wing aircraft. The owner of Southern Air had a very close friend who had approached him wanting to learn to fly in order to buy a small company aircraft for his business. This client was the owner of the largest food broking and distribution company in the country and was a very well-respected figure. Even I had heard of him. However, there was a problem. As this client was a very busy man and could not afford the time to go to a flying club, the flying club would have to go to him. The instructor would have to fit into the client's schedule and be available at short notice to deliver both ground and air lessons as and when required. There had been two previous instructors who had attempted this role and both had fallen foul of the client's sometimes short temper. This was sounding very much like a poisoned chalice and I was not tempted to give up my permanent full-time job for a part time, short-term contract. I thanked my interviewer and politely refused his offer, despite the generous remuneration on offer. The position was not for me. He seemed slightly taken aback and asked me to sit down and hear him out. The owner of Mercury had already agreed to give me unpaid leave and would guarantee that my job would be available when I returned. Also, his client happened to be expecting me at two o'clock that afternoon for a trial flight to see if we were compatible, which really meant, to see if he liked me or not. This changed things and I agreed to the trial flight and asked if he would let me know when his client arrived. He looked at me with an expression of exasperation. Had he not explained that they would expect me to fit into his schedule and not vice versa? I was to report at Fairoaks Airport in the new Piper. And now, if that was all, he had other matters to attend to.

I wandered back downstairs with the many questions I had meant to ask still running around my mind. What had I just agreed to and had I somehow been manoeuvred to a place that I did not want to be in? I went to the operations desk to inform them I would have to hand my afternoon students to another instructor. I looked up at the whiteboard and was astonished to see that my name had already been erased from the list. This confirmed that my future had already been decided, so my new student had better like me or I was in trouble. Still, first things first, I had to get the Piper refuelled and plan a route to Fairoaks, a small airfield just to the west of Heathrow which should take about thirty minutes' flying time. I looked at my watch which told me it was approaching midday, so I had better get a move on, especially as the aircraft was still in the hangar. It would take time to organise the movement of the other aircraft to make way for the Piper. Collecting all my flying paraphernalia, I headed off to the Southern Air hangar to find some kind engineers to help me get my aircraft out.

Walking alongside the hangar, I turned the corner and was astonished to see my aircraft sitting outside with two engineers cleaning and preparing it. This has never happened to me before and I went to thank them. My gratitude was politely brushed aside as they informed me that they had also refuelled the aircraft and completed the daily check. They had drained the tanks of any water contamination and would there be anything else I required? Scratching my head, I humorously asked if they could arrange a cup of coffee for my flight. After my walk-around, I was speechless when I saw that a cup had been placed in the aircraft's drinks holder. What was going on? I settled myself into this brand-new aircraft and admired all the new instruments and navigational aids. This was far more advanced than any other Piper I had flown before. As I taxied away, the two engineers stood and watched, probably to make sure I knew what I was doing, although it was more likely to make sure I had left in plenty of time to make my two o'clock appointment.

The weather was perfect as I climbed away from Shoreham and set course for Fairoaks. I had to fly around the Gatwick zone and then get permission to fly through the military airspace at Dunsfold. Finally, I had to talk to the approach controller at Heathrow to let him know that I would fly beneath the flight paths of aircraft landing at his airport. It was a very busy flight and as I finally turned onto finals at Fairoaks, I noted that I still had thirty minutes to spare before I was due to meet my new student. The taxi in was straightforward and I parked my shiny new aircraft outside the only clubhouse I could see. So far so good. I was in plenty of time. My next problem was how to find my student. I knew his name, but I had absolutely no idea what he looked like, so I set off to find someone who looked like a multi-millionaire pilot.

Entering the clubhouse, I felt a distinct lack of welcome from the few people who were standing and sitting around the reception desk. I approached someone who was obviously an instructor and held my hand out as I attempted to introduce myself. He left me with my hand hanging embarrassingly empty. I explained who I was and asked if he had heard of my student and if so, could he possibly describe him. I was curtly informed that he had heard of my student and that I would not need a description as I would know when he arrived. With that, he informed me that as I was not a member of the flying club, would I be so kind as to leave the premises. I was astounded at his rudeness. Flying is normally a very social activity and pilots will always try to help each other. Obviously, Fairoaks was the exception that proves the rule. Unsure as to what to do next, I made my way to the control tower to pay my landing fees and introduce myself. Hopefully, I would be a regular visitor from now on. I received a much more pleasant reception here and gleaned some local knowledge. Apparently, my student had started his training at the club I had just visited. He had not got on with their instructors and had cancelled his membership and here I was, an interloper taking business away from their club. The jigsaw pieces were falling into place. I asked where the best piece of sky to instruct in was as the local area was controlled airspace. His reply shocked me - Shoreham!

Wandering back to my aircraft, I was still none the wiser about how I was going to recognise my student. It was approaching two o'clock, and I was getting worried that I was going to miss my appointment. Suddenly, from between two hangars, a red Rolls Royce glided out onto the ramp and stopped beside my aircraft. A uniformed chauffeur swiftly jumped out and opened the rear door and out stepped an incredibly well-dressed man in his late fifties. This was my first meeting with Desmond Cracknell. Some people exude power and authority and as he strode towards me with a smile on his face and hand outstretched, I knew immediately that I would have to be at the top of my game if this was going to work out.

Here was a man who would not suffer fools and would expect the very best. I just hoped that I could live up to his standards.

Desmond, or Sir, or Mr Cracknell as I always addressed him, was a man always in a hurry. Time literally was money as far as he was concerned. Whilst this was fine in his world, it was not fine in mine. A pilot in a hurry will ultimately make a mistake and suffer the consequences. Desmond wanted to get into the aircraft and take off while I wanted to sit down and discuss just what flying he had already done and what he hoped to achieve from today's flight. This was our first and last stand-off. We both looked at each other. Here was I, a twenty-something-year-old flying instructor and here was one of the most successful men in the country. Something had to give. To his eternal credit, Desmond, who expected to be obeyed without question, blinked first and we headed off to the airport cafe for a chat and a cup of tea.

His story was fascinating. He had learned to fly in the Royal Navy in the early 1950s. He had flown some of the most powerful and dangerous of the last piston-engine fighter aircraft and had landed them safely on aircraft carriers all over the world. Nobody had mentioned that I was about to fly with a veteran and I felt slightly foolish. What on earth could I teach this man that he didn't already know? I voiced my concerns and he stopped me in my tracks. He had left the armed forces thirty years ago and apart from a few failed attempts at flying lessons with the local club, he had not been near an aircraft since. Also, as he rightly pointed out his Navy flying was as different from today's civil flying as it could be. All he knew how to do was take off, fly wherever a controller told him to and then, land. There was almost no navigation, very little radio communications and whatever he knew, he had forgotten. I was warming to Mr Cracknell. Between us, we decided that we would fly southwards towards the coast and just enjoy the flight. There would be no teaching except to explain anything in the aircraft he was unsure about. I would give him heights and headings and take care of the radio and navigation, I just wanted him to be able to enjoy flying again, something he had not done with the other instructors before me. The only restriction he gave me was that we must land by three thirty at the latest, as he had a very important meeting later that afternoon. With these parameters agreed upon, we settled ourselves into the aircraft. I had done the outside inspection to save time, although if we ever flew again, I would insist we did it together.

With Desmond at the controls, we taxied out, slowly. Although he was a little harsh on the brakes, all went well. We lined up and as they cleared us for take-off, the power was applied too quickly. This could easily result in a wild swing and I was ready to take control. The aircraft never left the centre line of the runway and we were soon climbing away with me just giving a speed and heading to fly. An hour later, we were flying along the south coast near Chichester and Lee-on-the-Solent, an area Desmond remembered well from his Navy days. Suddenly, I remembered that we had to be back in twenty minutes and we were at least thirty minutes away from Fairoaks. I had let Desmond down. It was my responsibility to get us back in time and I had failed him. I could have kicked myself. Apologising, I gave him a direct heading back to the airport and requested that we accelerate to the aircraft's maximum speed. He gave me a quizzical look and asked why we were going back so soon. Reminding him of his meeting and my assurance that we would be back in time, he laughed, "Let them wait, I haven't had this much fun in years." Eventually, we landed an hour later after I had talked Desmond through the approach and the landing. I hadn't touched the controls for the whole flight, which suited us both admirably.

The Rolls Royce was waiting where we had left it two hours ago and the chauffeur jumped to attention as we approached the car. Desmond asked us both to wait outside whilst he made a phone call from the car. A very rare luxury in those far-off days. Ten minutes later, the rear door opened and Desmond reappeared looking very business-like. He informed me all was settled and could I come to his office tomorrow morning. I was a little unsure what to say or do and so I just agreed. Maybe, he wanted me to start his ground school. As he returned to his car, he asked me to take care of his new toy. I must have looked confused as he pointed to the aircraft, "I've just bought the aircraft. I can't wait for you to teach me to fly it properly," he said and with that, he was gone. I stood there for a moment looking at the space where the Rolls Royce had been a few moments earlier. Finally, turning towards the aircraft, I guessed that I must have got the job. I flew back to Shoreham and parked back in front of the Southern Air hangar, to be met this time, by the chairman himself. As I climbed down from the wing, I received a slap on the back and an offer of a drink. Apparently, he had been trying to sell the aircraft to Desmond for the last few weeks and today was the first time he had enjoyed flying it and so he bought it.

Chapter 25

Progress at Last

It looked as though I had a new job, well at least for as long as it took to get Mr Cracknell his Private Pilot Licence. The next morning, I set off driving my beaten-up old car to Esher in Surrey, where Desmond had one of his offices. The company headquarters was in nearby Oxshott. However, there were also offices attached to Copsem Manor, the palatial home Desmond occupied. I drove my thirty-pound Skoda along the private drive and parked next to several Jaguars, BMW's and Desmond's Rolls Royce. I was shown into the house and directed to the offices attached to the principal residence. From there, I was further directed into a large office full of aviation paraphernalia. There were pictures of a young Desmond standing next to the most advanced fighter aircraft of a bygone era. Accepting the offer of a coffee, I unpacked the material I had brought along to start the ground school lectures that I assumed I would be required to present.

Exactly on time, Desmond appeared in the office to welcome me. However, this time, he had a scowl on his face, not a smile. He asked me to follow him and we made our way to the main entrance. Stopping, he pointed at my car and asked me what the hell was that thing doing parked in his drive. Stuttering, I apologised and assured him that in future, I would leave it on the road outside. Without saying another word, he turned and I followed him back to the office. Nothing else was said and we spent the next few hours going over the syllabus for the Private Pilot Licence and how we would fit in both the ground school and the flying. As expected, I would conduct all the ground school from this office and I would be expected to fit it in around his meetings. The flying schedule was to be agreed at the beginning of each week and with that, he was gone. Not sure what else to do, I thought the best thing was to get the Yellow Peril away as soon as possible before it could offend anyone else. As I was packing up my things, the receptionist came into the office and handed me an envelope. She gave me a warm, friendly smile before leaving as quickly as she had arrived. Opening the envelope, I discovered a set of car keys and a car brochure. There was also a brief note from Desmond asking me to drive this from now on. I could not quite believe what I was reading as now, it seemed, I had acquired a brand-new top-of-the-range Vauxhall. As I made my way back to my Skoda, there was my new car parked next to it. Realising that I could not drive both away a note had been placed on my windscreen informing me if I left my address on the Vauxhall's windscreen then the car would be delivered later that day. I had entered a different world and so far, I found it to be very satisfactory.

Over the course of the next few weeks, we settled into a routine of sorts: ground school at the Manor followed by flying lessons as and when we could fit them in. It made it easier when you happened to own the aircraft. The greatest benefit for me was that with only one student, I was able to spend a lot more time on studying for my own commercial licence. My number of hours were now approaching the magical seven-hundred and fifty, whereupon I could take my flying tests. The ground school was another matter. A lot of pilots in my position would book themselves in for an intensive course at a recognised school for two months before sitting the examinations. This was an excellent way of preparing for what were degree level exams in seven different subjects. You had to apply to sit the exams in the Angel, Islington, London and they were held over three days. Obviously, this was not an option available to me. I could not afford the ground course and also, I could not afford to take time off from my new position. The second option was to register for a correspondence course. The company, Avigation, would send the study material and the student would fill in a questionnaire each week and post it back to be marked. Avigation would then return the weekly exam with corrections and the mark you had attained. This was also expensive and very time-consuming and usually used as an addition to a shorter residential course. Therefore, this would not be suitable either. Most candidates were attending a two-year full time approved course and sat the exams as they went along.

There was one more way of passing these examinations and that was to borrow a friend's text books, get all his Avigation test papers together, erase the answers, which were luckily, in pencil and complete the whole thing yourself. This was a little like watching university students attend their lectures and reading their notes whilst they were at lunch, not a straightforward task. Each examination was three hours long and covered the subjects in great detail. We were expected to create a Mercator's navigational chart from scratch and then plot a route onto this chart. How would testing like that help deal with the reality of flying in the outside world? I did not know. These were academic exams, not the practical ones I had sat for my Private Pilot Licence. Therefore, whenever I was not teaching, I had my head in my books, or to be more precise, my friends' books. The exams had to be booked three months in advance. The cost was over one month's wages so literally, I could not afford to fail. The first day of the examinations arrived finding me feeling under prepared and nervous. This feeling was made a lot worse when I arrived at the examination hall and saw that all the other candidates knew each other and were huddled together in last-minute revision groups. To make matters worse, most of them wore the uniform of their flying school complete with blazers and ties. I was in jeans and a tee shirt.

The adjudicator arrived and we were all instructed to go to our allocated seats. Apparently, these details had been forwarded to the schools previously. Well, that was no help to me and I approached the very officious administrator and felt a little bit like Oliver Twist as I asked where I should sit. A short rebuke met my question and I was told that my school should have provided me with that information. As he turned to go, I informed him I was not applying through a school. He stopped and turned towards me, demanding my name as he began running his finger down the list of candidates. Stopping at my name, he stared back at me and asked where I was studying. "Anywhere I can," I said, a response which displeased him. However, he barked out a table number, turned on his heel and was gone. With my confidence slightly battered, I sat down and produced all the equipment that I had borrowed. My desk was awash with pencils, slide rules, circular navigation discs, rulers, protractors and the kitchen sink. There were no electronic calculators of any kind allowed, although to be fair, there were few such devices available in 1980. The next three days were sheer torture. I hated every single moment. All around me, I saw smart, well-prepared students churning out their well-prepared answers. In between exams, they all huddled together to discuss the last exam and prepare for the next one. Throughout the entire three days, literally nobody spoke to me. I tried starting a few conversations with absolutely no luck at all. These guys had been together for two years and were not interested in letting anyone in outside of their particular group. Well, that's going to work well for them on the flight deck of whichever airliner they fly with, I thought, as I resigned myself to a lonely three days.

Finally, the last exam was over and I was free at last. I felt an enormous surge of relief that I would never again have to see any of the arrogant people I had just spent the last three days stuck in a hall with. I was free to go and that feeling of relief was actually greater than the feeling of pride when two weeks later, an envelope dropped onto my mat. I had passed all of my exams, thank goodness. I would never have to go back to that dreadful examination hall. I still have nightmares about that place.

Back to my day job and I was very pleased with the progress Desmond was making. He had successfully passed all his ground school exams and his flying was coming along nicely. My only slight concern was his lack of an awareness of the restricted airspace accessible to us to fly in. This was understandable as it was something he had never needed to consider before. However, I knew that it presented a problem for him and I did my best to help him overcome this shortcoming. We had decided that we would do all the navigation and handling work from Shoreham as the airspace was much quieter and we could concentrate on the handling skills. All too quickly, Desmond had completed his solo flight and was well on his way to finishing the rest of his licence. As the weeks went by, he was finally ready to take his flying test, which he passed with flying colours.

As he taxied back in with his examiner, I could see from both their faces that my job was now complete. Desmond was the proud owner of a Private Pilot Licence and could now fly his new aircraft whenever he so desired, without my help. As I stood waiting for them to alight from the aircraft, I looked across at the car park. Next to my shiny new car sat a very familiar yellow object, now covered in bird droppings, as I had not used it for the past three months. We were about to be reunited. Banishing such self-centred thoughts, I congratulated my student on a job very well done before the owner of Southern

Air whisked him away, no doubt for a celebratory drink. They left me standing by an empty aircraft. Oh well, I knew this day would come and who needed a new car anyway. I went back to the flying club and wrote my name back onto the list of instructors.

My primary concern now was completing the rest of my commercial licence. The clock was now ticking, the ground and flying examinations had to be completed within a restricted time frame. I had three flying tests, a navigational test and a general flying test. Finally, I had to complete an instrument flying test and I was to take this in a very expensive twin-engine aircraft. I had very little money and the cost of these tests was well beyond my means. I had to find a way to reduce the cost. I decided that the best way to proceed was to take the two flying tests that I could complete in a single-engine aircraft on the same day. I could not afford any practice lessons. I would just have to book and turn up for the tests and hope for the best. These tests had to be conducted by a CAA flying unit examiner, the single-engine tests were to be taken at Bournemouth, the instrument flying test at London Stansted. I approached Mercury to ask if I could borrow an aircraft for the day to take the two tests. Unfortunately, they were reluctant to lose an aircraft for an entire day and I could understand why. I then remembered that Desmond's brand-new Piper was sitting in the hangar awaiting his next flight. Dare I ask him if I could borrow it? I thought long and hard. Was it an abuse of my association with him? Would he feel obliged to agree or would he think it rude of me to even ask? With my heart in my mouth, I rang his secretary to make an appointment to see him.

Arriving at Copsem Manor this time, I was sensible enough to leave my Skoda parked in the road. I was shown into the chairman's boardroom, somewhere I had not been before. Greetings completed, I was thanked once again for the instruction and asked what he could do for me. Nervously, as I hated asking for favours, I explained my predicament and wondered that if I supplied the fuel, could I possibly borrow his aircraft. His answer completely threw me. Which aircraft did I want to borrow? He had just bought himself a new one. This man did not hang around, which is probably why he was the owner of such a large and profitable company. I left with the assurance that I could use the Piper whenever I wanted, just check the day before to make sure he didn't need it. His last question as I left the room was to enquire which car I was now driving. My reply concerned him. He hoped that it was not back in his drive. Reassuring him that I had parked it in the road, his final words warning me that parking there was prohibited, were a little too late. I drove home with a parking ticket sitting on the empty seat next to me.

With use of an aircraft secured, I booked the two test flights at Bournemouth. I was in luck as they could fit in one test in the morning and the other in the afternoon. This would save me both time and money, the latter was now a real concern as I was approaching my overdraft limit and was still only earning two-thousand pounds a year.

The day of the tests arrived and at sunrise, I set off for Bournemouth. I wanted to make sure I was early to allow me time to familiarise myself with an airport I had never been to before. As my second test was a navigational exercise, I took the opportunity of a little local flying as I approached the Bournemouth control zone. I only had to pay for the fuel, the aircraft was free. Finally, happy that I knew the local landmarks, I joined the circuit, landed and taxied to the CAA's building. There were several other aircraft parked there and I noted that they were all painted in the colours of the various flying schools. Mine was the only private aircraft. Making my way to register for the tests, I recognised a few faces from the three days of ground examinations. I did not acknowledge any of them. An hour later, I was walking towards my aircraft with the examiner following closely behind. When I stopped at the gleaming Piper, I noticed his eyebrows rise. Obviously, he was not used to a private candidate. All checks completed, we took off and flew northwards for the general flying test. I was not concerned about this test. I knew I could fly well enough and luckily for me, all went as well as I could have hoped for. An hour later, we were shutting the aircraft down and I felt relief that the first test was over. The examiner informed me he would also take me for the navigational test later that afternoon and would I please prepare a route to Bristol and back via Salisbury. With that said, he was gone.

I spent the next few hours studying the map of the local area. I was determined that I was going to be as prepared as I could possibly be. This was by far the toughest of the two tests. No radio navigation was allowed and I knew that I had to fly with the utmost accuracy and be prepared to immediately identify any town. Added to this, I would be wearing a visor hood to restrict my view to the instruments only. I would then have to fly several headings and heights and half of the time, the main instruments would be blanked off with stickers. I would have to fly blind using only a very limited number of basic instruments and perform timed turns onto the required headings. After this exercise, which would last for twenty minutes, the hood would be removed and I would have five minutes to determine my exact position using only my map. It was going to be a tough ask.

The first part of the test went well. I was nicely on track towards Bristol when the dreaded hood was placed over my head. Apart from being very uncomfortable, it was also very disconcerting. The outside disappeared and left me in my own world with an ever-decreasing number of instruments to keep me company. Finally, I was down to a standby compass and very little else, when suddenly, the hood was removed. I had to blink a few times as the sunshine streamed into my face. I felt very disorientated which to be fair, was the entire purpose of wearing the hood. The examiner then asked me to identify our position, mark it on the map and hand it to him and with that, he started his stopwatch. I could feel my anxiety beginning to rise and had to physically make myself relax. Looking outside, all I could see were fields, nothing else, just fields. Wherever he had taken me was remote and there would be no straightforward way to enable me to identify where I was. I flew in a circle as I had taught my students to do whenever they were unsure of their position. I looked for anything that I could connect with the map on my lap, but there was nothing, literally nothing that stood out. Then I saw it. I blinked and looked again, making sure that I was not imagining it. There, on the side of the hill was the chalk white horse that had saved me on the return flight from Cardiff after my instructor's examination. I could hardly believe my luck. I had been redeemed. Trying not to look like the cat that had got the cream, I calmly picked up my map, marked our position exactly and handed the map to the examiner. He looked at where I had put my cross and nodded his satisfaction. He then lent forward and closed the throttle, I would now have to demonstrate an engine failure and forced landing. We were at two thousand feet, so I had a few moments to look around and choose a suitable field to put the aircraft down in. I demonstrated all the good practices that I had always taught my students, making sure to fly the aircraft first, thus ensuring that we were at the best gliding speed. Then, identify a suitable place to land and finally, once those things were assured, to have a look around to see if I could establish the source of the problem.

My luck was holding. I knew exactly where we were and I also knew exactly where Compton Abbas, the airfield I trained at, was located. I pointed out the little airfield hidden in the hillside and set the aircraft up on a final approach. Normally, on a practise forced landing, the instructor or examiner would allow the aircraft to descend to five hundred feet, the point where it became obvious if the aircraft could carry out a successful landing or not. We arrived at the five-hundred-foot point nicely placed and I prepared to apply full power and climb away. However, my examiner was having none of that. He had spoken to the control tower, who had cleared us for a touch-and-go. Surprised by this unexpected request, I still carried out a very acceptable landing and take-off. We climbed away and levelled back at two thousand feet. I knew now that he would expect me to fly back to Bournemouth. I knew roughly which way to fly but I was not sure of the exact track. The examiner then turned to me and informed me that the test was now complete and congratulations, I had passed. He then asked if I would mind if he flew us back to Bournemouth. He rarely flew these days and he would love to fly a brand-new aircraft. Apparently, the flying school aircraft were all very dated and no fun at all to fly. I considered his request for a split second before handing over control. For the next thirty minutes, I stared out of the side window with a huge grin on my face. It's better to be lucky than good, I thought to myself. After landing, we returned to the CAA building, where my examiner completed all the paperwork. He congratulated me on some of the best navigational skills he had seen. He was also very impressed that I had noticed Compton on the side of the hill. Apparently, he always chose that spot to fail the engine and only one in ten candidates spotted the airfield. I decided to keep quiet at that point. Clutching my papers, as I made my way back through the waiting room, I walked past the candidates I had seen earlier. Not one of them had a smile on their faces. Serves them right, I thought, as I made my way back to the Piper and set off for Shoreham.

I had now completed all my ground examinations and two out of the three flying tests. However, the greatest hurdle still stood in my way, the instrument flying test. This was, by far and away, the most difficult hurdle I had to overcome and it had to be completed in an approved twin-engine aircraft. I looked at the cost of hiring such an aircraft from an approved school. For the five hours of flight training and the test, they wanted more than I earned in two years. This was not an option. I had been teaching people to fly these aircraft and I was confident that I could handle one well enough to pass the Instrument Rating. The fundamental problem was finding an aircraft of which the CAA approved. Apparently, the only ones approved were those operated by the flying schools. They had a monopoly, which is why they could charge such exorbitant prices. I rang the CAA to enquire how I would go about getting an aircraft approved. The helpful assistant explained that I must supply the aircraft with screens that fitted on the windscreen in front of the pilot. Once airborne, these screens would be closed for the duration of the test and only opened again to allow the candidate to land the aircraft. I asked if there were any diagrams that he could send me and kindly, he agreed to do so.

The next thing I needed was an aircraft to fit these screens to. This was also a tricky problem. There were only a few approved to carry out the test. The aircraft had to fly adequately on one engine. This seemed obvious. However, there were several light twin-engine aircraft unable to maintain height on one engine alone. If an engine failed, the other engine merely slowed your descent down. I needed to find a Piper Aztec, a good workhorse that I had flown before and was a stable platform for instrument flying. There was an Aztec based at Shoreham that belonged to the airline British Island Airways. The pilot who flew it also flew the BAC 1-11 commercial airliner and was an amiable chap. I had also helped him out twice when he needed the aircraft positioning to Gatwick and back. Not one for letting a favour go unreturned, I approached him to ask if I could borrow the Aztec for an afternoon. He readily agreed and a deal was struck. Once again, I was lucky to only have to pay for the fuel, although in exchange, I would have to carry out several delivery flights to Gatwick and back. A small price to pay, I thought to myself.

I spent the next few days cutting out cardboard screens held together with speed tape to fit the Aztec. This was not as easy as it seemed. They had to obscure all forward views, be easy to fit once airborne and have a window in the screens that opened to allow the pilot to land. I tried to follow the blueprint as closely as I could. However, it was not type-specific and I had to adapt the design to fit the Aztec. Finally, after many hours of trial and error, I was satisfied with my screens. They may have looked like a five-year-old's attempt at origami but they stayed in place and were relatively easy to fit. Satisfied, I booked my test at Stansted. This was still going to be an expensive afternoon. The cost of the test alone was exorbitant and that was for the examiner only. Add together the cost of the fuel and the landing fees and it was clear that I needed to pass first time. On the day of the test, I once again made sure that I was early for my test as again, I wished to check out the lay of the land. This was the headquarters of the CAA Flying Unit, where all the test flying took place. I taxied in and shut down in front of the offices. I parked on the end of the line of aircraft, which once again were all decked out in the colours of various flying schools, and made my way to check in. They showed me into the briefing area where I would have to file a flight plan for the instrument route the examiner would give me. This was all very well run and slightly daunting. It resembled a small airline rather than an examination centre. I sat nervously awaiting my examiner's arrival, not sure what to expect as several smartly dressed airline captains, complete with four-stripe uniforms filed in and out of the room.

Suddenly, I heard my name being called and I jumped up to see who was calling my name. To my surprise, there stood a pilot in full uniform, complete with jacket and cap. He must have been in his late fifties and with a handlebar moustache and severe haircut, he looked a very formidable character. With no preamble, he asked for my credentials and all the aircraft's paperwork. He examined these in great detail and when he was finally satisfied, he gave me a route to plan and file. Finally, we made our way to my aircraft. It was on the very end of the line and as we approached it, the examiner stopped and stared. He demanded to know why I was not using an approved aircraft supplied by my flying school. I explained that I was not from a flying school and that I was here independently. He then wanted to know where I had completed my training for this test and again, I replied that I had undertaken no formal training, but I had taught myself. This did not seem to please him at all and for a moment, I thought he was going to turn and walk away. Instead, he watched me complete my walk-around and climb into the aircraft. He followed and shut the door behind him, immediately demanding to see the screens and my certificate of approval. I felt an icy hand grip my heart. What on earth was a certificate of approval? I had not been told of this and I quickly explained this to the examiner. I could see that he was losing patience with me. He curtly informed me I could not use an aircraft for this test without it first being approved. It had to have the proper screens fitted. He looked directly at me and demanded to know if I had screens. Trying my best to convince him I was not stupid enough to book the test without screens, I leant over to the back seats and produced my cardboard creation. His jaw dropped and again, I was convinced that he was about to open the door and walk away. Before he had the chance, I quickly showed him how well the screens fitted the aircraft and how the little door I had cut out, opened and shut. It was like a 'show and tell' at junior school - look what I made in the school holidays.

He became silent and leant over to open and shut my little window. He then demanded that I sit in the back whilst he checked out the security of the screens and made sure they would not collapse in flight and obstruct the flying controls. Finally, he asked me to take my seat again and I sat there not knowing if we were going to continue with the test or not. In the end, he handed me a piece of official paper which bore a temporary certificate of approval. I was back in business. The flight itself went well. Shortly after take-off, he failed an engine and I had to complete the rest of the flight on one engine. We flew the entire route with my cardboard screens preventing me from seeing beyond the instrument panel. We then flew a non-precision approach, followed by a go-around, followed by a precision approach to two hundred feet above the runway. At this point, he leant across to open the little window I had cut out of my screen. Unfortunately, he pulled at the wrong part of the screen and the whole thing fell into my lap. However, I could now see the runway and brushing the screen to one side, I completed a respectable one-engine landing. We taxied back to the ramp and I shut the aircraft down. We sat there in complete silence for at least five minutes as he completed page after page of official documents. Finally, he turned to me and demanded the return of the temporary certificate of approval he had issued before we departed. Theatrically, he tore this in two and placed both pieces into his briefcase. He then handed me the paperwork he had just completed and somewhat begrudgingly, congratulated me on passing the test. His parting words were that he admired my cheek for trying to beat the system but if I ever wanted to get anywhere in aviation, I needed to do it the proper way, with an approved school. To hell with that, I thought. I had finally done it! I had obtained my Commercial Pilot Licence and I had done it the hard way, completely independently. I felt so proud as I pointed the nose of the Aztec towards Shoreham and home. It would be a long time before the smile left my face.

Chapter 26

Turbulent Times

Although I had my Commercial Pilot Licence, or CPL, I still had to convince an airline that I was worth taking a chance on. They would still have to train me to fly their aircraft and it was a huge step up from flying a Piper to flying a Boeing. There was also the slight problem that this was 1980 and there was a recession in the airline industry. Nobody, literally nobody, was recruiting, even the back pages of *Flight International* magazine were empty. With the thought that any job was better than no job, I stayed instructing.

Mercury Flying Club was changing. We had moved out of the sumptuous surroundings of Southern Air and into a glorified garden shed. This I could just about accept. My main problem was that we now had a new chief flying instructor. The previous incumbent knew his craft back to front and had the backing and respect of everyone who knew him. We were all sad to see him retire. There were a couple of the instructors who had hoped to be promoted. They both deserved the job and would have been very good at it. Instead, we were all called into the office one morning to be introduced to our new boss. I try not to pre-judge people. I always try to be positive and wait for someone to confirm to me that they are unpleasant, rather than assume they are and wait to be proved wrong. After this individual had completed his introductory speech, I made him an exception to my rule. He had recently left the Royal Air Force, where he flew, as he would continually remind everyone, fast jets. When I asked which were the slow jets, I received an instant rebuke. Sometimes, it doesn't take me long to make enemies. He then referred to our fleet of aircraft as 'puddle jumpers' that any idiot could fly. His speech continued in this vein and he finished with a pledge to turn this ramshackle flying club into a proper, professional training school run with military precision and not civilian mediocrity. With that, he literally stood to attention, turned on his heel and left the room. I think even the owner of the club who had introduced him was a little taken aback and gave us all a sheepish smile and shrug of the shoulders as he followed his new appointee out of the door. After that, the whole morale of the club began to decline. Instructors became demotivated by his continual criticisms and students were put off by his brusque manner. I knew my days were numbered and I would have to find alternative employment.

Meanwhile, I still had my students to consider and as I held a full Instructor Licence, I did not need to seek approval from my new boss before sending someone solo or signing them off as ready for their flying tests. Despite this, the new chief would often appear and demand to take a lesson to check on a student's progress or try to insist that only he would send a pupil solo. Every time he interfered in this way it took me a while to restore my student's confidence.

Things came to an inevitable head one cold, grey day. I was due to fly a series of training flights around Southern England. The weather forecast was for low cloud and reduced visibility as a cold front approached. The student had booked the aircraft for the whole day and was hoping to complete his Twin-engine Rating as well as receiving some basic instrument flying. Unfortunately, the forecast was clearly unsuitable and I sat down to explain that we would have to reschedule for another day. He was happy with this and we made our way to the reception to rebook for another day. Unfortunately, the new boss entered just as we were asking the receptionist to cancel our flight and pencil in a new date. As soon as he heard our request, he strode over and demanded to know why I was cancelling this detail as the aircraft had been booked and I was wasting time and money postponing this flight. He said all of this in front of my student, in fact, in front of everyone in the room. Resisting the urge to respond, I asked if we could have a discussion somewhere more private. He loudly refused and insisted that I continue with the planned flight. I declined to do this and left the room clenching my fists behind my back. I needed to leave before a real conflict occurred. I heard him shouting as I was leaving, threatening me with losing my job. Staying as calm as I could, I simply walked away and took Roffey for a walk instead.

As I was returning to the clubhouse, I saw the aircraft I had been meant to fly taxiing out for take-off. Surprised, I went inside to enquire what was going on. One of the instructors informed me that the chief had made the decision to take the detail himself and they were continuing without me. I was furious. I had been undermined and humiliated in the most public manner. I felt he had made my position in the club untenable and when he returned, I intended to have it out with him and insist on an apology or I would offer my resignation. Tragically, when I returned the next day, I never had the chance to vent my anger, he was already dead. I later learnt the aircraft was attempting an approach into a small airfield in deteriorating weather. They had flown a precision radar approach to Birmingham Airport and broke off the approach to try to find their destination. The aircraft flew into a hill and both occupants were killed instantly. My anger dissolved into grief. I was stunned but not surprised. I had lost my student; he was just nineteen years of age. The pain was intense but nothing that could compare to his family's suffering. Unable to face anyone that day I turned around and drove home. Roffey received more than his usual dose of hugs that night.

There is a saying that things come in threes and it certainly was the case during this period. A few weeks later, one of the instructors was promoted and the club returned to normal. I was sitting in the new garden shed disguised as a flying club when a head popped around the corner informing me that the chairman of Southern Air wanted to see me. Following his secretary back into the building, we had recently vacated, I once again found myself sitting in front of the great man. There was little preamble this time and he came straight to the point. Did I know that Mr Cracknell had bought a new aircraft? I confirmed that I did. Did I know that he had bought a high performance, pressurised, twin-engine aircraft that could fly eight people over a thousand miles at twenty thousand feet? This, I did not know and I looked suitably impressed. This seemed far too advanced an aircraft for someone with just a Private Pilot Licence and no Instrument Rating. I voiced my concerns. The chairman looked at me as though I was slightly mad. Of course, this was why he had been supplying Desmond with a number of airline pilots to help him fly the aircraft - one of them even flew Concorde as his day job. Well, this all seemed satisfactory, so I asked why I was here. The chairman looked at me, sighed and replied that Desmond wanted a permanent, full-time pilot and for some strange reason, wanted that pilot to be me. He then went on to explain that he had tried his best to talk Desmond out of this as I had only just received my Commercial Pilot Licence and as far as he was concerned, I was far too inexperienced for such a position. They had argued the point until coming to a compromise. I would fly the new aircraft with the Concorde training captain in the other seat. He would assess me over five flights and would have the ultimate decision if I was good enough to become the company pilot. Was I interested and would I accept this condition? You bet your life I would and I hurried off to learn everything I could about the Cessna 340.

A week later, I reported to Gatwick on a cold and wet evening. We were due to fly to Newcastle and the weather was poor along the whole route with rain and thunderstorms at the destination. Welcome to the life of a commercial pilot, I thought, as we taxied out. The flight deck of this aircraft was so different to anything else I had ever flown. There were buttons, pumps and dials everywhere and I just hoped that I could remember what they all did, especially with a Concorde captain watching my every move. We launched into the sky and were immediately enveloped in cloud and turbulence. It took all of my concentration to keep the aircraft under control. Everything happened at twice the speed I was used to. For the first time, I had a weather radar and I used it to steer around the worst of the clouds. We came out of the tops of the clouds at twenty thousand feet using our de-icing systems to keep the wings clear of ice, a luxury I could only have dreamt of when I had flown back from Stornoway. The approach and landing into Newcastle were conducted in heavy rain and turbulence. I was so relieved when I managed a reasonable landing and we taxied in and escorted our passengers to the waiting limousines. We would be staying the night in a local hotel and flying back the next morning, so we returned to the aircraft for, I presumed, a debrief and to secure the aircraft for the night. Once the aircraft was secured, I asked how I had performed as he was obviously not going to say anything. He turned and looked at me, "I'm bloody glad you flew that sector, far too exciting weather for me." With that, we went off to find our hotel and hopefully, a bar. He flew the sector back to Gatwick in bright sunshine and calm winds and I guessed that is what Concorde captains can do, choose the sectors they wish to fly. We had a long chat after the passengers had departed and he said he would be talking to Southern Air later. I guessed they would be arranging another proving flight and with that, he was gone.

The next day, I received a telephone call from Desmond's secretary asking me to attend a meeting at Copsem Manor the next morning and I agreed to be there at nine o'clock. This time, I parked my battered old Skoda in Esher town centre, on a parking meter. Looking at the quality of the other cars around me, I left a note on the windscreen advising that I had not dumped the vehicle. I really did mean to collect it later. I walked the half mile back to the Manor House and was still thirty minutes early. I settled myself in the waiting area and decided what my bottom lines were if I was offered a full-time job. I knew that the two-thousand pounds I was being paid was unsustainable. I was getting deeper and deeper into debt just trying to pay my everyday bills and I still had a flying loan to pay back. If I got offered the job, I thought I would probably be asked what salary I was expecting. This was a very difficult question for me. Did he know how little I was being paid and if so, would that hamper my chances of getting substantially more? I had a figure of five-thousand pounds in my head as I was ushered into the boardroom. I had been expecting just Desmond to be there but instead, I was faced with three gentlemen I had never met before. They introduced themselves as the vice-chairman, the chief financial officer and the head of marketing. If you bear in mind that this was a one-hundred-million-pound company in the eighties, which would equate to at least five-hundred-million pounds today, I could not understand why these powerful men were bothering with such a lowly employee.

The interview started the moment I sat down. Questions were asked about my education, my flying career and my expectations should I be invited to join Food Brokers. This all seemed a bit heavy, especially when I was asked about the expected operating costs of each aircraft and if I saw potential for sub-letting the aircraft when they were not being used on Food Brokers' business. I mumbled something about getting back to them on that. In truth, it had never even occurred to me that we could put the aircraft out for charter work. Finally, I was asked if I could justify the company acquiring two aircraft and could each aircraft pay for itself. The only reply I could think of was that I did not have the required information to justify the purchases and besides, the aircraft were already bought so the justification must have been there at the time. I could see that I had not convinced any of them as to the need for a company pilot except for the fact they had two company aircraft with nobody to fly them commercially. Finally, they thanked me for my time and asked me to wait outside. Despondently, I returned to my seat in the ante room, convinced that I had blown my chance of a job. I should have been better prepared for their questions.

Twenty minutes later, I was called back into the boardroom and was fearing the worst. I made my way in, and this time was met by the chairman and chief executive officer himself. Desmond sat alone looking at the notes I presumed the others had written.

"Well, you spectacularly failed to impress my board," were his opening words. "Quite honestly, I expected more from you," were his closing ones, or so I thought. He continued to read what they had written. Finally, he looked up and addressed me directly, "I suppose it was my fault, throwing you to the lions without any warning."

He then went on to explain that the company's board did not want one aircraft, let alone two. They could see no need for them. Both aircraft were very expensive toys as far as the board members were concerned. Their view was that all executive travel could be done far more quickly and cheaply using commercial airlines. He went on to ask me if I agreed with them. I hesitated and he sighed, "Not you as well, surely?" Before I could reply, he went on, "Well, luckily for you, I own this company and my decision is all that matters." With that, he slid a contract across the desk to land in front of me asking me to read and sign it. I started the next day, with a salary of ten-thousand pounds a year, plus expenses, plus a brand-new car every three years. He asked me if the terms were acceptable. I replied that I was hoping for more, but as it was him, I would accept. Luckily, he had a sense of humour. I left quickly before he could change his mind. Heading for the parking meter where my time was expiring, I relaxed. This time I could afford the fine.

My contract also required me to fly commercially for Southern Air when not on company business. This suited me very well. I could be based at Shoreham, back in the building I enjoyed working from and get to fly a number of interesting aircraft. I would be given a weekly schedule from Food Brokers detailing all the flying required, the routes to be flown and the passenger details. Everything else was up to me, planning the flights, obtaining clearances to land at different airfields, catering the aircraft and anything else I could think of. If Desmond was on the flight, then he sat in the captain's seat and handled the aircraft, whilst I took care of the radio and navigation. If he was absent, I flew the aircraft and would take along a co-pilot to help out. Although the aircraft was certified to fly with just one pilot, the passengers felt more comfortable with two. I also flew the Cessna on charter flights for Southern Air, always as a single pilot as they did not want the additional expense of a second pilot.

One morning, I was preparing to taxi out to pick up some passengers from Gatwick to fly them to Wales. Parked next to the Cessna was a beautiful Dove, an aircraft that was owned by the chairman of Brighton & Hove Albion Football Club. The Dove, a small airliner from the fifties, capable of carrying fifteen passengers, had been fitted out in a luxurious executive interior and was the height of luxury. The aircraft had recently been fitted with a replacement engine and the owner was awaiting the arrival of a training captain to accompany him on a test flight. We began chatting and his plan was to test the aircraft and then fly down to pick his family up in Torquay. We discussed how the test flight would be conducted and what to expect. When I left to fill my aircraft with fuel, he was still awaiting the arrival of the test pilot. Thirty minutes later, I began my taxi out to the runway. Directly ahead of me was the Dove, taxiing slowly. I heard on the radio one of our instructors, Chris Cotterell, warning the tower that he could see blue smoke coming from the left engine of the Dove. The tower repeated this warning to the aircraft and they acknowledged the transmission. We all expected the Dove to return to the hangars but inexplicably it continued to taxi. I knew the test pilot personally and had the greatest respect for him and with that in mind, if he was happy to continue, then I assumed he knew what he was doing.

The pilot of the Dove requested take-off clearance and as the smoke had dissipated, this was granted. As the aircraft taxied onto the runway, I was next in line, so moved into the position he had vacated. I watched as they increased power and accelerated down the runway. It was a wonderful sight, such a large aircraft on the new tarmac runway. As the Dove accelerated down the runway, I could clearly see dark smoke once again coming from the left-hand engine and I immediately informed the control tower. The Dove's nose rose and the aircraft started to climb away. There was a hugely experienced pilot at the controls and he could deal with the failure. The Dove's nose continued to rise, far higher than it should have and then the aircraft began to bank towards the failed engine. I could not believe what I was witnessing and I shouted to the pilot to put in the correct rudder, yaw the aircraft back to level the wings and lower the nose to maintain a safe flying speed, all the things I taught my twin-engine students but of course, nobody could hear me. By this time, the aircraft was about one hundred feet above the ground, the engine had stopped smoking but the aircraft continued its bank until one wing was pointing directly at the ground. The aircraft's nose was still pointing skywards, desperately trying to claw its way into the sky and safety. However, the aircraft continued to bank until the inevitable stall occurred. From this height, there was only going to be one outcome. The beautiful aircraft rolled onto its side, the nose that only seconds ago, had been trying to pull the aircraft into the sky, dropped. There was no more lift available. The aircraft turned upside down and plunged nose down into the ground just beyond the end of the runway. Horrified, I watched as this majestic machine broke apart and burst into flames. There could be no survivors from the crash.

The airport was immediately closed and all flights were cancelled. I was instructed to return to Southern Air. I was wiping away the tears as I slowly taxied back. I had known both pilots, one of them I considered a friend. With a heavy heart, I shut the aircraft down and made my way back into the building, the sirens of the emergency services ringing in my ears. I was still unable to believe what I had just witnessed. How could such a pilot make this basic error?

I walked into the briefing area and was astonished to see the pilot I thought I had just seen die in the most horrific circumstances standing in front of me, looking as upset as I was. He had been delayed getting to the airfield. There were, of course, no mobile phones at that time and the owner had decided to conduct the test flight himself. I was still letting this sink in when the Southern Air chairman appeared and called me over. The family of the pilot was sitting in Torquay, awaiting the arrival of the Dove to bring them back to Shoreham. This was a high-profile man who had just lost his life and nobody wanted the family to hear the terrible news from a television or radio broadcast. I was asked if I felt up to flying down and picking them up. If I agreed, I was to say that there was a technical problem which had prevented the Dove's flight. I would have to land back at Shoreham on the short crosswind runway to avoid flying over the wreckage. Of course, I agreed and was airborne ten minutes later. It was by far the most distressing flight that I have ever had to undertake, although the objective was achieved and the family were informed of the tragedy in the privacy of their own home in Brighton.

The third of the three incidents occurred two weeks later, once again on a Southern Air charter. I was to fly a Queen Air piston-engine executive aircraft from Shoreham to Gatwick. From there I would pick up the owner of Southern Air and fly him to Jersey in the Channel Islands, along with two of his friends. As it was a Southern Air flight and not a Food Brokers' flight, I would be the only pilot. The weather was marginal, a late autumnal day with very low cloud bases everywhere. However, it was within limits and I took off for Gatwick. Making an instrument approach, I saw the runway lights at two hundred feet and completed a safe landing, taxiing to the General Aviation terminal to collect my passengers. As well as low clouds, there was icing around and I used my portable garden spray, do-it-yourself de-icing equipment to clear the aircraft of the ice it had accumulated on the short flight from Shoreham. Satisfied that all was well, I checked once again that the weather in Jersey was within limits. There was still a low cloud base but that was perfectly acceptable, so time to go.

We took off and climbed away. I had chosen a cruising altitude of six thousand feet, still in cloud but below the main icing level. We settled on a track towards Southampton and I was handed over to London control who would handle me until passing me over to the Jersey controller. After checking in with the controller, I noticed that the volume on the radio was decreasing and leaning forward to adjust the knob, I could see that a number of red flags had suddenly appeared on my flight instruments. As I reached for the emergency checklist, the autopilot dropped out with the accompanying warning alarm. Fly the aircraft was my first instinctive thought and I put the checklist down and began to try to work out what was happening. I had never experienced anything like this before. More red flags appeared as more of my instruments failed. I looked at my navigational aids and there were flags or bars across all of them, indicating that there was no electrical power keeping them running. It was time to declare an emergency and get as much help from air traffic as I could. Calling out a Mayday and trying to sound as calm as I could, I requested immediate vectors back to Gatwick for a radar approach. If they could talk me down, then I could get by without my navigational aids. I could just about fly the aircraft on the very limited air powered instruments I had left. There was no answer to my continued Mayday calls and it dawned on me to my horror that I had suffered a complete power failure and the aircraft's battery was now also dead. I had no radio, no instruments and no idea where I was.

At this point, the owner of Southern Air popped his head into the cockpit to inform me that his reading light had failed! I almost laughed ... almost. I informed him of our problems which he took surprisingly well and assured me that he would look after the passengers and make sure they adopted the brace position if and when I called for it. At least that was one thing less to worry about. My last known position was Goodwood, heading towards Southampton. I had to descend to get below the clouds. I could not continue to fly in cloud for too much longer without the risk of becoming disoriented and losing control of the aircraft. The South Downs were somewhere below me and I knew that if I descended now, there was a good chance I would hit a hill before I could clear the clouds. The best and only chance was to fly directly South for at least twenty minutes. This would ensure that I was flying over the English Channel.

From there, I could descend to break the cloud at around two hundred feet. Once clear of the clouds, I could turn northwards and fly towards the coast. I knew this part of the coastline extremely well and I hoped to be able to turn right and make my way along the coast until I reached Shoreham. Once I had Shoreham in sight, I could land without any aids or radio.

With my plan firmly in place, I slowed the aircraft as much as I dared. If we were going to hit anything, I wanted to do it as slowly as possible. Using the standby compass, I slowly turned to the south and at the same time, started the stopwatch I always carried. Twenty minutes later, I started a slow descent, all the time making sure I kept the wings level and the speed constant. We passed one thousand feet, still in thick cloud and a minute later, we passed five hundred feet, still in thick cloud. I reduced the rate of descent to barely one hundred feet a minute. If I had got my navigation wrong, I would soon find out, even if it was the last thing that I ever did. At two hundred feet, we were still in thick cloud and I could see nothing outside. I stopped descending and levelled off. If I continued heading south, I would infringe French airspace. I did not want to perform a turn below this height, so I gently nursed the aircraft back towards the English side of the Channel. Once on a northerly heading, I began descending once again, this time at about ten feet a minute. There was a real chance of us landing on water before we broke cloud and I had asked the passengers to put their life jackets on and adopt the brace position. I put some flap down and reduced the speed accordingly. If we landed on the water the slower the speed, the better. The landing gear could stay up. It was of no use on the water and anyway, it was lowered by an electrical motor and I had run out of electricity a long time ago. Still, we continued to descend, but there was nothing to see barring thick clouds up ahead. I tightened my seatbelt and awaited our certain contact with the water.

At just under one hundred feet, I thought I could see grey waves below. I stopped the descent and waited. There again, just to my left I could make out the waves, they were now incredibly close. I held my height and hoped the conditions would improve. Slowly, slowly, I could finally make out a very faint horizon in front of me and I could just about distinguish between sky and sea. Maintaining my height, I turned slightly to the east towards where I hoped to find Shoreham. Ten minutes later, I could practically make out a coastline, although it was impossible to identify which part of the coastline it was, especially from such a low height. Then I saw it. Out of the gloom ahead, pushing proudly into the sea, was Worthing pier. Relief flooded through me. I knew where I was and I could find my way to the runway from here. I knew the position of every building on the approach path. I started to consider my next problem, the landing gear. I could not lower it by the normal electrical motor and so with one hand trying to fly the aircraft, I started to wind the gear down manually with my other hand. Nobody had ever thought to teach me this trick. I wound until I could wind no more. I would never see the three green lights to indicate that the gear was safely locked down; I just had to hope that the dark space where three green lights should be, did not mean that our landing gear was still retracted, I would find out soon enough. I then tried to lower some more flaps for the landing, kicking myself when I realised that these were also driven by an electrical motor. I would have to land with what I had.

We were now just skimming above the waves. Unbelievably, the weather was still worsening. If I lost contact with the ground again, I would have to turn south and land on the waves as that was preferable to hitting something on the land and endangering more lives. We passed Worthing pier and I edged closer to the shoreline. I had grown up on Shoreham beach and as a child I had tried to catch lizards at an inland lagoon known as Wide Water. This was also directly in line with the runway at Shoreham. I held my breath and waited for the lagoon to appear out of the gloom. Suddenly, there it was. I had almost missed it. I immediately turned to the north and waited for a runway to appear. One minute later, I could make out some lights ahead. Thank goodness they had left the runway lights on; the airfield was surely closed with weather like this. At such a low height and high speed, I had to increase the normal landing speed to compensate for having no landing flaps. Everything happened very fast. We were over the threshold of the runway, so I closed the throttles and stamped on the brakes as soon as I could feel the wheels touching down. We came to a stop with half the runway still remaining. I could hear my passengers clapping as I turned the aircraft on the runway and began to taxi back. Emergency vehicles came rushing towards me, blue lights flashing and sirens wailing. They turned and escorted me back to the Southern Air hangar. I would have a lot of explaining and form filling to do after this little adventure, not least landing without permission, one of the most heinous crimes a pilot can commit. Still, that was for later. For now, I was just glad to be alive and by the sound of it, so were my passengers.

The subsequent enquiry into the whole sorry affair exposed the company we had leased the aircraft from as fraudulent. They had removed half of the instruments that had back up pneumatic power and replaced them with the cheaper electrical instruments. This had worked without causing any problems until I had inadvertently overloaded the electrical system by the full use of all the systems on the aircraft, including the de-icing system. On take-off from Gatwick, the main electrical circuit had fused and the aircraft had to rely totally on the aircraft battery. The system to warn the pilot of this failure had been disarmed and the battery failed after only twenty minutes. After that, well you know the story.

I supplied a full written report and the leasing company was prosecuted for criminal negligence. Personally, I was told off by the Southern Air engineers for applying too much braking after landing, all three tyres had suffered flat spots. Sometimes, our worlds were intertwined and at other times, I wondered if we even occupied the same planet. Engineers! Who needed them? I later found out that as far as the London area air traffic controller was aware, I had ditched into the sea. He had seen my radar return begin to fade and then disappear. The coast guard had been notified and they were waiting for conditions to improve before launching a search and rescue operation. On hearing the news that my aircraft was missing, one of the instructors had asked the controller at Shoreham to leave the runway lights on. He thought that if I was in trouble, I would try to make my way back to the airfield I knew so well. The first time the control tower knew about my landing was when they saw me turn around on the runway. The weather had prevented them from observing my descent and touch-down. This had been far too much excitement as far as I was concerned and I hoped for smoother times ahead.

Chapter 27

Food Brokers Flying

Flying the Food Brokers' aircraft was, thankfully, a lot less exciting. The aircraft was nearly new and properly maintained. Each week, I would receive a flying schedule, the trips were becoming more frequent and more interesting. At this time, the company owned several racehorses and we flew all over the country to watch them race. If a horse was running at a track nearby, we would take the little Piper and literally land at the racecourse itself. If the meeting was further afield, we took the Cessna and usually chose an airfield close by. We needed a lot more runway with the bigger aircraft. The company itself was expanding rapidly and the clients ranged from northern Norway to Italy and Spain. Slowly, I got to know the other members of the board as I flew them around the network. After a few months, the vice chairman approached me after a busy day flying around Europe. He apologised for having given me such a hard time at my interview and admitted that he had been wrong. The company aircraft was turning out to be an invaluable business asset. He was especially impressed with the fact he could now get home far more often. If a meeting went on longer than expected, missing the last commercial flight home often meant spending a night away. Now, his meetings were not run on an airline's schedule that we could not control. We also flew our customers around the country and into Europe, another bonus. Everything was going well, so well that Desmond asked me to think about an upgrade. We needed a bigger and faster aircraft. I used our other aircraft, the Piper to fly around local aircraft dealerships to see what was available.

It was surprising how varied the receptions were that I received when I approached the different dealerships. Few took a twenty-something year old customer turning up in a Piper terribly seriously. I was looking at aircraft that cost close to a million pounds. I was not given the time of day by two brokers. Undeterred, I continued to consider what type of aircraft could fly our expanding network. There really was only one answer, the King Air, the very aircraft I had pretended I flew in Sonoma. Here, I was now seriously considering buying one on behalf of my company, a situation that I could never have even dreamt of just two years ago! Eventually, I went back to the Food Brokers' board and suggested that we upgrade to a King Air and I had found a very good contender. Engineers from Southern Air were dispatched to thoroughly check the aircraft and after a clean bill of health, the aircraft was purchased and sent to the paint shop to re-emerge resplendent in our brown livery. The conversion course was relatively straightforward, the fundamental difference being that the King Air had jet engines turning the propellers rather than the much less powerful piston-engine in the Cessna. We now had an aircraft that could reach almost thirty thousand feet and cruise at nearly three hundred miles an hour. I was a very happy pilot. I just hoped that the salesmen who would not give me the time of day would rethink their attitude.

With this new aircraft, complete with a small galley and toilet facilities, we had the capability for longer range and multi-sector flights. We flew the executives of the major supermarkets to meetings with our clients. Very few other operators in the market had this capability. We flew mainly from Gatwick now as Shoreham and Fairoaks were not open late into the night and they only had limited customs facilities. I was now only flying the King Air, fortunately for me, as I was just too busy to fly any other aircraft. Our new aircraft lived up to its reputation in every way. It was fast, reliable, flew above most of the weather and the passengers loved it.

Everything looked set for a long and happy association with our new aircraft until one evening when we were flying back from Edinburgh, Desmond was in the captain's seat and we had just reached our cruising height of twenty-two thousand feet. The cabin was full and as the sun was setting, I left the cockpit to check on the passengers and to distribute the drinks and food that I had loaded before take-off. We were due to land at Gatwick around eight o'clock in the evening, in time for one of our passengers to make a flight connection to Italy. The mood in the cabin was cheerful. We had treated them to a golf day and the celebrations had been going on long before they boarded the aircraft.

Returning to the cockpit, I noticed that we were still a long way from the beacon we were navigating to. This did not seem right. I checked the radio equipment, re-tuned the box and once again, checked on the distance to go. It was still counting down at a very slow rate. Becoming more concerned, I cross-checked with other beacons, each one confirmed that our ground speed was unusually low, just over one hundred miles an hour. The weather forecast was for a strong headwind all the way to Gatwick and I had allowed for this in my flight planning. However, if my ground speed was correct, then the headwind must be at least twice as strong as forecast. It was a crystal-clear night, no clouds anywhere and I could see for miles. On the nose, the city of Manchester stood out, as did Liverpool to our right. The trouble was, they did not seem to be getting any nearer. I checked all the aircraft instruments. All seemed well and the powerful engines were humming away, so no problems there. Looking above us, we could see the commercial airliners streaming ahead of us as if we were suspended in time and space. I asked air traffic control for a wind check; airliners had equipment capable of giving accurate wind values. As usual there were no other aircraft flying at our level; pure jet aircraft flew above thirty thousand feet. The wind readouts were more or less as predicted, which only added to my confusion. I then heard an aircraft descending into Manchester reporting a wind increase of over one hundred and twenty miles an hour passing through our level. We were in a low-level jet stream, no wonder we were going nowhere fast, or should that be slow? Gathering more information, it appeared that the jet stream ranged from fifteen to thirty thousand feet, with severe turbulence forecast below this funnel of wind. We did not have the capability to climb above the jet stream and I did not fancy descending into severe turbulence, so we stayed where we were.

As we droned on into the teeth of the gale, I could see Desmond getting more and more frustrated. He kept looking up at all the aircraft overtaking us and eventually, he turned to me and announced, "We need a jet" and with that he lapsed into a moody silence for the rest of the endless flight. We arrived at Gatwick nearly two hours later and with not a lot of fuel left. At one point, I was even considering diverting to Birmingham to refuel. I also had a very unhappy chairman. On top of everything, our Italian passenger had missed his connection. Unfortunately, he was the president of an Italian chocolate company that Desmond had been trying to impress and get to sign a contract to supply the confectionery into the UK. Think Ferrero Rocher and you will get an idea of just how big a deal this was. A very unhappy Desmond slid into the rear seat of the waiting Rolls Royce and was gone without a thank you or goodbye, an unheard-of omission. After the passengers had departed, I returned to the aircraft to do the usual housework, cleaning and restocking of the bars from the supply I kept in my company car. Then, I refuelled the aircraft. I liked everything to be ready, just in case of a last-minute change of plan. Nobody wanted to turn up to watch the pilot cleaning out the previous day's mess. I felt deflated, almost like it was my fault that the forecasters had got the wind so wrong. I had given Desmond a flight time back to Gatwick and I had let him down. He had based all his timings on my estimate and I had made him look amateurish in front of one of his most important clients. Mr Ferrero would have to spend the night in the local Hilton because of my failure to get him to his connecting flight on time. Powerful men like this dislike being let down and I had put the whole negotiations under threat. Dejectedly, I locked the aircraft up and left to drive home. I expected a call the next morning and it would not be good news.

I heard nothing for the next three days. There were no flights scheduled. I was used to getting a daily update from the company. I sat at home and worried about my future. Had I let Desmond down to the extent that he would lose one of the most lucrative contracts he had ever negotiated? Roffey and I went for some long walks together. He was a wonderful listener. On the fourth day, my phone rang. Desmond wanted to see me in his office. My fate was about to be revealed. An hour later and I was being ushered into the chairman's boardroom. After being asked to take a seat, I apologised for the flight the other evening. This immediately brought a flurry of expletives. However, his anger seemed to be directed towards the aircraft and not myself. He explained how frustrated he felt that we were being overtaken by so many of the airliners. What was the point of having a company aircraft when it was quicker to fly with the commercial airlines? I could see his point. However, he had forgotten all the arguments about privacy and flexibility. I rightly gauged that this was not the time to remind him of these benefits. He finished up by saying that he wanted a new aircraft and this time, he wanted an executive jet. I was told to find him one and with that the meeting was over.

Chapter 28

Into the Jet Age

I was nearly twenty-five years old. I had held a Commercial Pilot Licence for just over a year and was now in the market for a business jet. The whole thing seemed surreal. Fortunately for me, I had upgraded my licence to the Air Transport Pilot Licence which enabled me, on paper at least, to captain a jet aircraft. As far as I knew, nobody had ever captained an aircraft like this at such a young age. I knew that to find such an aircraft was beyond my experience level and I sought the help of Southern Air. Returning to Shoreham, I asked for an appointment with the chairman. I knew that since my flight with Southern Air's owner, they held me in high esteem. I also knew that the chairman still thought of me as a bit of an upstart. He had flown a multitude of aircraft for the airlines and knew that the protocol was becoming a first officer for many years before being allowed anywhere near a jet captain's seat. This process could take over twenty years in some airlines.

I was shown into his office and invited to take a seat. Coffee was ordered and after the minimum of formalities, he enquired as to the purpose of my visit. I knew that the tables were now turned. It was not him interviewing me for a job, it was me interviewing him. He had played his games previously and now it was my turn. I asked him various questions about his company's experience with executive jets, especially regarding maintenance and operations. I knew that Southern Air had no pure jets on their fleet and so I offered him the prospect of being able to acquire one. All I needed was the help of his engineers to find me the right aircraft. I could see the look of astonishment on his face. He had serious doubts that I could fly a jet aircraft with my limited experience and he told me so in no uncertain terms. If Food Brokers wanted a jet, then they needed to employ a jet pilot, not a trumped-up flying instructor! I thanked him for his time and left. Unfortunately, I could see his point. Who on earth would sell me an executive jet when I had absolutely no jet experience? The problem was that I could not gain jet experience without flying one. I went downstairs to consider my options, when suddenly, the chairman reappeared and sat down next to me. He apologised for being rude. He had been taken by surprise and had reacted accordingly. He had also been on the telephone to Desmond to confirm that we intended to upgrade to a business jet. He asked me to leave it with him and he would find out which aircraft were on the market and arrange a viewing. As he got up to leave, he asked me if I knew anything about a rusting yellow Skoda that had been abandoned in his car park. I promised to have it removed as soon as possible.

A week later, Desmond and I flew up to Hatfield in the Piper. We had an appointment to see a Cessna Citation and a Learjet, both being sold by the same agent. These were both small jets, four passengers plus two pilots, small but quick, especially the Learjet. We taxied to the dealership's private apron and parked next to the two aircraft which had been prepared for our inspection. Desmond was impatient to inspect both aircraft, so leaving him to it, I went to find the salesman. By the time I returned with a very hopeful salesman, Desmond was sitting back in our Piper. This confused me. Surely, he had not already decided which aircraft he wanted to buy? It was either that or something was wrong. I left the salesman standing by the Learjet and went to find out what was going on. Standing on the wing, I opened the door and told Desmond that the salesman was waiting for us. He looked at me and demanded why I was wasting his time. He wanted a proper jet, not a toy. I had to admit that both these jets were much smaller than our King Air, but they were also twice as fast. I also reminded him he and the Southern Air chairman had arranged this viewing, not me. There was no time for any further discussion. Desmond was already getting ready to start the aircraft. I hurried back to a very confused and bemused salesman and apologised. Five minutes later, we were on our way back to Fairoaks and the drawing board. On the flight back, Desmond had outlined his requirements. He wanted an aircraft that he could stand up and walk around in, with a proper toilet, not a bucket and he wanted ten seats including a settee which could be converted into a bed. Well, that ruled out the aircraft we had just seen. Desmond, it seemed, wanted a small airliner. All I had to do now was to find him one. My greatest concern was that I would never be allowed to fly such an aircraft and I realised I would be finding him an aircraft that would be putting me out of a job.

At Gatwick, occasionally, we parked next to a Hawker Siddeley HS 125 business jet. I had noticed how often Desmond would look longingly at this aircraft. It was a top-of-the-line aircraft used almost exclusively by the major international companies and banks. These aircraft had everything that Desmond required. They had the same interior dimensions you found in an airliner but with fewer seats. I set about finding one that was in our price range.

Eventually, I found a company at Stansted, known as Tal Air, which operated an HS 125 Executive Jet and who might be prepared to sell it. I drove over to inspect the aircraft. I had no intention of letting Desmond anywhere near it until I was certain it fulfilled all his requirements. Arriving at Tal Air's headquarters, I was impressed with the whole setup which was very professionally run. They introduced me to the Chief Pilot, Captain Ron Handfield, who was very welcoming. He showed me around the aircraft and explained the performance and operational versatility. Again, I was impressed. Leaving the aircraft, we went to his office where he kept the relevant sales brochure. We went through all the aircraft's paperwork and I examined the maintenance history. Everything looked to be in order. My next question seemed to stop him in his tracks. Could we possibly go for a demonstration flight? He recommended that we wait until Food Brokers' company pilot was here. There was little point in me sitting in the cabin whilst he flew the aircraft. Here we go, I thought to myself, more reverse ageism as I produced my flying licence and handed it over. He studied the document and passed it back with a huge grin on his face at the same time congratulating me on having made it so far so quickly. When I explained to him that we wanted to operate the aircraft as we operated the King Air with Desmond in the captain's seat, he shook his head and informed me that this was not possible. Because of the size and complexity of the aircraft, it required two qualified pilots to fly it. This was a game changer as there was no way Desmond would buy an aircraft that he could not fly himself. Reluctantly, I stood up to leave. As I did so, Captain Ronnie, as affectionately, I came to know him, asked if I would still like a demonstration flight? Surprised, as the sale was now definitely not going ahead, I asked him if he was sure. Taking an aircraft like this into the sky was not cheap. With a twinkle in his eye, he explained that the company did not know the sale had been cancelled, so let's have some fun and with that, I followed him out of the office heading back to the aircraft.

We did an external inspection with Captain Ronnie pointing out the important aspects of the airplane. I could feel my excitement growing. This aircraft could climb to forty-three thousand feet, higher than most commercial airliners and cruise at five hundred and fifty miles an hour. It was an awesome machine. Could I really be allowed to fly such an aircraft with my very limited experience? We climbed aboard and I was asked to go to the flight deck whilst he closed the passenger door. I settled myself into the co-pilot's seat and looked in awe at all the dials and buttons, half of which I had never seen before and had very little idea what they did. A moment later, Captain Ronnie appeared and asked what I was doing in that seat. I felt foolish. Of course, there was a proper co-pilot standing behind him. What on earth had I been thinking? I jumped out of the seat as quickly as I could, apologising to the third pilot. There was a pull-down jump seat behind the two pilots and that is where I was expected to sit. Not a bit of it, I was instructed to sit in the Captain's seat; the third pilot would occupy the jump seat. She was just coming along for the ride.

Captain Ronnie explained that he was a fully qualified type and instrument rating examiner for the HS 125 and could fly the aircraft from either seat, although today I would do all the flying whilst he watched. I could not believe what I was hearing and before it had fully sunk in, both jet engines were running and they cleared us to taxi out. There was very little noise inside the flight deck but I knew from experience that outside, the noise would be intense. These were noisy aircraft. Under careful instruction, we made our way to the runway. All the checks had been carried out and to my surprise, they cleared us for an immediate take-off with a clearance to climb to six thousand feet on an easterly heading. As I applied full power, the aircraft leapt forward accelerating faster than I had ever experienced before. In what seemed like seconds, I was told to rotate to fifteen degrees nose-up and we were away. Climbing to six thousand feet would at least give me some time to settle down, well at least I thought it would. Just over a minute later, I heard Captain Ronnie warning me that we had one thousand feet to go until we levelled off. What would normally take four minutes on the King Air or ten minutes on the Piper had been reduced to a minute. I pushed the nose of the aircraft down to avoid going through our cleared level and we all floated upwards out of our seats because of the negative gravity force. Thank goodness we did not have passengers on board. Levelling off, I had to reduce the power, otherwise our speed would quickly increase towards the maximum allowable. I felt like this was my first solo all over again. I was so far behind the aircraft that I might as well have been on the jump seat after all.

Watching all of this was Captain Ronnie who I noticed had another huge grin on his face. Maybe, I didn't like him after all. They cleared us for a further climb and I increased the power. The aircraft leaped forward like a horse that had its backside whipped. This aircraft was a true stallion. I wrestled some control back as we levelled again at twenty thousand feet. We had been airborne just five minutes, unbelievable. We flew up the east coast towards Norwich, before descending over the North Sea. The beautiful seaside town of Southwold flashed under the wing, not that I had much time to admire the view. Thirty minutes later, we were on the approach back into Stansted. Amazingly, Captain Ronnie allowed me to fly the approach and carry out the landing, talking me through it as we went. With a lot of luck, I managed my first jet landing, inflicting no damage on the aircraft or its occupants. As we shut down, I was literally breathless with the excitement and thrill of handling such a beautiful aircraft. As always, Captain Ronnie was smiling and I even received a clap on the shoulder and a resounding, "Well done." If he knew how far behind the aircraft I had been at almost every moment, his congratulatory gestures may have been more restrained. I was being naïve, of course nothing got past him - a fact I was soon to appreciate.

Returning to the office, the realisation that we would not be buying this aircraft tempered my excitement. Although it was within the price range I had been given, the fact that it needed two pilots was surely a deal breaker. It was unthinkable that Food Brokers would operate an aircraft that Desmond could not occasionally fly himself. Ronnie and I discussed this and the fact that the CAA would also have an issue with me flying the aircraft because of my lack of jet experience. Sadly, I accepted that this had been a step too far and thanked everyone involved for their time and trouble. It was time to go back to the drawing board. As I drove my company car home, I knew that I'd had a taste of something that I desperately wanted to experience again. How could I possibly get more opportunities to fly an HS 125?

The answer came very early the next morning when I received a phone call from Ronnie. Would I be prepared to go through five hours of simulator training to establish if I could fly the HS 125 as a captain? I thanked him but reminded him that even if I was successful, Desmond still could not fly the aircraft. I could almost hear his smile as he reassured me that he had a plan for that. Enquiring about the cost, he assured me that if we bought the aircraft, they would include the cost of the simulator in the price. If I failed to pass the simulator course, then we could discuss that if and when it happened. I told him I would get back to him later that day. It was time to speak to the Boss. After discussions, it became apparent that although this was probably a waste of time, financially, there was no risk to Food Brokers. They gave me the permission to attend the simulator course and we would go from there. I informed Ronnie and we set a date for a ground school and simulator course. He asked me to drive over to Stansted to collect all the study material and to meet the simulator instructor, a wonderful chap named Tony Angel. I spent the next two weeks with my head in the technical manuals and feeling reasonably satisfied that I understood how the aircraft worked, I turned up for the conversion course. This comprised three intensive days of ground lectures followed by written examinations and, as all went well, I felt ready and prepared when the next stage of my training arrived.

I was in the captain's seat, with Captain Ronnie in the co-pilot's seat. As this was a training flight, no other people were allowed. We taxied out and were given an immediate take-off clearance as there was a Boeing 737 on short finals. Stupidly, I accepted the clearance instead of waiting for the Boeing to land. Just as we rotated there was an enormous bang, the aircraft swung violently to the left and as far as I could see every light and bell on the flight deck either lit up or rang. The shock was intense. It overloaded my senses and for an instant, I could not think straight. Recovering, my previous training took over and I stopped the aircraft rolling into the ground. I had seen the consequences of not applying the correct inputs at Shoreham the previous year. Carefully raising the nose, I tried to coax the aircraft into a safe climb, everything else could wait until we had enough height. Eventually, we were climbing safely away and I engaged the autopilot. I went through the memory drills to shut down the left engine and extinguish the fire. Finally, I pulled the checklist from the pouch next to my seat and went through the rest of the emergency drills. Then I declared an emergency and asked the air traffic controller for an immediate return to Stansted. Completing the rest of the after-take-off checklist, I immediately actioned the approach and landing checklist. The fire seemed to be out but I could take no chances. I had to get back on the ground as soon as possible. Flying on one engine, the aircraft was much more difficult to control. Every movement of throttle caused the aircraft's nose to swing one way or another due to power being available on one side of the aircraft only. The landing was just about safe. At least we were back on the ground being rapidly followed by the emergency services. We finally came to a stop. The engine, far from being extinguished, was still burning fiercely and so I ordered an immediate evacuation, shutting everything else down before I climbed out of my seat.

"That's great, let's go get a coffee," was Ronnie's only remark. Personally, I was just pleased we were only flying the simulator, although it was so realistic that you totally forgot that you were not in the real aircraft.

On all my previous types of aircraft, I had learned to fly, well … the aircraft. There were obvious limitations to this as you could not deliberately start an engine fire, fail major systems or set off an explosive device. In the simulator, which replicates the aircraft in every way, the examiner can do all of those things and more. My first session was all about how to fly the aircraft, taxiing, take-offs, climbs, descents, approaches and landings. All great fun and exactly what you would do in the real aircraft. However, the next four sessions were a series of failures, fires and emergencies. Each session required all of my flying abilities and skills, such as they were. I would come out of the simulator drained and sometimes disheartened when things had not gone well. It was a different kind of training environment or at least I thought so and I was so relieved when it was all over.

The next day, I received a telephone call asking me to attend a meeting with the CAA's Flying unit at Stansted and then for an evaluation flight on the HS 125. Confused, I rang Ronnie to ask if he knew anything about this. Unsurprisingly, he had arranged the whole thing. Apparently, if I qualified, not only on the HS 125 but also as a type rating examiner, then I could fly the aircraft as commander in either seat. This would allow Desmond to sit in the captain's seat. Astounded, I reminded Ronnie that I had only flown the aircraft once, although after five, four-hour sessions in the simulator, I felt comfortable flying the aircraft. He advised me to take the flying test. The worst that could happen would be that I failed my Examiner's Licence. If so, I could still fly the King Air.

Only slightly reassured, I presented myself at the test centre a week later, the same place I had taken my Instrument Rating in the Aztec with the dodgy screens. I registered and sat in the waiting room for the examiner to arrive. I really did not know what to expect, apart from the fact that I would have a check ride in the simulator followed by a flight in the real aircraft. What could possibly go wrong? I immediately knew the answer when I looked up after hearing my name called. Standing there was the same examiner who had collapsed the screens on my Instrument Rating flight, the same person who had advised me to follow the established training route. As soon as he recognised me, I knew that it would be a long day and I was correct.

After four hours in the simulator and an hour flying the aircraft, I sat waiting whilst the powers-that-be decided my fate. I had literally no idea if I had performed well enough to gain a type rating, let alone an Examiner's Rating. My heart was in my mouth as they summoned me into an anteroom to hear my fate. The look on the examiner's face told me all I needed to know. I had not passed. They gave me a long debrief and I received a full breakdown of what had gone well and what had not. Disappointed but not surprised, I stood up to leave, thanking him as I left, not sure where to go from here. He asked me to sit down. Apparently, there was more to come. I was handed back my licence, which had now been endorsed with a HS 125 Captain's Rating. He explained that after I had flown the aircraft for fifty hours, I could upgrade to the Examiner's Licence and with that, I was dismissed. At least, I had no cardboard screens to dispose of this time.

Walking back to Tal Air, I found a very excited Captain Ronnie waiting to congratulate me. Confused, I asked him how he knew - I had only found out myself moments ago. He smiled and tapped the side of his nose. I never found out. The next day, we bought the aircraft and immediately had it painted in the brown and white colours of Food Brokers. Desmond was ecstatic. He now owned a real aircraft, as he called it. Initially, he flew with Captain Ronnie until I had accumulated the necessary fifty hours flying experience. I took the Examiner's Licence test again and became a fully qualified examiner. Sadly, we had to say goodbye to Ronnie and Tal Air. We were now a private jet company and I had still not reached my twenty-fifth birthday.

We could now fly higher than most of the commercial aircraft we used to stare up at and they would now do the same to us. We cruised at the same speed and all of our passengers loved the aircraft. The only voice of caution came from our chief financial officer. The cost of running the aircraft was eye watering; it consumed fuel at an alarming rate. Added to the cost of fuel were the maintenance costs and the landing and handling fees too, both of which were very high. We could no longer use Shoreham or Fairoaks as we needed much longer runways. There was only one alternative. We moved our entire operation to Gatwick.

Chapter 29

Moving to Gatwick and the Beehive

If the accountants thought operating aircraft from small general aviation airfields was expensive, they were in for the shock of their lives when we moved to Gatwick. Being based at an international airport had many advantages. We no longer had to rush back before the airfield was closed and customs was also available on a twenty-four-hour basis. However, the downside was that the costs were spiralling and it was my job to try and keep them under control. Food Brokers was only using the aircraft for a fraction of the time it could be flying. We needed to charter the aircraft for the whole enterprise to make some economic sense. I was called to a meeting a few months after we took delivery of the aircraft. The entire board was present and the accountants took great delight in highlighting the costs involved in operating the aircraft. After thirty minutes of facts and figures, they asked me to give a presentation as to how we could recover some of these overheads and start making the aircraft pay for itself. Fully expecting such a request, I had prepared a presentation detailing why we could not charter the aircraft. I had previously warned Desmond about it before we took delivery. We operated the aircraft on a Private Operating Certificate with an alleviation, allowing Desmond to fly with me in my role as training captain.

The only alternative to this was to apply for an Air Operator's Licence and to create a commercial company along the same basis as the airlines. To achieve this, we would have to create a company that had an operations office at Gatwick. We would need to create an operation manual for flight and cabin crew. We would need to employ a chief Pilot, an operations manager and a cabin crew manager. We would need to have a flight operations inspector appointed by the CAA to oversee all of this. Before any of this could happen, we would need to create a new company and apply for the Air Operator's Licence. This would be a huge and costly task, well beyond my experience level. I had explained that this was a step too far and we were already very lucky that we could operate the aircraft on a private certificate, to do so commercially was unthinkable. I sat down feeling very pleased with myself. I had produced all the technical requirements in a clear and concise manner. I looked around the table and I could see that the directors were nodding their heads in agreement. They realised that setting up a small airline was a non-starter. We would have to continue to operate as a private company. It would be unrealistic to charter the aircraft. And then … everything changed. Why I was surprised was, in hindsight, the only surprising thing.

Desmond spoke for the first time from his seat at the end of the table. He asked me to find an office at Gatwick and at the same time, to compile all the manuals required and to employ an operations manager. He further instructed that I be appointed as chief pilot and then hire more pilots able to fly the aircraft on commercial operations. I had three months to get the new company off the ground and operating. With that bombshell he asked if there was anything else that required his attention. Nobody spoke and so without further ado, he was gone, leaving behind a silent room. The chief accountant came over to enquire if I was alright. The look on my face must have given him cause for concern. Putting his arm around my shoulder, he asked if it was possible to achieve any of what Desmond had just demanded. I stared down at all of my notes which I thought had produced a very persuasive argument against just such a venture. With a lot more conviction than I felt, I replied that anything was possible, it was just highly improbable.

I left the meeting with mixed feelings. I had been given the opportunity to create a new company. It would be a daunting prospect and the chances of success were slim. However, now was not the time for doubts, it was time for action. The first thing to do was the obvious one, create and register the new company, FB Air Services. The next was to find an office at Gatwick, not such a straightforward task. Finally, I had to find a commercial and operations director. I had someone in mind, my best friend Pete Brown. I registered our new company and persuaded Pete to join us. We located a small office in what was the original terminal building at Gatwick, an Art Deco building known as the Beehive. All we had to do now was write the various operation manuals and seek approval for our Air Operator's Licence, a hugely daunting task that took many months. Fortunately, I had obtained copies of other operators' manuals which gave me a template from which to create our own. Just under six months later, I was ready to present our application to the CAA seeking their approval.

The next stage was a detailed inspection of our aircraft, our office, our staff and our operations manuals. We would then have to undergo a series of proving flights with our newly appointed flight operations inspector. After doing all that, we would have to await a decision. I was not optimistic. One of the main stumbling blocks was the employment of a chief pilot. Normally, this position would be held by a highly experienced captain, with a normal requirement of a minimum number of flying hours of five thousand and I barely had two thousand. Employing a new chief pilot would be very expensive and make the entire project commercially unviable, unless they got rid of me, something I was keen to avoid. We made a date for our appointed flight operations inspector to examine our application at our new office. All that had to be done now was to employ new pilots and air hostesses and keep our fingers crossed. Employing pilots was not a problem, as sadly there were, a number of unemployed air crew due to the economic downturn. This time, it was my turn to place an advertisement in the back pages of *Flight International* magazine. How times had changed. The response was astounding and in my first week at the new office, I went through at least one hundred applications. These varied from low-hour student pilots to highly experienced airline captains. Choosing who to interview was a daunting task. My father, who had retired the previous year, fancied flying the HS 125, an aircraft very similar to the BAC 1-11 he flew in the early 1960s. After an extensive interview I had employed my first pilot, I still needed another two.

A week before the interviews started, I had booked a last-minute flight to Spain, a few days in the sun before the serious work began. The airline was Air Cymru, a start-up charter airline operating the BAC 1-11, basically a larger version of our aircraft. During the flight, I asked one of the cabin crew if I could visit the flight deck to say hello. Smiling, she went to ask the captain if he would allow a visit. She came back a couple of minutes later full of apologies. Apparently, the captain never allowed visitors, even if they were fellow pilots. Fair enough, I thought, it's his aircraft. An hour later, I stood up to retrieve something from the overhead locker, at the same time as one of the crew tried to pass with a tray of drinks. We collided and everything from the tray ended up on my seat. Whilst the seat was being dried and cleaned, they allowed me to sit on the only spare seat on the aircraft, the jump seat on the flight deck. I was made to feel very unwelcome and was given strict instructions not to speak to either pilot. After sitting for a while, I asked if it would be alright if I asked for a coffee. Hearing my voice, the captain turned around and blue in the face, he ordered me to leave the flight deck immediately. I had disobeyed his direct order. Sheepishly, I spent the rest of the flight standing in the galley, getting in the way of the cabin crew, only taking my wet seat for landing. A week later, Air Cymru went into administration and all their staff, sadly, were made redundant.

A number of the applicants we selected for the interviews had not included a photograph and one of the first candidates to walk through the door was none other than my Air Cymru captain. He did not recognise me, but I had certainly not forgotten him. My first question was that as we were an executive operation, passengers often requested to visit the flight deck. Would he allow such visits and if so, would he make a passenger feel welcome? He looked directly at me and assured me he encouraged such visits. I pressed a little more and asked if a passenger's seat had become unusable, would he be happy to have that passenger on the flight deck? Slowly, I could see recognition dawn on his face. Without a word from me, he stood up and showed himself out. A wise man once said of aviation, 'be careful who you upset on the way up, you may meet them again on the way down'. I felt sad that this highly experienced pilot had lost the opportunity to fly again. Hopefully, he had learned his lesson, though I doubted it.

Two weeks later, we had everything in place, well as much as we could think of. The office sparkled, our first-generation computers sat impressively on the desks and I hoped that the inspector would not ask me how they worked as I had absolutely no idea. We proudly exhibited our new manuals on the shelves and all the required paperwork was on display, awaiting approval. We sat nervously waiting for him to arrive. Everything we had worked so hard for hinged on the next few hours. If we failed to obtain our Air Operator's Licence, it would spell the end for the new company and it would probably cost me my job. Exactly on time, there was a knock on the door and in walked our newly appointed inspector. At first, I thought there may have been a mistake. He was only five or six years older than I was, not at all what I had expected. He was also friendly. I had been used to very officious CAA officials most of whom seemed to be more interested in stopping flying rather than encouraging it. This was a breath of fresh air. He seemed impressed with what he saw and settled himself down to go through our manuals. Apprehensive, I left him to it and settled myself in the adjoining office. Less than five minutes later, his head appeared around the corner to inform me that there was a problem and he could not proceed with our application. This was potentially devastating news for us. If our application was rejected this quickly, it did not bode well. I followed him back into the office to hear our fate.

Apologising, he explained that there had been a clerical error. He was only qualified on propeller aircraft and had never flown a jet. Only a fully qualified pilot could act as the flight operations inspector for a company. He then informed me he had spoken to his office to report the mistake and that there were no HS 125 inspectors available for the next six months. We would have to wait until one had the time to approve our operation. This was terrible news. We had everything ready to go and a six-month delay would spell disaster for us. Thinking quickly, I asked him if he obtained a type rating on the HS 125 could he then become our inspector? He agreed that he could. However, he reminded me that he only flew small aircraft and that the CAA would not pay for a type rating on a jet. This was a catch twenty-two situation. He could not approve us without a type rating and he could not get a type rating without the CAA's approval. I had really warmed to our inspector and I also did not want to wait six months until they could find a replacement, so I made an impulsive offer. Would he be interested in becoming qualified on the aircraft? This seemed to take him aback and he explained that the CAA would not pay for his conversion. He was too junior to get a jet rating. Luckily, I had the simulator booked at Stansted later in the week to carry out conversion courses on our own new pilots. I offered him a free place on the course and a check flight at the end of the simulator course. He looked stunned and repeated that he had no jet experience. I explained that neither did I a few months ago and if I could do it, I was sure he could. Three weeks later, I signed his licence as an HS 125 captain and a week later, he signed our approval as a jet operation company. He had gone through everything with a fine-tooth comb during his conversion course. We were in business! FB Air Services was now licensed to carry fare paying passengers. All we had to do now was find customers willing to charter our aircraft. Luckily, this was Pete's remit and I could go back to regular Food Brokers flying whilst he arranged the charters.

Getting business in 1985 was difficult. Companies were cutting back on staff and expenses and they saw an executive jet as an unnecessary luxury. We had the occasional charter which helped to contribute to the operating costs. However, we needed a big contract to justify the expense of creating this new company.

Chapter 30

The Early Charters

We now had an operator licence and with that, came enormous overheads. We had an office, new employees and a very thirsty aircraft. We desperately needed to get the aircraft to start earning its keep. We were uncertain of the best way to break into the mainstream market which was small with several established operators. When in doubt, Pete and I headed to the golf course for a quick nine holes after a long day in the office.

Golf over and with the ever-faithful Roffey at my side (he made finding my wayward golf shots so much easier), we stopped at the pub for a swift couple of pints. The Six Bells is a classic British pub, dating from the seventeenth century and was popular with aircrews, being so close to Gatwick. We entered the busy lounge and found ourselves a table in the corner. Discussing the upcoming tour and our chances of successful contract, I left Roffey to his own devices. Sometime later, when our beers needed refreshing, I noticed Roffey was no longer lying by my feet. He rarely left my side so I was a little concerned at his absence and as we needed another beer, I set off to find both. The beer part was straightforward, the dog part not so. Eventually, I spotted my missing canine friend sitting by a large open fire being fussed by a very attractive woman. Retrieving

Roffey, I apologised for his intrusion and led him back to our table. Roffey had other ideas and after he had disappeared for the third time to join his new friend, Pete and I were invited to join their party. We discovered that Roffey's new best friend was called Liz and she and her two friends worked as cabin crew for British Caledonian. The night went well and we agreed to meet again the next time she was in the country. Roffey came along too, as I was sure she was more interested in him than me. After a few more dates, I plucked up the courage to ask her the big question, "Would you like to ... fly with me as an executive air hostess on the HS 125?" Luckily for me, she said yes.

Not so luckily for her and not far into our new ad hoc agreement, Liz happened to be on a late-night flight back into Gatwick with Desmond and I flying the aircraft. Our passengers were the board members of the largest supermarket in the UK, all high-powered executives returning from a fact-finding trip to Jerez in Spain. The flight had gone very well, the drinks were flowing and Liz had served up a wonderful supper. Everyone was very relaxed and enjoying themselves until the point that I tried to lower the undercarriage for landing.

The landing gear refused to come down and lock into place, not something you want especially late at night after a long day. There were definitely only two green lights when there should have been three, indicating that all three wheels were not down and locked. We were too close to the ground to run through a complicated checklist and so we flew a go-around. Flying with Desmond was basically like a single pilot operation. He flew the aircraft but had little input as far as checklists went, so I was essentially on my own. We entered a holding pattern, not a straightforward thing to do with only a navigation needle and a stopwatch. Whilst making sure we stayed flying in the correct place, I completed the checklist and tried to lower the landing gear on the alternate system. Still no luck. By now, our fuel was getting a little low and we had to make a decision soon or we would have no option but to land on the available wheels. I asked the control tower if we could do a low flypast for them to check if they could see if all our wheels were down which they agreed to do. We positioned onto final approach and flew down the runway at fifty feet whilst they shone a light on us. It was not good news. One of our main wheels was jammed, half down and half up. We flew another go-around and went back into the holding pattern.

Whilst all this was going on, I had spoken to Liz and asked her to prepare the aircraft and passengers for an emergency landing. The look on her face told me everything. I suspected she was wishing that she had never set eyes on Roffey in her local pub that night! I knew that I was very unlikely to get another date if we got through this. Stoically, Liz calmed the passengers, who understandably were very nervous. I found out later that the aircraft's whisky stock sadly did not survive the flight.

Then we received instructions to divert immediately to Stansted, a quieter airport that also had full emergency services standing by. Gatwick did not want their runway blocked if our undercarriage failed. Looking at our fuel which by now was dangerously low I politely refused their offer. We barely had enough fuel to land at Gatwick let alone fly to Stansted. Liz had everyone practising the crash position: lean forward, heads down, arms over the head and knees together. She had to remind me I did not need to do that. A little humour goes a long way. I was now in control of the aircraft and Desmond had tightened his lap and shoulder harness to their full extent. I performed two high gravity turns to encourage the gear to lock down but still no luck. As we passed two hundred feet, I could hear Liz shouting at the passengers to "Brace, Brace" and to keep their heads down. The whisky was working its magic and there seemed to be no panic. It was our right main wheel that was refusing to cooperate and my plan was to keep that wing as high as possible for as long as possible. Only when we ran out of flying speed would I try to allow the gear to meet the runway. On the flight deck, we had a series of warnings and flashing lights telling us that our gear was not down. Tell me something I don't know, I grimaced to myself. Around eighty miles an hour, our right wheel touched the runway. Everyone held their breath. We slowed down and the aircraft did its best to go off the right side of the runway. The gear was definitely not fully down. Eventually, we came to a stop with the right wing low and the nose pointing at the side of the runway, but apart from that, all appeared to be well. I had to make a quick decision to either evacuate the passengers through the emergency exits or sit quietly and think of another plan. I chose the latter. There was no immediate threat to the aircraft or its occupants. We had shut the engines down and there was no obvious damage apart from the gear. By this time, a multitude of flashing blue lights, very disconcerting both for the passengers and myself, surrounded us.

Our maintenance company, Dan Air and their wonderful engineers, saved the day. They quickly had support under our wing in case the gear failed completely. Checking the extension arm, they discovered that the locking mechanism had failed. They suggested that they jacked the wing up slightly, push the gear down manually and insert the ground locking pin. This would be much quicker and safer than trying to tow the aircraft off the runway. Ten minutes later, I restarted the engines and slowly taxied back to our parking stand. I could hear the laughter and clapping from the cabin. Liz had done a wonderful job. As they all disembarked, I was pleased to see that they were being met by limousines, not one of them was in any fit state to drive. Finally, there were just the two of us left in the aircraft and I apologised profusely. This was not what I had in mind when I had asked Liz to fly with me. My apology must have had the right impact as we have now been married for thirty-three years and she even still flies with me!

The next day, we flew the aircraft to Stansted. The gear stayed down with the locking pins in place, a little noisier than usual but quite safe. The aircraft had the failed locking mechanism changed and everything was back to working as it should. Time to fly back to Gatwick. As the flight had no passengers, I took Roffey along for the ride. He still loved to fly with me. One of his favourite things was to sit in one of the pilot's seats and look out. He didn't mind when we put a pair of headsets on him to complete the picture. We only did this on the ground of course. It was still fun and made everyone smile. On this occasion, we had landed back at Gatwick and we were being given parking instructions by a man waving two large bats over his head. Quickly the co-pilot jumped out of his seat as we were parking and Roffey took his place. We put his headset on and watched as he became fascinated by the man with the bats. I sank low in my seat so that all the poor ground controller could see was a Golden Retriever apparently, taxiing an aircraft on his own. After shutting down the controller entered the flight deck, I thought I was in for a hard time. Instead, he was still laughing and asked if we could put Roffey back into the seat whilst he fetched his camera.

Unfortunately, I agreed and the next week was horrified to see a picture of Roffey on the front page of the *Gatwick News*. This would not go down well with the authorities and sure enough, the very next day I was summoned to the CAA head office for an explanation of the photograph. Entering our flight inspectors office, he asked me to clarify why a dog was sitting in the flight deck, apparently, by himself. He then asked me two very specific questions. Did my dog have a flying licence? Did he have a security pass? What could I possibly say? He had neither and I tried to explain that I was taxiing the aircraft, even though you could not see me in the photograph. Ignoring my explanation, he laid down two documents. Surely, I could not lose my Air Operator's Licence so soon after having it granted. Gingerly, I picked up the documents. I could barely believe what I was holding. The first was a perfect copy of a flying licence in Roffey's name; the second was a security pass with his photograph on it. Laughing, the inspector told me to make sure Roffey had both in his possession when he next flew and to make sure there were no more front-page headlines.

A week later, we were flying a charter flight into RAF Marham, a frontline Royal Air Force base in East Anglia. The Cold War was still at its height and to get permission to land at Marham had taken two weeks. The application required the names of all passengers, their passport details and a letter of intent from the company we were visiting. The RAF also required a copy of my flying licence and logbook. Eventually, we received the required permission. Also, there was a landing and departure slot to which we had to adhere to strictly. I had every intention of complying, especially as they had larger aircraft with guns attached. On the approach my thoughts drifted back to an earlier era nearly fifty years before, the last time one of my family, Flight Sergeant Jack Eades had made the same approach to this airfield.

In his diary on the first of January 1941, Jack wrote the simple words, 'I wonder?' In that same diary on the twenty-third of February his mother had written: 'My darling son, Jack. How I loved you. Oh dear, what shall I do?'.

Jack's Wellington Bomber had flown back from a raid over Germany on a single engine. That engine failed just a mile from the runway and safety. Tragically, no one on board survived. His diary remains one of my most treasured possessions.

Fortunately, this time it was a normal approach and landing, albeit an emotional one for me. A fleet of military vehicles escorted us to our parking bay. The passengers were whisked away and the three of us began preparing the aircraft for our departure later that day. Suddenly, a very large military limousine pulled up at the steps of the aircraft. Two sergeants stepped into the aircraft and informed me that the station commander wanted to see me in his office. This was highly unusual and it was with a certain amount of dread that I climbed into the back of the car.

Minutes later, I was being escorted down a long corridor. What on earth had I done wrong? Mentally, I checked off everything that had been required of us. As far as I could see, we had fully complied. After a knock, swiftly followed by the command, "Enter," I was standing in front of the station commander who was fully resplendent in uniform. This was clearly not a social visit. I was asked to confirm my name, which I did. Inviting me to take a seat, the entire atmosphere changed and he offered me refreshments. I thought this was a little over the top. Do they do this for every visiting aircraft, I wondered? If so, it would not give them much time to monitor the Russians. Eventually, all became clear. Upon receiving my request to visit, the Ministry of Defence had run a background check and they had come up with another Eades. This of course was my Uncle Jack. After his aircraft had crashed just short of the runway here at Marham, the crew were buried at the local church. I was then invited to visit the graveyard and tour the airfield. This was followed by lunch in the officers' mess. My co-pilot and our air hostess were also invited. So followed a memorable, albeit emotional, day. At last, I had the chance to pay my respects to my uncle. The fact that I could now do this as one aviator to another gave me an immense feeling of pride. Hopefully, nobody noticed as I wiped away the tears.

A few weeks later, on another charter flight, we landed at Leeds on a wet and blustery day. The approach onto the relatively short runway was difficult. The wind rocked the aircraft and a sudden wind shift as we touched down resulted in a longer landing distance than I had anticipated. Feeling a certain amount of relief that we were safely down, we taxied onto the apron and shut the aircraft down. In the wild weather, the co-pilot escorted our passengers to the waiting cars. Fortunately, the airport authorities had been kind enough to send a Land Rover to take us to the terminal. Walking behind our aircraft to fit the engine covers, I looked at the runway we had just landed on. To my utter surprise and horror, I saw a huge aircraft appear from the cloud base; a landing from this position was unthinkable, as there was insufficient runway remaining. Despite this, the aircraft continued its landing and touched down directly in front of me. The moment the wheels were on the runway, the pilot applied full brakes and reverse thrust. He then lost control of the aircraft. All this happened in apparent slow motion; I could not believe what I was witnessing. The runway at Leeds, as well as being short, ended with a drop into a valley below. If the Tristar overran the runway it would drop into the valley with catastrophic consequences. As I stared, the nose of the aircraft swayed from side to side. To see such a large aircraft in such trouble was traumatising. I ran to the Land Rover and told the driver to follow the aircraft. If there was going to be a crash, we needed to be there as quickly as possible. We drove directly onto the runway and followed the Tristar as it continued its erratic path. Eventually, we saw the aircraft swerve violently to the right and leave the runway just before the drop into the valley below. As it left the runway, the nose wheel collapsed and the aircraft came to a sudden halt in the muddy ground. With its nose on the ground and its tail in the air, the crew began an emergency evacuation. Slides appeared from the aircraft's doors that were still usable and we helped as many passengers as we could as they made their way down the slides. Incredibly, there were only minor injuries to crew and passengers. The airport was closed for the rest of the day whilst the emergency services dealt with the aftermath of the accident. Obviously, our return flight was cancelled which was just as well as it took a few days for my hands to stop shaking. A few years later, I found myself flying with the captain of the stricken aircraft. Aviation is often a very small world.

Chapter 31

The 'Out of My Tree' Tour

Our biggest break came when we bid for and were unexpectedly awarded the contract to fly U2 on their legendary 'Out of My Tree' tour, more widely known as the 'Joshua Tree' tour. The band was and still is, one of the biggest in the world. The year was 1986 and the band were putting on their first and some say, most successful tour. Rumours were rife in the executive jet world that the tour organisers were looking to charter an aircraft for the entire tour, a costly but equally very lucrative contract for the successful company. We were still the new kids on the block. The established operators were used to getting all the large contracts, leaving us to pick up the crumbs. We were happy to do this. We had made some very good contacts in the food business and some of the largest supermarkets regularly chartered our aircraft. However, we were still looking for our breakthrough into the mainstream charter world.

Initially, I had been reluctant to bid for the tour. It was a very costly and time-consuming business to put together a detailed bid for a three-month tour and I thought our chances of success were slim to the point of being non-existent. Pete Brown had a very different idea though. He would not entertain the idea that anyone else could possibly get the contract. Between the two of us, we were just about in the ballpark. Over a beer, we decided to submit a bid. Pete would do all the hard work - a lot of it in his own time - whilst I looked after the day-to-day business of keeping the aircraft flying. Around this time, we managed another quick nine holes of golf, an activity that would have a huge bearing on the success of our bid in the weeks to come, something that would have been impossible to predict. Pete put together a very detailed and we thought, competitive bid. We travelled to London to meet the tour organisers. It was very important that we could work together successfully as there were certain to be many obstacles to overcome during the three-month tour. Luckily, they seemed to like the fact that we were so much younger than our competitors and our outlook seemed to fit in with theirs. We were thanked for our time. They would be in touch in due course. This normally meant thank you, but no thank you. We were not hopeful.

We were informed that the outcome of the tenders would be announced the following week. Would we make sure that we were contactable at all times in case they had any last-minute questions. This sounded more promising. Maybe, just maybe, we actually were in with a chance. The days ticked by and we sat by the phone waiting and hoping. We were both lucky enough to have car phones, a very rare luxury in the eighties. I kept the battery for the phone, which was similar in size to a car battery, in the car's boot. You could remove both the phone and the battery from the car and use them as a makeshift mobile phone. The major drawback of this device was carrying around the huge battery. Undaunted and tired of waiting for a phone call, Pete and I decided that we required another nine holes of golf. Collecting our four-legged ball finder, we arrived at the course. It took a little while to remove the phone battery, connect it to the phone and strap the whole thing onto a set of golfing wheels. We had to make sure we were contactable. Pulling this contraption behind us, we received many strange looks from other golfers. Few had seen the world's largest mobile phone making its way around a golf course, followed by a Golden Retriever.

The sun was setting as we arrived at the final green. The phone remained ominously silent. Pete was about to putt first when we both heard a strange sound. Looking around, we could not identify what or where the sound was coming from. Pete settled over his putt once more. Suddenly, I realised that our mobile phone was ringing; I had never taken an outdoor call before. Snatching up the receiver, I answered in my best executive voice. It was the call we had been waiting over a week for. I stood there listening intently as the tour manager explained that he wanted us to fly the tour.

However, there was a problem. Another operator had undercut our price by five percent. If we could match this price, the contract was ours. My immediate instinct was to agree until Pete reminded me that to do so could result in us losing money. I hesitated. Was it best to accept? The publicity would be wonderful but on the other hand, if we lost money, it could have serious consequences for our company. Whilst we were deliberating, the tour manager asked where we were as he could hear background noises. When I explained and informed him that we were on the last green and about to putt, he came up with a solution. He asked how long Pete's putt was. I said about six feet. "How about if Pete makes the putt, we go with your original quote. If he misses, you match the competitor's price." I was stunned. Did people really do business this way? I asked Pete what he thought. He laughed, assuming it was a joke. The voice on the handset assured me it was no joke and he trusted us to let him know if the putt was successful, after all he was about to trust us with the safety of U2. Without thinking it through, I agreed. It seemed appropriate somehow.

Pete looked astonished. Putting, like the rest of his game was not one of his strengths. But it was too late now as I had agreed to the challenge and so Pete crouched over the ball readying himself for the most expensive stroke he would ever make. My job was to comment on the putt, which I did. The whole thing was surreal. Pete struck the ball far too hard and it raced towards the hole. If it missed, it would run off the green entirely and we were doomed. Unbelievably, however, it hit the hole, jumped into the air, ran around the cup and finally disappeared into the hole. From the tension, dread and then excitement in my voice, there could be no doubt as to the outcome and we were rewarded with the contract. Even Roffey, who usually sat quietly, entered the celebrations. We had hit the big time. The proper work was about to start.

The next few weeks were all about sorting out our involvement with the finer details of the tour. The band decided that they wanted the aircraft repainted with the name of the tour across the fuselage. We also had to have a lock made especially for the aircraft's door. The band would be leaving a lot of personal effects in the aircraft throughout the tour. Planning went on week after week. We could leave nothing to chance. Finally, we were ready. The first day of the tour arrived and we sat waiting by the aircraft for the band's arrival. The press were there in force packing the whole of the executive terminal with onlookers, cameras and the paparazzi. If this was a taste of things to come, then it was going to be one hell of a tour.

Our aircraft was parked directly outside the terminal, resplendent in its new paint scheme. Our air hostess had everything ready, champagne on ice, smoked salmon starters already plated and waiting to be served. The co-pilot for the first week of the tour was my father, recently retired from British Caledonian. He was enjoying his new job (although having his son as the captain must have felt strange). The plan was to fly to Turin, where we would stay for two days and then on to Rome. As we waited a fleet of cars suddenly swept into view, followed by flashing camera lights and general pandemonium. Pete went to meet and greet the band whilst I waited at the foot of the aircraft stairs with our hostess. Finally, after much fanfare, the band and their manager boarded the aircraft. We were all set. I really did not know what to expect when I was introduced. Luckily, they all seemed very friendly. It was going to be a fun tour.

The flight to Turin was uneventful. Everyone on board was enjoying the flight and Bono joined us on the flight deck for our descent into Turin. The views over the Alps were incredible. The same excited scenes we left behind at Gatwick were replicated at Turin. Eventually, the band were whisked away by a series of limousines. There was a concert the next day and we were keen to get to our hotel. As part of the contract, it had been agreed that the three crew members would stay in the same hotel as the band. This would make it easier for us to meet up with the tour directors each evening to plan for the next day's flight. Fortunately for us, we had two days off in Turin and so after checking in, we were invited to a pre-tour party being held at the hotel. As expected, it was a lavish affair with everyone having a great time. My night was going particularly well until the tour manager approached me late in the evening to inform me of a change of plan. They had decided that we would fly the band to Milan early the next morning for a photo shoot before returning to Turin later that day. He wanted the aircraft to be ready in the morning for an eight o'clock departure. This was not good news. It left us only a few hours to get some rest. We would have to be up at five o'clock in the morning to get a taxi to the airport and prepare the aircraft. Finding my father and our hostess - who was enjoying the attentions of more than one admirer - I suggested we all leave and get as much sleep as possible.

As the alarm went off in the early hours, I realised just how tired I felt. I hoped the others felt better than I did. We met in the lobby and dropped our room keys off in the box provided. We set off for the airport. I went immediately to the operations room to file a flight plan for the short flight to Milan. My father went to refuel the aircraft and get it ready for our departure. Melanie, our hostess went in search of provisions. It was all a bit of a rush, not at all what I had wanted. After completing all the formalities, I went to join my father in the aircraft to prepare for the flight. Walking across the tarmac, I noticed he was standing by the aircraft door looking confused. He had been there for at least twenty minutes and the door was not even opened. I quickened my pace. Obviously, there was something very wrong. As I arrived at the aircraft, my father, clearly angry, threw the aircraft's key towards me and pronounced that it would not work. This was terrible news. If we couldn't open the door, well it didn't bear thinking about. I tried the key for myself and looked down at it and to my horror, saw a label for Room 225. I asked my father why he was trying to open the aircraft with his room key. Angrily, he replied that it could not possibly be his room key, as he had dropped that off at the hotel. My blood ran cold as I realised what had happened. In his rush to leave, my father had mistakenly put the aircraft keys in the drop off box at the hotel and kept his room key. The Joshua Tree tour for us, was about to come to a very premature end.

The hotel was an hour's drive away and the band would be arriving in twenty minutes. A heavy-duty padlock firmly locked the door. Our only hope was to find a hacksaw to remove it. Running back to the terminal and our handling agent, my broken Italian did not portray the seriousness of our predicament. I then noticed an Alitalia maintenance van parked opposite the building. The engineers inside were U2 fans who had come to watch their departure. Fortunately, they spoke English and even more fortunately, they had a drill that could cut through metal. I promised to introduce them to the band if they could open the aircraft's door. It seemed a fair trade off and less than ten minutes later, we had the door open just as the fleet of cars made its way to the aircraft's steps. The band looked slightly bemused as they were introduced to a group of Italian engineers but signed the offered pieces of paper with their usual good grace. Luckily, the rest of the day went well, not that my father saw much of it as he fell back to sleep on the aircraft's sofa.

I stayed with the tour for that first week and then reluctantly, had to return to Gatwick, to look after the flying for Food Brokers. We were now using a chartered aircraft. We were also in negotiations for the next tour for U2. This time, they wanted a much larger aircraft, the BAC 1-11, an airliner capable of carrying around one hundred and twenty passengers. They also wanted the executive version with all the trimmings. I made a tentative approach to the CAA and asked them if we could operate an aircraft this size. After much negotiation, they agreed that if I could get five hundred hours flying on the aircraft, we could add it to our Air Operator's Licence. This was another question. How could I fly the aircraft for five hundred hours if we could not operate the aircraft until I had those hours?

The answer presented itself one day when I was talking to our engineering company at Gatwick, Dan Air. They had been amazing ever since we signed the contract for them to carry out the servicing on our aircraft. They treated us if we were one of their own. I got chatting to one of their BAC 1-11 pilots and explained our predicament. He immediately advised me to write to Dan Air's chief pilot. They were short of pilots for summer. What better way to get the required experience? So, I became a part-time Dan Air pilot, the difference between executive flying and the bucket and spade holiday charter flights could not have been more of a contrast.

I now had my hands full. I was still flying Food Brokers' staff around on a chartered aircraft as well as flying my socks off for Dan Air to get the required five hundred hours on the aircraft. I also had to keep a very close eye on the U2 tour, occasionally flying out to operate a sector. It was heady stuff, a million miles away from my first flights at Shoreham less than five years ago. Could all of this really have been crammed into such a brief space of time?

Unbeknownst to me, my career in executive aviation was coming to an end. The contracts I had hoped to fulfil were becoming more and more difficult to achieve. There were new players coming into the market. Tony Ryan, the owner of a small Irish company, was trying to establish a foothold in the UK market. Personally, I thought he had very little hope. Ryanair had little chance of success. We bravely continued to bid for new contracts. We then came up against a company called Highland Express as we bid for more contracts in the entertainment world. Their owner seemed to know what he was doing. Sadly, we lost out on one of the contracts we desperately needed. At the time, we were not sure how Highland Express could bid so low. They must have a very solid financial backer. As we discovered to our cost, that's exactly what they did have! A few months later, they changed their name to Virgin Atlantic and Richard Branson became a household name.

I now had a decision to make. As I was flying airliners for Dan Air, should I risk it all to go back to the executive charter world or should I try to make my way with the airlines?

Gloomily, I felt I had to choose the latter. My thinking at the time was that this would be a safer and quieter way to earn a living, how wrong this was to prove to be.

I joined British Airways in 1987 to fly the Boeing 747, quite a step up from the HS 125 and BAC 1-11. I had no idea at the time that this phase of my career would prove just as exciting, challenging and unpredictable as my career in the executive world. A year after joining British Airways, my face made the front page of every newspaper in the UK and many international newspapers as well.

That is a story still to be told but for now, I bade a sad farewell to all that I knew and had grown to love. Luckily, I did not need Pete to drive me to Heathrow to start this new adventure. I knew my own way this time.

THE END ... FOR NOW

STILL IMPROVING,
The sequel, coming soon.

Photo Gallery

Flying High

Friends for over sixty years and still going strong. Pete Brown
(right) and me, complete our pre-flight checks.

1981 – Food Brokers' first turboprop, the King Air.
A painting commissioned by my mother.

Relaxing as I fly the King Air - Wonderful times!

Liz and I celebrating Christmas 1985.

Pete Brown next to our HS 125 as the U2 tour begins.

The future, in retro. The aircraft I was destined to fly for a record breaking thirty-four years.